HOME ELECTRONICS

Other Publications:

MYSTERIES OF THE UNKNOWN

TIME FRAME

FIX IT YOURSELF

FITNESS, HEALTH & NUTRITION

SUCCESSFUL PARENTING

HEALTHY HOME COOKING

UNDERSTANDING COMPUTERS

LIBRARY OF NATIONS

THE ENCHANTED WORLD

THE KODAK LIBRARY OF CREATIVE PHOTOGRAPHY

GREAT MEALS IN MINUTES

THE CIVIL WAR

PLANET EARTH

COLLECTOR'S LIBRARY OF THE CIVIL WAR

THE EPIC OF FLIGHT

THE GOOD COOK

WORLD WAR II

HOME REPAIR AND IMPROVEMENT

THE OLD WEST

HOME ELECTRONICS

TIME-LIFE BOOKS
ALEXANDRIA, VIRGINIA

Fix It Yourself was produced by
ST. REMY PRESS

MANAGING EDITOR	Kenneth Winchester
MANAGING ART DIRECTOR	Pierre Léveillé

Staff for *Home Electronics*

Series Editor	Kathleen M. Kiely
Editor	Brian Parsons
Series Art Director	Diane Denoncourt
Art Director	Francine Lemieux
Research Editor	Elizabeth Cameron
Designers	Nicolas Moumouris, Solange Pelland
Editorial Assistants	Fiona Gilsenan, Michael Mouland
Contributing Writers	Margaret Caldbick, Chris Cockrill, James Fehr, Harriett Fels, Patrick Godon, Karen Haughian, Jay Herringer, Joan Irving, Emer Killean, Yves Lacroix, Grant Loewen
Contributing Illustrators	Gérard Mariscalchi, Jacques Proulx
Technical Illustrator	Robert Paquet
Cover	Robert Monté
Index	Christine M. Jacobs
Administrator	Denise Rainville
Coordinator	Michelle Turbide
Systems Manager	Shirley Grynspan
Systems Analyst	Simon Lapierre
Studio Director	Daniel Bazinet
Photographer	Maryo Proulx

Time-Life Books Inc. is a wholly owned subsidiary of
TIME INCORPORATED

FOUNDER	Henry R. Luce 1898-1967
Editor-in-Chief	Jason McManus
Chairman and Chief Executive Officer	J. Richard Munro
President and Chief Operating Officer	N. J. Nicholas Jr.
Editorial Director	Ray Cave
Executive Vice President, Books	Kelso F. Sutton
Vice President, Books	George Artandi

TIME-LIFE BOOKS INC.

EDITOR	George Constable
Executive Editor	Ellen Phillips
Director of Design	Louis Klein
Director of Editorial Resources	Phyllis K. Wise
Editorial Board	Russell B. Adams Jr., Dale M. Brown, Roberta Conlan, Thomas H. Flaherty, Lee Hassig, Donia Ann Steele, Rosalind Stubenberg, Henry Woodhead
Director of Photography and Research	John Conrad Weiser
Asst. Director of Editorial Resources	Elise Ritter Gibson
PRESIDENT	Christopher T. Linen
Chief Operating Officer	John M. Fahey Jr.
Senior Vice Presidents	Robert M. DeSena, James L. Mercer
Vice Presidents	Stephen L. Bair, Ralph J. Cuomo, Neal Goff, Stephen L. Goldstein, Juanita T. James, Hallett Johnson III, Carol Kaplan, Susan J. Maruyama, Robert H. Smith, Joseph J. Ward
Director of Production Services	Robert J. Passantino

Editorial Operations

Copy Chief	Diane Ullius
Production	Celia Beattie
Library	Louise D. Forstall
Correspondents	Elizabeth Kraemer-Singh (Bonn); Maria Vincenza Aloisi (Paris); Ann Natanson (Rome).

THE CONSULTANTS

Consulting Editor **David L. Harrison** served as an editor for several Time-Life Books do-it-yourself series, including *Home Repair and Improvement*, *The Encyclopedia of Gardening* and *The Art of Sewing*.

Evan Powell is the Director of Chestnut Mountain Research Inc. in Taylors, South Carolina, a firm specializing in the development and evaluation of home appliances. He is a contributing editor to several do-it-yourself magazines, and is the author of two books on home repair.

William J. Hawkins is Senior Editor of Consumer Electronics/Computers for *Popular Science* magazine. As a consultant, he has appeared on radio and television in the United States and Canada. He has written several books on computers.

John Banks, special consultant for Canada, owns the Audio Centre and the Video Centre in Montreal, specializing in high-quality home entertainment equipment. He is a regular consultant on radio and television.

Michael R. MacDonald is a technical director for television production. He also operates a computer consulting company and is a freelance photographer.

Steven J. Forbis was a writer and editor for Time-Life Books' *Home Repair and Improvement* series. He writes about home electronics for several magazines, and is editor of *Prodigy Service*, an interactive electronic entertainment network, for Trintex, Inc.

Library of Congress Cataloging-in-Publication Data
Home electronics
    p. cm. – (Fix it yourself)
  Includes index.
  ISBN 0-8094-6252-4
  ISBN 0-8094-6253-2 (lib. bdg.)
1. Household electronics--Maintenance and repair--
Amateurs' manuals.   I. Time-Life Books.
II. Series.
TK9965.H59   1988
621.381   88-8576

For information about any Time-Life book, please write:
Reader Information
Time-Life Customer Service
P.O. Box C-32068
Richmond, Virginia
23261-2068

HOW TO USE THIS BOOK

Home Electronics is divided into three sections. The Emergency Guide on pages 8-11 provides information that can be indispensable, even lifesaving, in the event of a household emergency. Take the time to study this section *before* you need the important advice it contains.

The Repairs section — the heart of the book — is a comprehensive approach to troubleshooting and repairing electronic units. Pictured below are four sample pages from the chapter on receivers, with captions describing the various features of the book and how they work. If the volume control in your receiver is abrupt or scratchy, for example, the Troubleshooting Guide will offer a number of possible causes. If the problem is a dirty or faulty potentiometer, you will be directed to page 24 for detailed, step-by-step directions for cleaning, testing and replacing the potentiometer.

Each job has been rated by degree of difficulty and the average time it will take for a do-it-yourselfer to complete. Keep in mind that this rating is only a suggestion. Before deciding whether you should attempt a repair, first read all the instructions carefully. Then be guided by your own confidence, and

Introductory text
Describes basic principles of the electronic unit, most common breakdowns and basic safety precautions.

Exploded and cutaway diagrams
Locate and describe the various components of the electronic unit.

Troubleshooting Guide
To use this chart, locate the symptom that most closely resembles your electronic unit problem, review the possible causes in column 2, then follow the recommended procedures in column 3. Simple fixes may be explained on the chart; in most cases you will be directed to an illustrated, step-by-step repair sequence.

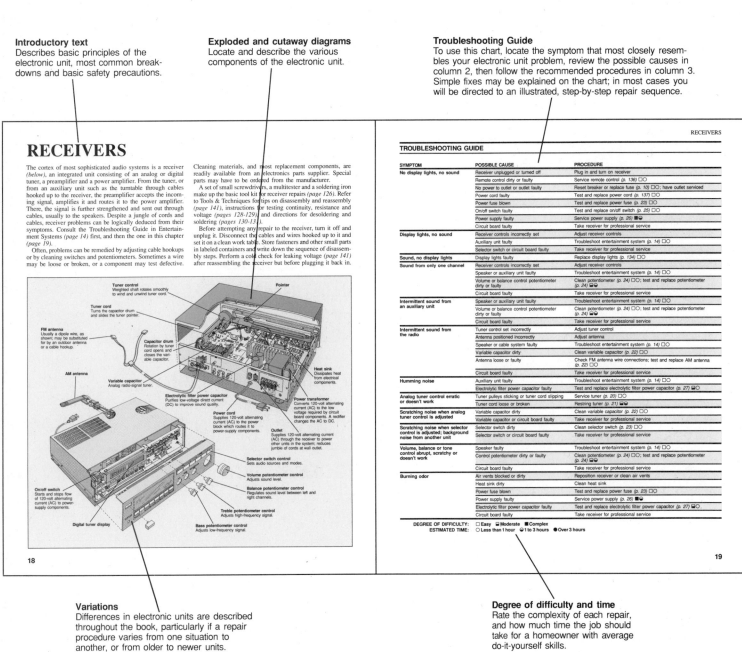

Variations
Differences in electronic units are described throughout the book, particularly if a repair procedure varies from one situation to another, or from older to newer units.

Degree of difficulty and time
Rate the complexity of each repair, and how much time the job should take for a homeowner with average do-it-yourself skills.

CONTENTS

the tools and time available to you. For more complex or time-consuming repairs, such as servicing the power supply or replacing the electrolytic filter power capacitor, you may wish to take the receiver for professional service. You will still have saved time and money by diagnosing the problem yourself.

Most repairs in *Home Electronics* can be made with a set of screwdrivers, a multitester and a soldering iron. Any special tool required is indicated in the Troubleshooting Guide. Basic tools — and the proper way to use them — are presented in Tools & Techniques *(page 126)*. If you are a novice at home

repair, read this section and the chapter called Entertainment Systems *(page 12)* in preparation for a job.

Repairing an electronic unit is easy and safe if you work logically and follow the tips and precautions. Before beginning, turn off power to the unit and unplug it. Disconnect the cables and any ground wire hooked up to it and set it on a clean work table. Store fasteners and other small parts in labeled containers and write down the sequence of disassembly steps. Perform a cold check for leaking voltage *(page 141)* after reassembling the unit but before plugging it back in.

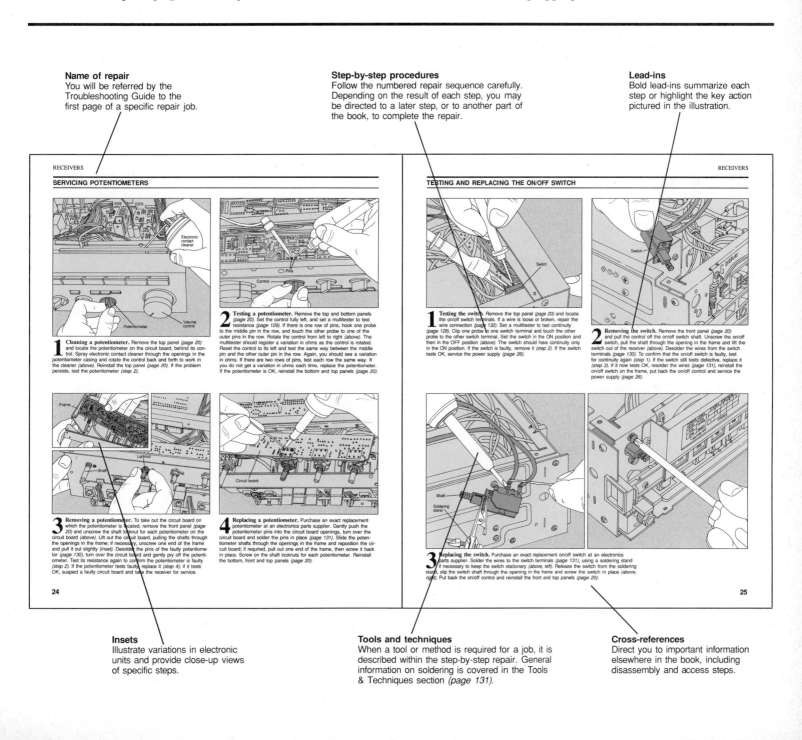

Name of repair
You will be referred by the Troubleshooting Guide to the first page of a specific repair job.

Step-by-step procedures
Follow the numbered repair sequence carefully. Depending on the result of each step, you may be directed to a later step, or to another part of the book, to complete the repair.

Lead-ins
Bold lead-ins summarize each step or highlight the key action pictured in the illustration.

Insets
Illustrate variations in electronic units and provide close-up views of specific steps.

Tools and techniques
When a tool or method is required for a job, it is described within the step-by-step repair. General information on soldering is covered in the Tools & Techniques section *(page 131)*.

Cross-references
Direct you to important information elsewhere in the book, including disassembly and access steps.

EMERGENCY GUIDE

Preventing home electronics problems. The electronic units in your home are expertly designed for years of safe, worry-free use. With proper care and maintenance, most of them can last a lifetime — outdated only by newer, more sophisticated units. Yet, even with the latest in engineering technology, emergency situations can occur; it's usually only then that we pay belated respect to the electrical current coursing through the intricate circuits housed in these machines.

Although rare, electrical emergencies are the most likely and serious threat to the user of an electronic unit. You can easily prevent most electrical emergencies by proper installation, use and maintenance of the machine. Familiarize yourself with the owner's manual that came with the unit; if you have misplaced it, order a new one from the manufacturer.

The repair of electronic units need not be any more dangerous than their routine use. Indeed, a repair procedure that is properly performed can prevent hazardous conditions. The list of safety tips at right covers basic guidelines for the maintenance and repair of any electronic unit; consult the chapters on individual units for more specific advice.

Electrical shock and fire are life-threatening emergencies that can happen in even the most safety-conscious of homes. Deprive fire of its sneak attack by installing smoke alarms judiciously throughout the house. Have the correct fire extinguisher on hand to snuff out a blaze before it gets the upper hand, and learn how to use it before you need it *(page 11)*. If you must rescue someone stuck to an electronic unit by live current, do not touch him; use a wooden broom handle or wooden chair to push him free *(page 10)*. Keep medical emergency numbers posted by the telephone, and do not hesitate to use them; in most areas, dial 911 in case of a life-threatening emergency.

Prepare yourself to handle emergencies before they occur. Read the Troubleshooting Guide on page 9, which places emergency procedures at your fingertips. It lists quick-action steps to take and refers you to the steps on pages 10 and 11 for detailed instructions. Also review Tools & Techniques *(page 126)*; it provides invaluable information on repairing electronic unit components and on the safe use of tools.

Get technical help when you need it. If you are in doubt about the safety of an electronic unit or about the nature of a repair, have the unit checked out by a professional service technician. And even in non-emergency situations, an inspector from your utility company or fire department can answer questions concerning the condition and proper use of your home's electrical system.

SAFETY TIPS

1. Before attempting any repair in this book, read the entire procedure. Familiarize yourself with the specific safety information presented in each chapter.

2. Read Entertainment Systems *(page 12)* to understand the interrelationship of electronic units that are hooked up together. Refer to Tools & Techniques *(page 126)* for instructions on the proper use of tools and on getting help when you need it.

3. Never use or work on electronic units under wet conditions. Make sure grounding wires are properly connected.

4. Turn off and unplug the electronic unit before a repair. Disconnect the cables and any ground wire hooked up to it *(page 12)*. Set it on a clean work table that is well lit; do not touch any internal component you cannot see.

5. Remove watches and jewelry before starting a repair. Cover the electronic unit if you take a break while working. Store tools safely; do not set them down inside the unit.

6. Cover the power-supply components *(page 138)* with a nonconductive shield as a precaution during voltage tests. Avoid touching anything but the contact points being tested.

7. Never look directly at the laser in a compact disc player that is plugged in and turned on; it can cause eye damage.

8. Wear eye protection when making repairs inside a television. Prevent injury from picture-tube implosion by asking a qualified service technician to dispose safely of an old set.

9. When making outdoor repairs to antenna and cable systems, work on a dry, calm day. Work with a helper, or at least within earshot of someone else. Do not service any system near overhead utility lines.

10. Use only replacement components of the same specifications as the originals. Consult the manufacturer of the electronic unit or a reputable electronics parts supplier.

11. Perform a cold check for leaking voltage *(page 141)* after reassembling an electronic unit but before plugging it back in. If in doubt about the safety of a repair, have a qualified professional service technician check it.

12. Avoid running power cords under carpets or through heavily trafficked areas. Do not use extension cords. Never splice power cords or remove the grounding prong from a three-prong plug. Do not alter the larger prong on a polarized plug.

13. Keep food and beverages away from electronic units, and make sure air vents remain unobstructed and dust-free.

14. Unplug electronic units and disconnect external antenna connections from the television before going on vacation.

15. Install surge suppressors to protect computers and other sensitive electronic units from voltage spikes.

16. Locate and label your home's electrical service panel.

17. Install smoke detectors and fire extinguishers in your home.

18. Post emergency, utility company and repair service numbers near your telephone.

TROUBLESHOOTING GUIDE

PROBLEM	PROCEDURE
Fire in unit, power cord or wall outlet	Call fire department
	Use fire extinguisher rated for electrical fires *(p. 11)*
	Shut off power at service panel; then, unplug unit power cord from wall outlet *(p. 10)*
	If flames or smoldering continue, leave house and wait for fire department
Unit power cord or plug sparking or hot	Shut off power at service panel; then, unplug unit power cord from wall outlet *(p. 10)*
Unit gives off sparks or shocks user	Unplug unit power cord from wall outlet or shut off power at service panel *(p. 10)*
	Locate and repair cause of sparks or shock, or take unit for professional service
Smoke coming from unit	Unplug unit power cord from wall outlet or shut off power at service panel *(p. 10)*
	Take unit for professional service
Burning or other peculiar odor coming from unit	Turn off unit and unplug unit power cord from wall outlet *(p. 10)*; wait until odor dissipates before servicing unit
	Locate and repair cause of odor or take unit for professional service
Unit is excessively hot	Turn off unit and unplug unit power cord from wall outlet *(p. 10)*
	Check unit air vents and clean air vents *(p. 11)* if necessary
	Reposition unit with air vents unobstructed
Unit is flooded	Do not touch unit or any plumbing fixture; dry yourself if you are wet
	Shut off power at service panel; then, unplug unit power cord from wall outlet *(p. 10)*
	Dry unit with absorbent cloth and hair dryer *(p. 11)*
Beverage or other foreign material spilled into unit	Unplug unit power cord from wall outlet *(p. 10)*
	Dry unit with absorbent cloth and hair dryer if wet; or clean the components *(p. 11)*
Electrical shock	If person is immobilized by live current, push him away from source with wooden broom handle or wooden chair *(p. 10)*
	Check whether victim is breathing and has pulse. If not, begin artificial resuscitation or cardiopulmonary resuscitation (CPR) if you are qualified. Otherwise, place victim in recovery position *(p. 10)* and call for help
Electrical burn	Soak injury in cold water and cover with sterile gauze if severe
	Seek medical attention immediately, since electrical burns can cause internal injury
Power failure	Turn off all units that have motors, to prevent overloading electrical system when power is restored
	Keep emergency supplies on hand, including a flashlight or candles
	Leave a light on so that you will know when power is restored
Lightning storm	Unplug all electronic units or use a surge suppressor to protect them
	Stay away from windows, doors, fireplaces, radiators, stoves, sinks and pipes
Utility line down	Call utility company, police or fire department
	Treat every fallen line as if it were live with electricity. Stay far away from the line and anything it touches, including fences, trees and antennas
Antenna fallen against utility line	Do not touch units hooked up to antenna
	Do not attempt to dislodge antenna
	Call utility company, police or fire department

SAFETY SYMBOLS ON ELECTRONIC UNITS

 Operation warning. A triangle with an exclamation mark warns the user to consult the owner's manual *before* operating the unit.

 Voltage warning. A triangle with a lightning bolt warns of a potential electrical shock hazard. Usually, this symbol can be found on the back or bottom of the unit. If the symbol is posted on an internal component, do not touch the component; electrical current may be stored in it even though the unit is turned off and unplugged.

 Laser warning. A triangle or square with a sunburst symbol warns of possible danger from a laser. This symbol may be found on the back or bottom of a compact disc player. Never look directly at an operating laser; its intense light can cause permanent eye damage.

CUTTING OFF ELECTRICAL POWER

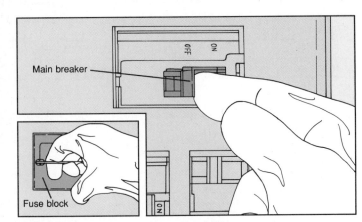

Shutting down power at the service panel. If the floor around the service panel is wet, stand on a dry board or a rubber mat, or wear rubber boots. Wear heavy, dry rubber gloves and use only one hand; keep the other hand in your pocket or behind your back. At a circuit breaker panel, flip off the main breaker *(above)*. As an added precaution, use your knuckle; that way, any shock will jerk your hand away from the panel. At a fuse panel, grip the main fuse block by its handle and pull it out *(inset)*. If the fuse panel has a shutoff lever, shift it to the OFF position.

Pulling the power cord plug from the wall outlet. If the floor around the wall outlet is wet, or if the wall outlet itself is sparking or burning, do not touch the power cord or the electronic unit. Instead, shut off power at the service panel *(left)*. Otherwise, disconnect the power cord plug. Protect your hand with a thick, dry towel or a heavy work glove. Without touching the wall outlet or the electronic unit, grasp the power cord several inches from the plug and pull the plug out of the wall outlet *(above)*. Locate and repair the problem before using the electronic unit or the outlet again.

RESCUING A VICTIM OF ELECTRICAL SHOCK

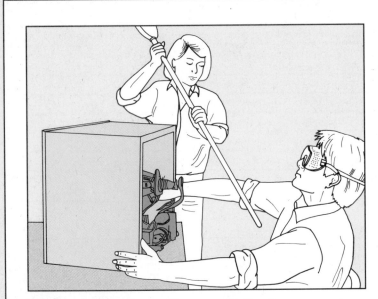

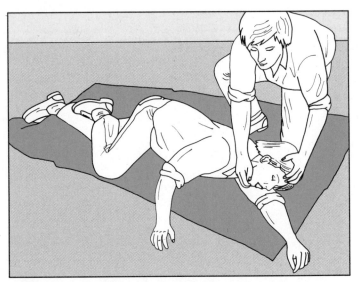

Freeing someone from a live current. Usually a person who contacts live current will be thrown back from the source. But sometimes muscles contract involuntarily around a wire or component. Do not touch the victim or the unit. Pull the power cord plug from the wall outlet *(step above, right)* or shut off power at the main service panel *(step above, left)*. If the power cannot be cut immediately, use a wooden broom handle or wooden chair to knock the person free *(above)*.

Handling a victim of electrical shock. Call for help immediately. Check the victim's breathing and heartbeat. If there is no breathing or heartbeat, give mouth-to-mouth resuscitation or cardiopulmonary resuscitation (CPR) only if you are qualified. If the victim is breathing and has not sustained back or neck injuries, place him in the recovery position *(above)*. Tilt the head back with the face to one side and the tongue forward to maintain an open airway. Keep the victim calm and comfortable until help arrives.

CONTROLLING AN ELECTRICAL FIRE

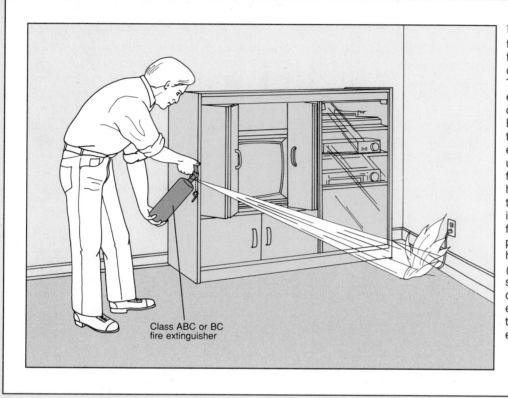

Using a fire extinguisher. Call the fire department immediately. If there are flames or smoke coming from the walls or ceiling, leave the house to call for help. To snuff a small, accessible fire in an electronic unit or at the wall outlet, use a dry-chemical fire extinguisher rated ABC or BC. Stand near an exit, 6 to 10 feet from the fire. Pull the lock pin out of the extinguisher handle and, holding the extinguisher upright, aim the nozzle at the base of the flames. Squeeze the two levers of the handle together, spraying in a quick side-to-side motion. Keep spraying until the fire is completely extinguished. Watch carefully for "flashback," or rekindling, and be prepared to spray again. You may also have to shut off power at the service panel *(page 10)* to remove the source of heat or sparking causing the fire. Find the cause of the fire and remedy it before using the electronic unit or the outlet again. Have the fire department examine the area even if the fire is out.

Class ABC or BC fire extinguisher

CLEANING UP SPILLS AND DIRT

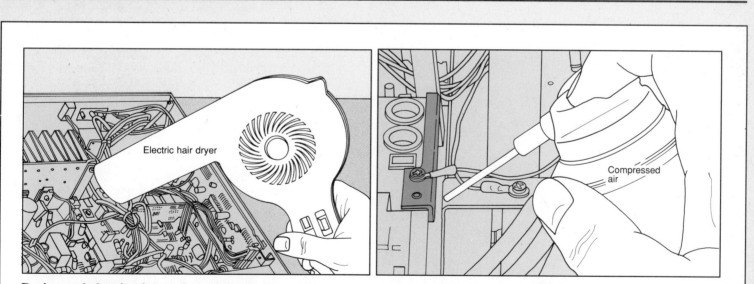

Electric hair dryer

Compressed air

Drying and cleaning internal components. Turn off the electronic unit and unplug it from the wall outlet. Disconnect its cables and any ground wire hooked up to it *(page 12)*. Set the unit on a clean work table. Refer to the chapter on the electronic unit for instructions on reaching the internal components. Using a clean, lint-free, absorbent cloth, carefully soak up pools of liquid. Dry the internal components thoroughly using a hair dryer set on the no-heat or low-heat position *(above, left)*; aim with slow, sweeping motions to avoid heating up a component. To remove sticky dust or dirt particles from components, spray them with short bursts of compressed air *(above, right)*. Use foam swabs to clean components; apply denatured alcohol to metal or plastic, rubber-cleaning compound to rubber, and electronic contact cleaner to circuit boards and switches. Finally, lubricate moving parts by applying light machine oil to metal and white grease to plastic. Perform a cold check for leaking voltage *(page 141)* after reassembling the electronic unit but before plugging it back into the wall outlet.

ENTERTAINMENT SYSTEMS

It may boast a top-of-the-line compact disc player and video-cassette recorder, or just a modest receiver, turntable and speakers, but a typical entertainment system *(below)* is an investment in leisure that can cost thousands of dollars. While each additional unit adds new entertainment options, it also complicates system hookups and problems diagnosis.

Thanks to solid-state circuitry, electronic problem are rare and can be logically deduced from their symptoms. Refer to the appropriate chapter to troubleshoot your telephone system *(page 100)* or your computer and printer *(page 110)*. But consult the Troubleshooting Guide in this chapter *(page 14)* first before referring to the chapter covering a specific audio or video entertainment unit.

To answer questions about the set-up or cable hookups for your entertainment system, check the owner's manual that came with each unit or consult the manufacturer. As a general rule, most units perform best if the cables between them are kept as short as possible, reducing electrical resistance and interference that weaken the audio or video signal; if the cable is coaxial, this is less of a worry. An exception is the turntable, which is highly sensitive to vibration and signal interference; position it at least 3 feet away from the speakers.

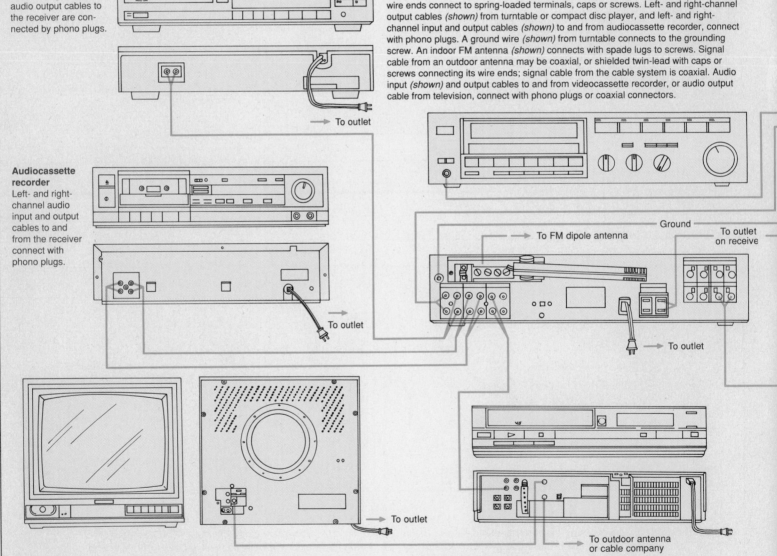

Compact disc player
Left- and right-channel audio output cables to the receiver are connected by phono plugs.

Audiocassette recorder
Left- and right-channel audio input and output cables to and from the receiver connect with phono plugs.

To outlet

Receiver
Speaker cables *(shown)* provide left- and right-channel audio output to speakers. The wire ends connect to spring-loaded terminals, caps or screws. Left- and right-channel output cables *(shown)* from turntable or compact disc player, and left- and right-channel input and output cables *(shown)* to and from audiocassette recorder, connect with phono plugs. A ground wire *(shown)* from turntable connects to the grounding screw. An indoor FM antenna *(shown)* connects with spade lugs to screws. Signal cable from an outdoor antenna may be coaxial, or shielded twin-lead with caps or screws connecting its wire ends; signal cable from the cable system is coaxial. Audio input *(shown)* and output cables to and from videocassette recorder, or audio output cable from television, connect with phono plugs or coaxial connectors.

Ground
To FM dipole antenna
To outlet on receive
To outlet

To outlet

To outdoor antenna or cable company

Television
Signal cable from an outdoor antenna may be coaxial, with a screw-on or push-on connector, or shielded twin-lead, with spade lugs connecting to a matching transformer; signal cable from the cable system is coaxial. Video and audio input cable *(shown)* from the videocassette recorder, and audio output cable to the receiver, may be connected by phono plugs or coaxial connectors.

Videocassette recorder
Signal cable *(shown)* from an outdoor antenna may be coaxial, with a screw-on connector, or shielded twin-lead with a matching-transformer; signal cable from the cable system is coaxial. Video output cable *(shown)* to the television, and audio output cable *(shown)* to the television or receiver, have phono plugs or coaxial connectors.

Many entertainment system problems can be resolved by adjusting cable hookups. Always turn off the units before tampering with their cables. If you must disconnect a cable, tag it first, noting at each end the specific terminal to which it connects; if there is more than one wire or connector at the end of the cable, tag each one. Cable connections at a splitter box, which routes a signal to more than one unit, should be labeled as carefully as those at the entertainment system units.

To tame the profusion of power cords in an entertainment system, install a grounded multiple-outlet plug in the wall outlet. Some are available with a voltage spike protector, which can shield sensitive electronic equipment from power surges. First check your fuse box or circuit breaker panel to make sure the circuit can handle the load, especially if other household appliances will be running at the same time. Do not use extension cords; reposition the units instead, if necessary.

Once you eliminate cable hookups as the source of a problem, service the unit itself. First refer carefully to the Emergency Guide *(page 8)* and Tools and Techniques *(page 126)*. Then consult the unit's chapter; pay special attention to the introduction and familiarize yourself with the exploded diagram before beginning work.

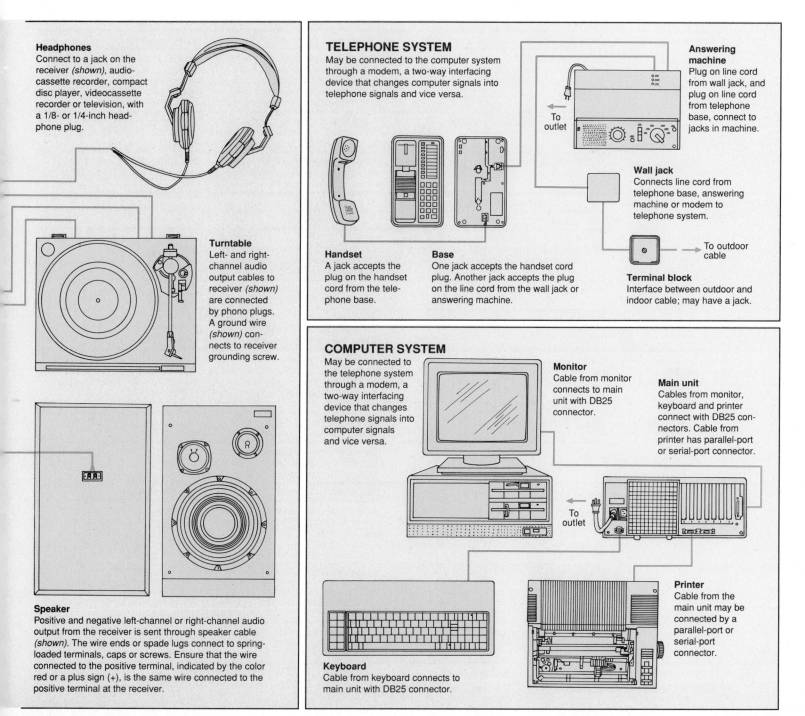

Headphones
Connect to a jack on the receiver *(shown)*, audio-cassette recorder, compact disc player, videocassette recorder or television, with a 1/8- or 1/4-inch headphone plug.

Turntable
Left- and right-channel audio output cables to receiver *(shown)* are connected by phono plugs. A ground wire *(shown)* connects to receiver grounding screw.

Speaker
Positive and negative left-channel or right-channel audio output from the receiver is sent through speaker cable *(shown)*. The wire ends or spade lugs connect to spring-loaded terminals, caps or screws. Ensure that the wire connected to the positive terminal, indicated by the color red or a plus sign (+), is the same wire connected to the positive terminal at the receiver.

TELEPHONE SYSTEM
May be connected to the computer system through a modem, a two-way interfacing device that changes computer signals into telephone signals and vice versa.

To outlet

Answering machine
Plug on line cord from wall jack, and plug on line cord from telephone base, connect to jacks in machine.

Handset
A jack accepts the plug on the handset cord from the telephone base.

Base
One jack accepts the handset cord plug. Another jack accepts the plug on the line cord from the wall jack or answering machine.

Wall jack
Connects line cord from telephone base, answering machine or modem to telephone system.

To outdoor cable

Terminal block
Interface between outdoor and indoor cable; may have a jack.

COMPUTER SYSTEM
May be connected to the telephone system through a modem, a two-way interfacing device that changes telephone signals into computer signals and vice versa.

Monitor
Cable from monitor connects to main unit with DB25 connector.

Main unit
Cables from monitor, keyboard and printer connect with DB25 connectors. Cable from printer has parallel-port or serial-port connector.

To outlet

Keyboard
Cable from keyboard connects to main unit with DB25 connector.

Printer
Cable from the main unit may be connected by a parallel-port or serial-port connector.

TROUBLESHOOTING GUIDE

SYMPTOM	POSSIBLE CAUSE	PROCEDURE
AUDIO ENTERTAINMENT SYSTEMS		
No display lights, no sound	Receiver and/or other unit unplugged or turned off	Plug in and turn on receiver and/or audiocassette recorder, turntable or compact disc player
	Remote control dirty or faulty	Service remote control *(p. 136)* □○
	No power to outlet or outlet faulty	Reset breaker or replace fuse *(p. 10)* □○; have outlet serviced
	Receiver, audiocassette recorder, turntable or compact disc player faulty	Service receiver *(p. 18)* or audiocassette recorder *(p. 28)* or turntable *(p. 42)* or compact disc player *(p. 52)*
Display lights, but no sound	Receiver and/or audiocassette recorder, turntable or compact disc player controls set incorrectly	Adjust receiver and/or audiocassette recorder, turntable or compact disc player controls; in particular, check receiver volume and tape-monitor controls
	Receiver, audiocassette recorder, turntable or compact disc player faulty	Adjust receiver selector control to other modes. If there is sound, service audiocassette recorder *(p. 28)*, turntable *(p. 42)* or compact disc player *(p. 52)*; if no sound, service receiver *(p. 18)*
Sound from only one speaker channel	Receiver controls set incorrectly	Adjust receiver controls; in particular, check balance control
	Cable hookup faulty between speaker and receiver or between receiver and audio-cassette recorder, turntable or compact disc player	Adjust receiver selector control to other modes. If there is sound from both speaker channels, check cable hookups between receiver and audiocassette recorder, turntable or compact disc player *(p. 16)* □○; if there is still sound from only one speaker channel, check cable hookups between speakers and receiver *(p. 16)* □○
	Audiocassette recorder, turntable or compact disc player faulty	Adjust receiver selector control to other modes. If there is sound from both speaker channels, service audiocassette recorder *(p. 28)*, turntable *(p. 42)* or compact disc player *(p. 52)*
	Speaker or receiver faulty	Reverse receiver left- and right-channel cable connections. If no sound from same speaker, service speaker *(p. 60)*; if no sound from other speaker, service receiver *(p. 18)*
Sound intermittent or distorted from the radio	Receiver tuner control set incorrectly	Adjust receiver tuner control
	Antenna positioned incorrectly	Adjust antenna
	Cable hookup faulty between speaker and receiver or between receiver and antenna or cable system	Adjust receiver selector control to other modes. If sound is OK, check cable hookups between receiver and antenna or cable system *(p. 16)* □○; if sound not OK, check cable hookups between speakers and receiver *(p. 16)* □○
	Antenna or cable system faulty	Adjust receiver selector control to other modes. If sound is OK, service antenna or cable system *(p. 76)*
	Speaker or receiver faulty	Reverse receiver left- and right-channel cable connections. If sound not OK from same speaker, service speaker *(p. 60)*; if sound not OK from other speaker, service receiver *(p. 18)*
Sound intermittent or distorted from the audiocassette recorder, turntable or compact disc player	Cable hookup faulty between speaker and receiver or between receiver and audio-cassette recorder, turntable, or compact disc player	Adjust receiver selector control to other modes. If sound is OK, check cable hookups between receiver and audiocassette recorder, turntable or compact disc player *(p. 16)* □○; if sound not OK, check cable hookups between speakers and receiver *(p. 16)* □○
	Audiocassette recorder, turntable or compact disc player faulty	Adjust receiver selector control to other modes. If sound is OK, service audiocassette recorder *(p. 28)*, turntable *(p. 42)* or compact disc player *(p. 52)*
	Speaker or receiver faulty	Reverse receiver left- and right-channel cable connections. If sound not OK from same speaker, service speaker *(p. 60)*; if sound not OK from other speaker, service receiver *(p. 18)*
Humming, buzzing or rumbling noise	Speaker vibrating or too close to turntable	Reposition speakers
	Cable hookup faulty between speaker and receiver, or between receiver and antenna or cable system, or between receiver and audiocassette recorder, turntable or compact disc player	Adjust receiver selector control to other modes. If sound is OK, check cable hookups between receiver and antenna or cable system *(p. 16)* □○ or between receiver and audiocassette recorder, turntable or compact disc player *(p. 16)* □○; if sound not OK, check cable hookups between speakers and receiver *(p. 16)* □○
	Ground wire hookup faulty	Check ground wire hookups *(p. 17)* □○
	Antenna or cable system (radio), or audio-cassette recorder, turntable or compact disc player faulty	Adjust receiver selector control to other modes. If sound is OK, service antenna or cable system *(p. 76)* or audiocassette recorder *(p. 28)*, turntable *(p. 42)* or compact disc player *(p. 52)*
	Speaker or receiver faulty	Reverse receiver left- and right-channel cable connections. If sound not OK from same speaker, service speaker *(p. 60)*; if sound not OK from other speaker, service receiver *(p. 18)*

DEGREE OF DIFFICULTY: □ Easy ◫ Moderate ■ Complex
ESTIMATED TIME: ○ Less than 1 hour ◖ 1 to 3 hours ● Over 3 hours

TROUBLESHOOTING GUIDE

SYMPTOM	POSSIBLE CAUSE	PROCEDURE
VIDEO ENTERTAINMENT SYSTEMS		
No display lights, no picture and no sound	Television or videocassette recorder unplugged or turned off	Plug in and turn on television and videocassette recorder
	Cable converter unplugged	Plug in converter
	No power to outlet or outlet faulty	Reset breaker or replace fuse (p. 10) □○; have outlet serviced
	Television or videocassette recorder faulty	Service television (p. 68) or videocassette recorder (p. 88)
Display lights, but no picture and no sound	Television or videocassette recorder controls set incorrectly	Adjust television and videocassette recorder controls; in particular, check channel selector controls
	Television or videocassette recorder faulty	Turn off videocassette recorder and tune in television. If still no picture and no sound, service television (p. 68); if there are picture and sound, service videocassette recorder (p. 88)
Picture, but no sound	Television or receiver controls set incorrectly	Adjust television and receiver controls; in particular, check television and receiver volume controls and receiver tape-monitor control
	Audio cable hookup faulty between television and videocassette recorder, or between one of these units and receiver	Check audio cable hookups between television and videocassette recorder, and between receiver and television or videocassette recorder (p. 16) □○
	Receiver faulty	Adjust receiver selector control to other modes. If no sound, service receiver (p. 18)
	Television or videocassette recorder faulty	Turn off videocassette recorder and tune in television. If still no sound, service television (p. 68); if there is sound, service videocassette recorder (p. 88)
Sound, but no picture	Television or videocassette recorder controls set incorrectly	Adjust television and videocassette recorder controls; in particular, check television brightness and contrast controls
	Video cable hookup faulty between television and videocassette recorder	Check video cable hookups between television and videocassette recorder (p. 16) □○
	Television or videocassette recorder faulty	Turn off videocassette recorder and tune in television. If still no picture, service television (p. 68); if there is picture, service videocassette recorder (p. 88)
Sound from only one speaker channel	Television or receiver controls set incorrectly	Adjust television and receiver controls; in particular, balance controls
	Audio cable hookup faulty between television and videocassette recorder, or between receiver and television or videocassette recorder, or cable hookup faulty between receiver and speaker	Adjust receiver selector control to other modes. If there is sound from both speaker channels, check audio cable hookups between television and videocassette recorder and between receiver and television or videocassette recorder (p. 16) □○; if there is still sound from only one speaker channel, check cable hookups between receiver and speakers (p. 16) □○
	Television or videocassette recorder faulty	Turn off videocassette recorder and tune in television. If there is sound from both speaker channels, service videocassette recorder (p. 88); if still sound from one speaker channel, service television (p. 68)
	Speaker or receiver faulty	See audio entertainment systems (p. 14)
Picture and sound intermittent or distorted	Antenna positioned incorrectly	Adjust antenna
	Cable hookup faulty between antenna or cable system and television or videocassette recorder	Check cable hookups between antenna or cable system and television or videocassette recorder (p. 16) □○
	Antenna or cable system, television or videocassette recorder faulty	Service videocassette recorder (p. 88), television (p. 68) or antenna or cable system (p. 76)
Picture intermittent or distorted	Video cable hookup faulty between television and videocassette recorder	Check video cable hookups between television and videocassette recorder (p. 16) □○
	Television or videocassette recorder faulty	Turn off videocassette recorder and tune in television. If still no picture, service television (p. 68); if there is picture, service videocassette recorder (p. 88)
Sound intermittent or distorted	Audio cable hookup faulty between television and videocassette recorder, or between receiver and television or videocassette recorder, or cable hookup faulty between receiver and speaker	Adjust receiver selector control to other modes. If sound is OK, check audio cable hookups between television and videocassette recorder, and between receiver and television or videocassette recorder (p. 16) □○; if sound not OK, check cable hookups between receiver and speakers (p. 16) □○
	Television or videocassette recorder faulty	Turn off videocassette recorder and tune in television. If still no sound, service television (p. 68); if there is sound, service videocassette recorder (p. 88)
	Speaker or receiver faulty	See audio entertainment systems (p. 14)

DEGREE OF DIFFICULTY: □ Easy ▣ Moderate ■ Complex
ESTIMATED TIME: ○ Less than 1 hour ◑ 1 to 3 hours ● Over 3 hours

SERVICING CABLE HOOKUPS

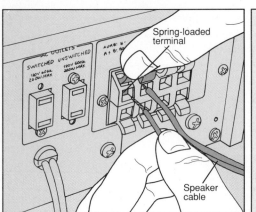

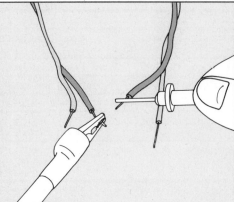

Checking speaker cable connections.
Press the tabs *(far left)* or loosen the caps or screws and remove the cable wire ends or spade lugs from the speaker and receiver terminals. If a wire end or spade lug is damaged, repair it *(page 132)*. Set a multitester to test continuity *(page 128)*. Clip one probe to a wire and touch the other probe in turn to each wire at the other end *(near left)*; there should be continuity only once. Test the other wire the same way. If the cable tests faulty, replace it *(page 131)*. If the cable tests OK, reconnect it. Press the tabs and insert the wires; at cap or screw terminals, wrap the wires clockwise and tighten them.

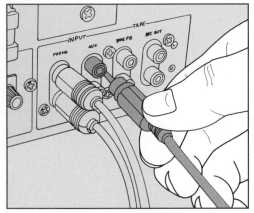

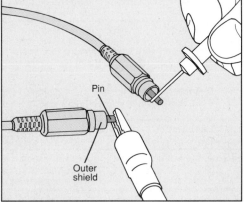

Checking phono cable connections. Pull the plugs out of the jacks on both units *(far left)*. If the center pin or outer shield is damaged, replace the plug *(page 133)*. Clean the plugs and jacks *(page 17)*. Set a multitester to test continuity *(page 128)*. To test each plug, clip one probe to its center pin and touch the other probe to its outer shield; there should be no continuity. If either plug tests faulty, replace it *(page 133)*. To test the cable, clip or touch a probe to each center pin *(near left)*, then to each shield; there should be continuity both times. If the cable tests faulty, replace it *(page 131)*. Push each plug firmly into its jack.

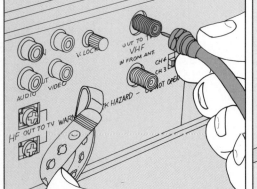

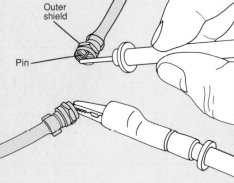

Checking coaxial cable connections. Unscrew or pull off the connectors at both ends *(far left)*. If the center pin or the outer shield is damaged, replace it *(page 133)*. Clean the connectors and terminals *(page 17)*. Set a multitester to test continuity *(page 128)*. To test each connector, clip a probe to the center pin and touch the other probe to the outer shield; there should be no continuity. If a connector tests faulty, replace it *(page 133)*. To test the cable, clip or touch a probe to each center pin *(near left)*, then to each shield; there should be continuity both times. Replace a faulty cable *(page 131)*. Screw or push each connector onto its terminal.

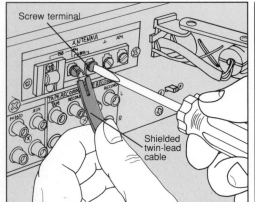

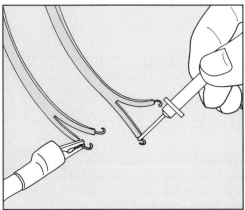

Checking shielded twin-lead cable connections. Loosen the caps or screws *(far left)* and remove the cable wire ends or spade lugs from the terminals on both units. If a wire end or spade lug is damaged, repair it *(page 132)*. Set a multitester to test continuity *(page 128)*. Clip one probe to a wire at one end of the cable and touch the other probe in turn to each wire at the other end *(near left)*; there should be continuity once—and only once. Test again at the other wire. If the cable tests faulty, replace it *(page 131)*. If the cable tests OK, reconnect it. Wrap the wires clockwise around the terminals and tighten the caps or screws.

CLEANING CONNECTIONS

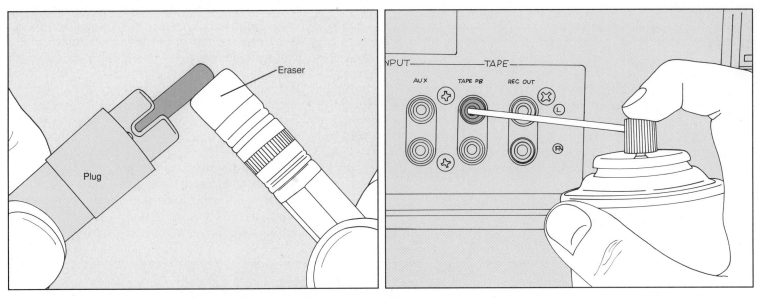

Cleaning cable connectors and unit terminals. To clean a plug connector, use the eraser end of a pencil. Rub thoroughly around the outer shield and along the center pin *(above, left)*; apply only moderate pressure to avoid bending the pin. Clear away particles by spraying electronic contact cleaner or compressed air into the connector, or use a foam swab moistened with denatured alcohol. Use the pencil eraser as well to clean any accessible contact points on the terminal. To clean inside the terminal, spray short bursts of electronic contact cleaner or compressed air through the opening *(above, right)*.

SERVICING GROUND WIRE CONNECTIONS

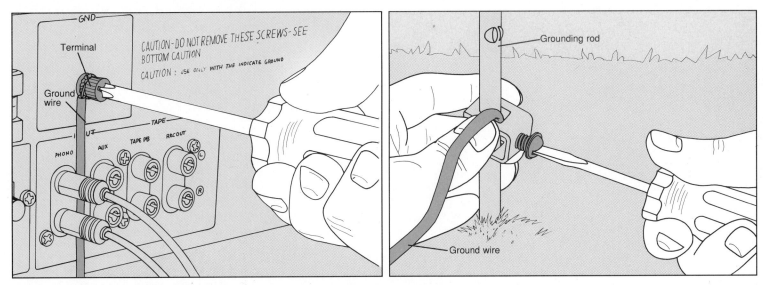

Checking indoor and outdoor ground connections. Carefully inspect ground wire connections, both to troubleshoot problems and as a preventive measure. A loose or damaged ground wire can be an annoying source of humming noise. It can also be a hazard in the event a circuit is shorted or a cable is struck by lightning. Tighten a loose turntable ground wire at its terminal on the receiver *(above, left)*. Tighten the outdoor ground wire from the antenna system discharger or grounding block at the discharger or the grounding block, as well as at the grounding rod *(above, right)*. Repair any damaged wire end or spade lug *(page 132)*. To test a ground wire, set a multitester to test continuity *(page 128)*, disconnect one end of the wire and touch a probe to each end of the wire. If the ground wire does not have continuity, replace it *(page 132)*. Be sure to run an outdoor ground wire in the shortest and straightest possible path.

RECEIVERS

The cortex of most sophisticated audio systems is a receiver *(below)*, an integrated unit consisting of an analog or digital tuner, a preamplifier and a power amplifier. From the tuner, or from an auxiliary unit such as the turntable through cables hooked up to the receiver, the preamplifier accepts the incoming signal, amplifies it and routes it to the power amplifier. There, the signal is further strengthened and sent out through cables, usually to the speakers. Despite a jungle of cords and cables, receiver problems can be logically deduced from their symptoms. Consult the Troubleshooting Guide in Entertainment Systems *(page 14)* first, and then the one in this chapter *(page 19)*.

Often, problems can be remedied by adjusting cable hookups or by cleaning switches and potentiometers. Sometimes a wire may be loose or broken, or a component may test defective.

Cleaning materials, and most replacement components, are readily available from an electronics parts supplier. Special parts may have to be ordered from the manufacturer.

A set of small screwdrivers, a multitester and a soldering iron make up the basic tool kit for receiver repairs *(page 126)*. Refer to Tools & Techniques for tips on disassembly and reassembly *(page 141)*, instructions for testing continuity, resistance and voltage *(pages 128-129)*, and directions for desoldering and soldering *(pages 130-131)*.

Before attempting any repair to the receiver, turn it off and unplug it. Disconnect the cables and wires hooked up to it and set it on a clean work table. Store fasteners and other small parts in labeled containers and write down the sequence of disassembly steps. Perform a cold check for leaking voltage *(page 141)* after reassembling the receiver but before plugging it back in.

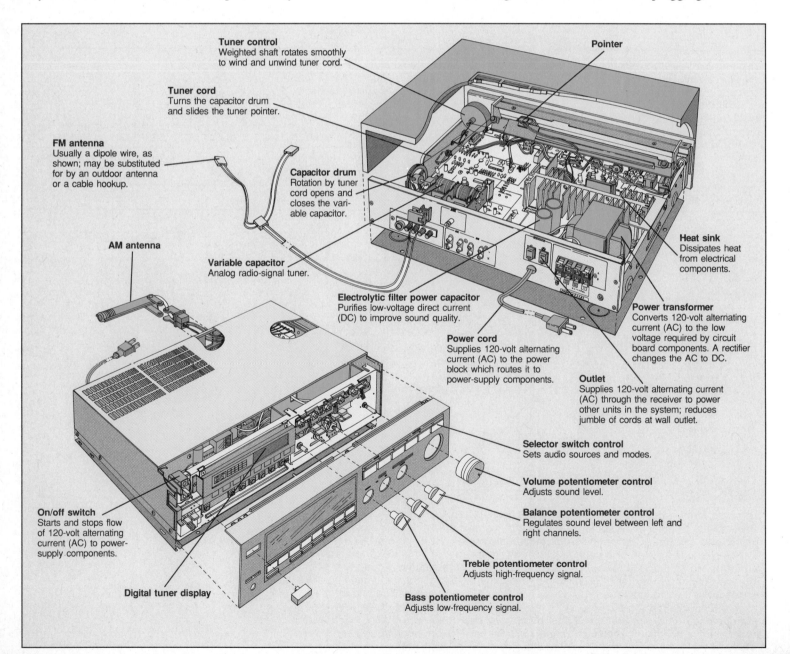

Tuner control
Weighted shaft rotates smoothly to wind and unwind tuner cord.

Pointer

Tuner cord
Turns the capacitor drum and slides the tuner pointer.

FM antenna
Usually a dipole wire, as shown; may be substituted for by an outdoor antenna or a cable hookup.

Capacitor drum
Rotation by tuner cord opens and closes the variable capacitor.

AM antenna

Heat sink
Dissipates heat from electrical components.

Variable capacitor
Analog radio-signal tuner.

Electrolytic filter power capacitor
Purifies low-voltage direct current (DC) to improve sound quality.

Power transformer
Converts 120-volt alternating current (AC) to the low voltage required by circuit board components. A rectifier changes the AC to DC.

Power cord
Supplies 120-volt alternating current (AC) to the power block which routes it to power-supply components.

Outlet
Supplies 120-volt alternating current (AC) through the receiver to power other units in the system; reduces jumble of cords at wall outlet.

Selector switch control
Sets audio sources and modes.

Volume potentiometer control
Adjusts sound level.

On/off switch
Starts and stops flow of 120-volt alternating current (AC) to power-supply components.

Balance potentiometer control
Regulates sound level between left and right channels.

Digital tuner display

Treble potentiometer control
Adjusts high-frequency signal.

Bass potentiometer control
Adjusts low-frequency signal.

TROUBLESHOOTING GUIDE

SYMPTOM	POSSIBLE CAUSE	PROCEDURE
No display lights, no sound	Receiver unplugged or turned off	Plug in and turn on receiver
	Remote control dirty or faulty	Service remote control (p. 136) □○
	No power to outlet or outlet faulty	Reset breaker or replace fuse (p. 10) □○; have outlet serviced
	Power cord faulty	Test and replace power cord (p. 137) □○
	Power fuse blown	Test and replace power fuse (p. 23) □○
	On/off switch faulty	Test and replace on/off switch (p. 25) □○
	Power supply faulty	Service power supply (p. 26) ■◒
	Circuit board faulty	Take receiver for professional service
Display lights, no sound	Receiver controls incorrectly set	Adjust receiver controls
	Auxiliary unit faulty	Troubleshoot entertainment system (p. 14) □○
	Selector switch or circuit board faulty	Take receiver for professional service
Sound, no display lights	Display lights faulty	Replace display lights (p. 134) □○
Sound from only one channel	Receiver controls incorrectly set	Adjust receiver controls
	Speaker or auxiliary unit faulty	Troubleshoot entertainment system (p. 14) □○
	Volume or balance control potentiometer dirty or faulty	Clean potentiometer (p. 24) □○; test and replace potentiometer (p. 24) ◪◒
	Circuit board faulty	Take receiver for professional service
Intermittent sound from an auxiliary unit	Speaker or auxiliary unit faulty	Troubleshoot entertainment system (p. 14) □○
	Volume or balance control potentiometer dirty or faulty	Clean potentiometer (p. 24) □○; test and replace potentiometer (p. 24) ◪◒
	Circuit board faulty	Take receiver for professional service
Intermittent sound from the radio	Tuner control set incorrectly	Adjust tuner control
	Antenna positioned incorrectly	Adjust antenna
	Speaker or cable system faulty	Troubleshoot entertainment system (p. 14) □○
	Variable capacitor dirty	Clean variable capacitor (p. 22) □○
	Antenna loose or faulty	Check FM antenna wire connections; test and replace AM antenna (p. 22) □○
	Circuit board faulty	Take receiver for professional service
Humming noise	Auxiliary unit faulty	Troubleshoot entertainment system (p. 14) □○
	Electrolytic filter power capacitor faulty	Test and replace electrolytic filter power capacitor (p. 27) ◪○
Analog tuner control erratic or doesn't work	Tuner pulleys sticking or tuner cord slipping	Service tuner (p. 20) □○
	Tuner cord loose or broken	Restring tuner (p. 21) ◪◒
Scratching noise when analog tuner control is adjusted	Variable capacitor dirty	Clean variable capacitor (p. 22) □○
	Variable capacitor or circuit board faulty	Take receiver for professional service
Scratching noise when selector control is adjusted; background noise from another unit	Selector switch dirty	Clean selector switch (p. 23) □○
	Selector switch or circuit board faulty	Take receiver for professional service
Volume, balance or tone control abrupt, scratchy or doesn't work	Speaker faulty	Troubleshoot entertainment system (p. 14) □○
	Control potentiometer dirty or faulty	Clean potentiometer (p. 24) □○; test and replace potentiometer (p. 24) ◪◒
	Circuit board faulty	Take receiver for professional service
Burning odor	Air vents blocked or dirty	Reposition receiver or clean air vents
	Heat sink dirty	Clean heat sink
	Power fuse blown	Test and replace power fuse (p. 23) □○
	Power supply faulty	Service power supply (p. 26) ■◒
	Electrolytic filter power capacitor faulty	Test and replace electrolytic filter power capacitor (p. 27) ◪○
	Circuit board faulty	Take receiver for professional service

DEGREE OF DIFFICULTY: □ Easy ◪ Moderate ■ Complex
ESTIMATED TIME: ○ Less than 1 hour ◒ 1 to 3 hours ● Over 3 hours

ACCESS TO THE COMPONENTS

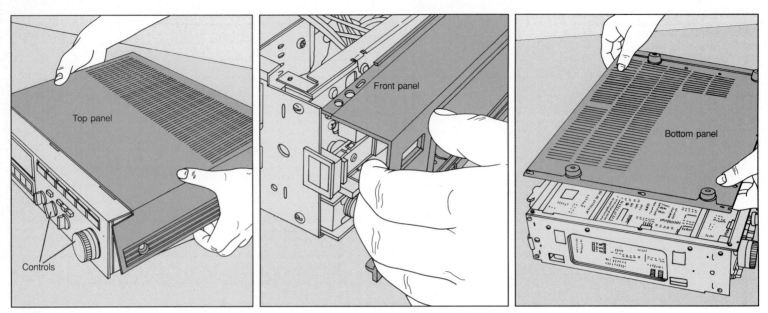

Removing and reinstalling top, front and bottom panels. Turn off the receiver, unplug it from the wall outlet and disconnect the cables and ground wire hooked up to it *(page 12)*. Top panel screws are usually located on the sides, and sometimes on the back or bottom. Unscrew the top panel, slide it out from under any lip on the front panel and lift it off the receiver frame *(above, left)*. Pull off or unscrew any controls too large to fit through the front panel. Front panel screws may be at the top, sides or bottom. Unscrew the front panel and gently pry it away from the frame *(above, center)*. Turn over the receiver. The bottom panel screws are on the edges and sometimes in the feet. Unscrew the bottom panel and lift it off the frame *(above, right)*. After working on the receiver, reverse this sequence to reinstall the panels, then cold check for leaking voltage *(page 141)*. Reconnect the cables *(page 16)* and ground wire *(page 17)*, plug in the receiver and turn it on.

SERVICING THE DIAL TUNER

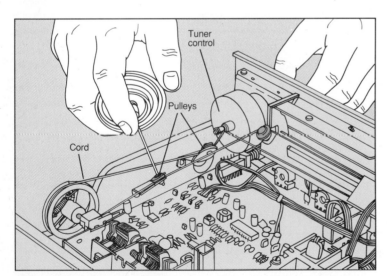

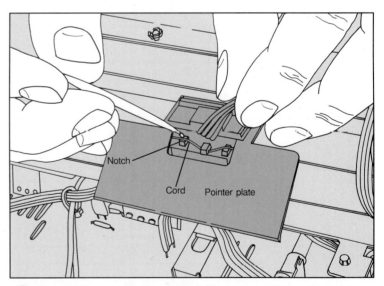

1 **Lubricating the pulleys and rail.** Remove the top panel *(step above)*. Rotate the tuner control, checking the motion of the tuner cord and the tuner pointer inside the receiver. If the tuner cord is loose or broken, restring the tuner *(page 21)*. If the tuner cord does not travel easily, spray a tiny amount of silicone-based lubricant on the axles of the tuner pulleys, avoiding contact with the tuner cord. Work in the lubricant by rotating the tuner control *(above)*. Use a clean cloth to rub a little of the same lubricant on the pointer rail. If the tuner cord travels easily but the tuner pointer does not slide smoothly, reset the pointer *(step 2)*. When the tuner cord travels easily and the tuner pointer slides smoothly, reinstall the top panel *(step above)*.

2 **Resetting the pointer.** Unhook the tuner cord from the notches or clips on the pointer plate. Rotate the tuner control fully in one direction, then slide the pointer by hand fully in the same direction. Rethread the tuner cord snugly through the notches or clips on the pointer plate. Secure the tuner cord to the pointer plate by applying a small dab of nail polish to each notch *(above)* or by pressing down the clips with a small screwdriver. Reinstall the top panel *(step above)*.

RESTRINGING THE DIAL TUNER

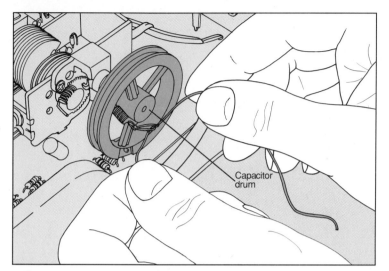

1 **Tying on cord at the capacitor drum.** Remove the top panel *(page 20)* and check inside the receiver for a sketch of the tuner cord route. If there is no sketch, draw one as complete as possible, noting the sequence and the direction and number of turns the tuner cord makes around each component. If the tuner cord route cannot be determined, consult the receiver manufacturer, or attempt to retrace the route using a replacement tuner cord of about the same length. Undo the knots securing the damaged tuner cord to the capacitor spring and remove the cord. Purchase the required length of tuner cord at an electronics parts supplier. Knot one end of the tuner cord to the capacitor spring *(above)*, then loop it around the capacitor drum. To keep the capacitor drum stationary, turn it fully in the direction of the loop.

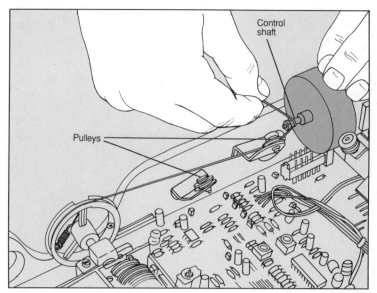

2 **Wrapping cord around the tuner control shaft.** Following the direction and number of turns noted in the sketch, wrap the tuner cord tautly around the tuner pulleys on the route to the tuner control shaft; if you are proceeding without a sketch, start by assuming once around each pulley in the same direction as the initial loop around the capacitor drum. Wrap the tuner cord around the tuner control shaft the direction and number of turns noted *(above)*. In most instances, at least two or three turns are required in the same direction as the initial loop around the capacitor drum, to allow the pointer to travel the full length of the tuner dial.

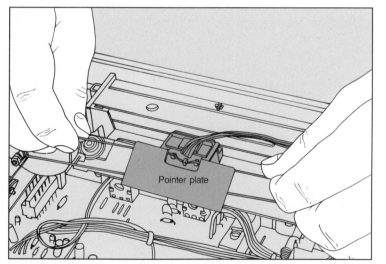

3 **Threading cord through the tuner pointer.** Pull the tuner cord across the back of the front panel, feeding it under the pointer plate. Still following the direction and number of turns noted in the sketch, wrap the tuner cord tautly around the tuner pulley at the end of the dial farthest from the tuner control shaft. Slide the pointer by hand as close as possible to the tuner control shaft. Pull the tuner cord to the pointer and thread it through the notches or clips on the pointer plate *(above)*. Finally, wrap the tuner cord around the tuner pulley at the end of the dial closest to the tuner control shaft and pull the cord back to the capacitor drum, wrapping it around any other pulleys indicated in the sketch.

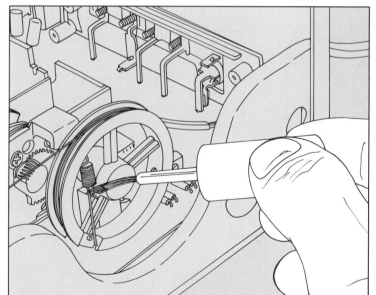

4 **Tying off cord at the capacitor drum.** Wrap the tuner cord once around the capacitor drum in the direction opposite to the initial loop. If the new tuner cord ends up much shorter or longer than the old tuner cord, retrace the route taken and look for errors. If the new tuner cord ends up about the same length as the old tuner cord, tie the cord to the capacitor spring, cut off any excess and apply a small dab of nail polish *(above)*. Rotate the tuner control to ensure that the capacitor blades can open and close fully and that the pointer can travel the full length of the tuner dial; if required, reset the pointer *(page 20)*. Reinstall the top panel *(page 20)*.

SERVICING THE VARIABLE CAPACITOR

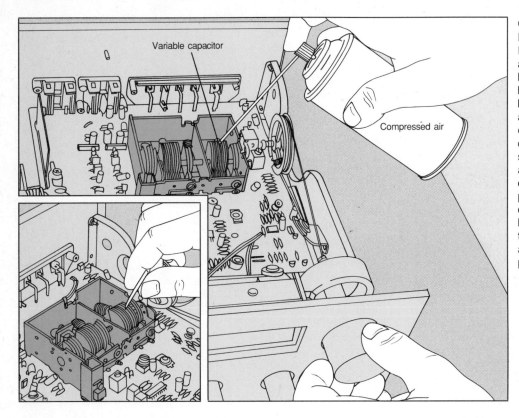

Cleaning a variable capacitor.
Remove the top panel *(page 20)*. Rotate the tuner control as shown, and inspect the variable capacitor blades for dirt or dust. To clean the blades, spray them carefully with short bursts of compressed air *(left)*, or apply a small amount of tuner cleaner or electronic contact cleaner. Use tuner cleaner and electronic contact cleaner sparingly, however; they tend to leave a slight sticky residue that traps dirt and dust. If necessary, gently use a toothpick or a folded sheet of paper to dislodge particles from between the blades *(inset)*. To dislodge particles that are difficult to reach, try using a vacuum cleaner. Reinstall the top panel *(page 20)*.

SERVICING THE AM ANTENNA

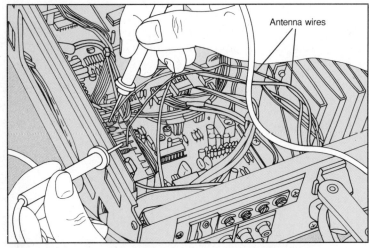

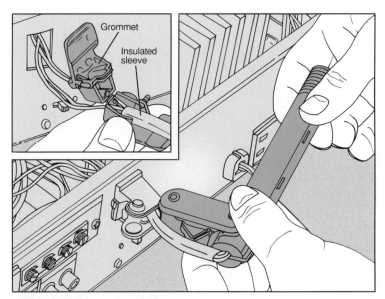

1 **Testing the antenna.** Remove the top panel *(page 20)* and locate the antenna wire terminals on the circuit board. If a wire is loose or broken, repair the wire connection *(page 132)*. Set a multitester to test continuity *(page 128)*. Touch one probe to one antenna wire terminal on the circuit board and touch the other probe in turn to each of the other antenna wire terminals *(above)*. The multitester should register continuity at least once. Repeat this step to test each terminal against each other terminal. If the multitester does not register the correct results, replace the antenna *(step 2)*. If the multitester shows that the antenna is OK, reinstall the top panel *(page 20)*.

2 **Replacing the antenna.** If the circuit board is not coded to the antenna wire colors, note the wire contact points. Desolder the wires from the circuit board *(page 130)* and pull the antenna off the grommet *(above)*. Pry the grommet off the back panel, open it and slip out the wires *(inset)*. Order an exact replacement antenna from the receiver manufacturer. Slide the open grommet onto the wires, pressing it against the insulated sleeve. Close the grommet and thread the wires through the opening in the back panel. Fit the grommet into the back panel and push the antenna onto the grommet. Solder the wires to the circuit board *(page 131)*. Reinstall the top panel *(page 20)*.

REPLACING THE POWER FUSE

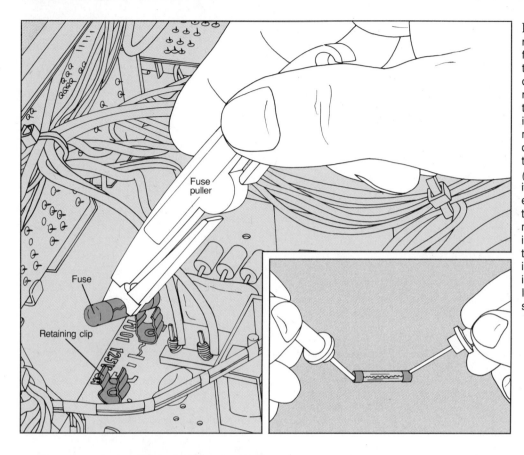

Removing and testing the fuse. Turn off the receiver and unplug it from the wall outlet. If the fuse is externally mounted in the back panel, turn the fuse cap counterclockwise and pull the fuse out of its casing. If the fuse is located inside the receiver, remove the top panel *(page 20)*. Grasp the fuse with a fuse puller and gently pry it out of its retaining clips *(left)*. To test either fuse, set a multitester to test continuity *(page 128)*. Touch one probe to the cap at one end of the fuse and touch the other probe to the cap at the other end *(inset)*. If the multitester does not register continuity, purchase an exact replacement fuse at an electronics parts supplier. If the multitester registers continuity, reinstall the fuse: If the fuse is mounted in the back panel, insert it into the casing, screw the cap into the back panel, plug in the receiver and turn it on. If the fuse is located inside the receiver, gently push it into the retaining clips and reinstall the top panel *(page 20)*. If the fuse blows repeatedly, service the power supply *(page 26)*.

SERVICING THE SELECTOR SWITCH

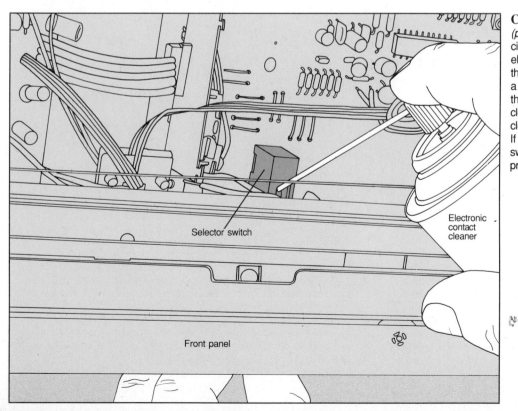

Cleaning the switch. Remove the top panel *(page 20)* and locate the selector switch on the circuit board behind the selector control. Using electronic contact cleaner, direct the nozzle through the opening in the switch casing. Spray a short burst of cleaner into the switch and rotate the selector control fully clockwise and counterclockwise a number of times to work in the cleaner *(left)*. Reinstall the top panel *(page 20)*. If the problem persists, suspect a faulty selector switch or circuit board and take the receiver for professional service.

SERVICING POTENTIOMETERS

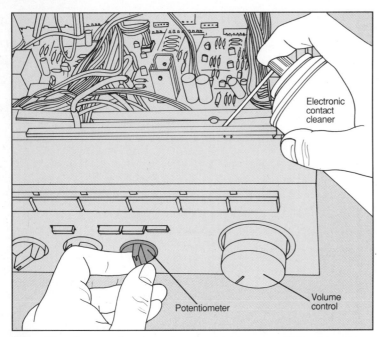

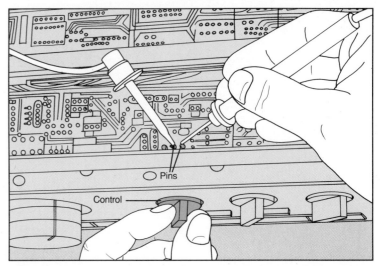

1 **Cleaning a potentiometer.** Remove the top panel *(page 20)* and locate the potentiometer on the circuit board, behind its control. Spray electronic contact cleaner through the openings in the potentiometer casing and rotate the control back and forth to work in the cleaner *(above)*. Reinstall the top panel *(page 20)*. If the problem persists, test the potentiometer *(step 2)*.

2 **Testing a potentiometer.** Remove the top and bottom panels *(page 20)*. Set the control fully left, and set a multitester to test resistance *(page 129)*. If there is one row of pins, hook one probe to the middle pin in the row, and touch the other probe to one of the outer pins in the row. Rotate the control from left to right *(above)*. The multitester should register a variation in ohms as the control is rotated. Reset the control to its left and test the same way between the middle pin and the other outer pin in the row. Again, you should see a variation in ohms. If there are two rows of pins, test each row the same way. If you do not get a variation in ohms each time, replace the potentiometer. If the potentiometer is OK, reinstall the bottom and top panels *(page 20)*.

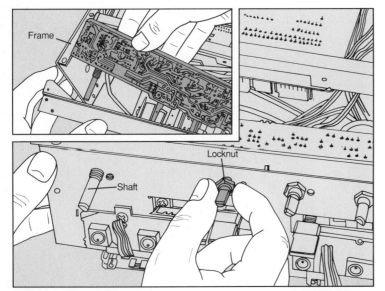

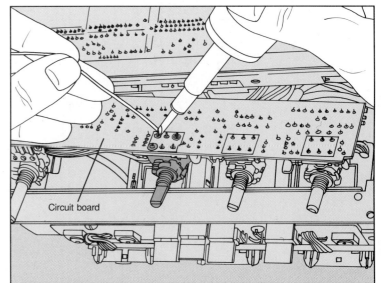

3 **Removing a potentiometer.** To take out the circuit board on which the potentiometer is located, remove the front panel *(page 20)* and unscrew the shaft locknut for each potentiometer on the circuit board *(above)*. Lift out the circuit board, pulling the shafts through the openings in the frame; if necessary, unscrew one end of the frame and pull it out slightly *(inset)*. Desolder the pins of the faulty potentiometer *(page 130)*, turn over the circuit board and gently pry off the potentiometer. Test its resistance again to confirm the potentiometer is faulty *(step 2)*. If the potentiometer tests faulty, replace it *(step 4)*; if it tests OK, suspect a faulty circuit board and take the receiver for service.

4 **Replacing a potentiometer.** Purchase an exact replacement potentiometer at an electronics parts supplier. Gently push the potentiometer pins into the circuit board openings, turn over the circuit board and solder the pins in place *(page 131)*. Slide the potentiometer shafts through the openings in the frame and reposition the circuit board; if required, pull out one end of the frame, then screw it back in place. Screw on the shaft locknuts for each potentiometer. Reinstall the bottom, front and top panels *(page 20)*.

TESTING AND REPLACING THE ON/OFF SWITCH

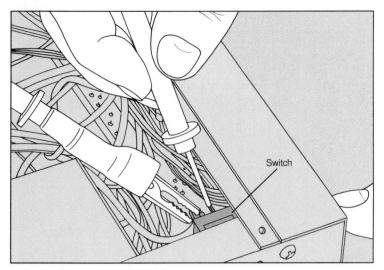

Switch

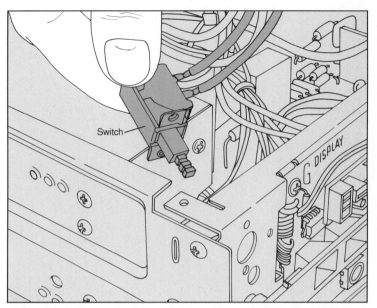

Switch

1 **Testing the switch**. Remove the top panel *(page 20)* and locate the on/off switch terminals. If a wire is loose or broken, repair the wire connection *(page 132)*. Set a multitester to test continuity *(page 128)*. Clip one probe to one switch terminal and touch the other probe to the other switch terminal. Set the switch in the ON position and then in the OFF position *(above)*. The switch should have continuity only in the ON position. If the switch is faulty, remove it *(step 2)*. If the switch tests OK, service the power supply *(page 26)*.

2 **Removing the switch**. Remove the front panel *(page 20)* and pull the control off the on/off switch shaft. Unscrew the on/off switch, pull the shaft through the opening in the frame and lift the switch out of the receiver *(above)*. Desolder the wires from the switch terminals *(page 130)*. To confirm that the on/off switch is faulty, test for continuity again *(step 1)*. If the switch still tests defective, replace it *(step 3)*. If it now tests OK, resolder the wires *(page 131)*, reinstall the on/off switch on the frame, put back the on/off control and service the power supply *(page 26)*.

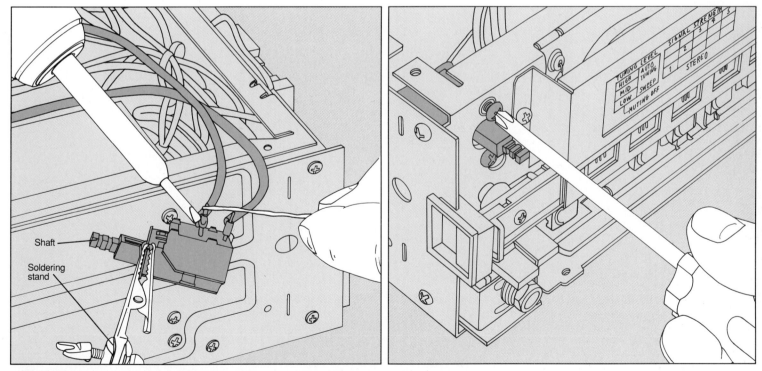

Shaft

Soldering stand

3 **Replacing the switch.** Purchase an exact replacement on/off switch at an electronics parts supplier. Solder the wires to the switch terminals *(page 131)*, using a soldering stand if necessary to keep the switch stationary *(above, left)*. Release the switch from the soldering stand, slip the switch shaft through the opening in the frame and screw the switch in place *(above, right)*. Put back the on/off control and reinstall the front and top panels *(page 20)*.

SERVICING THE POWER SUPPLY

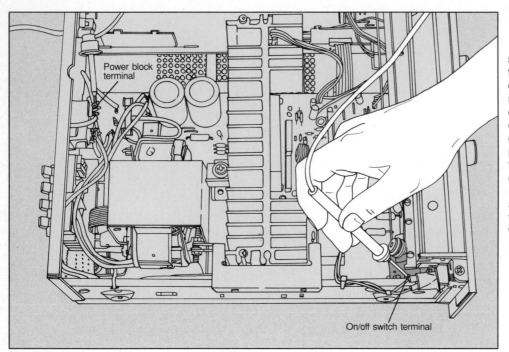

Power block terminal

On/off switch terminal

1 **Testing between the on/off switch and the power block.** Remove the top panel *(page 20)* and identify the power supply components *(page 138)*. Locate the contact points for the two wires that connect the on/off switch terminals to the power block terminals. If a wire is loose or broken, repair the wire connection *(page 132)*. Set a multitester to test continuity *(page 128)*. Clip one probe to one contact point for a wire and touch the other probe to the contact point at the other end of the wire *(left)*. The multitester should register continuity. Repeat this step for the other wire. If the multitester does not register continuity for a wire, replace the wire *(page 132)*. If the multitester registers continuity for each wire, test the wires between the power block and the fuse *(step 2)*.

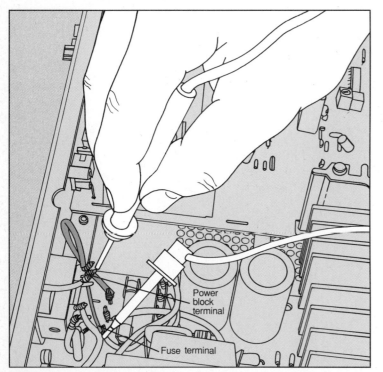

Power block terminal

Fuse terminal

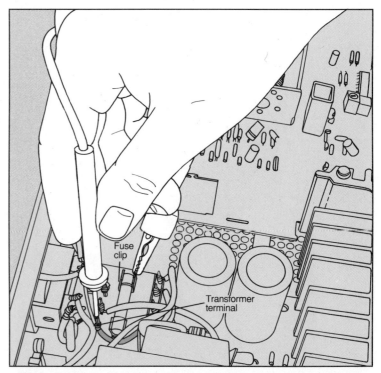

Fuse clip

Transformer terminal

2 **Testing between the fuse and the power block.** Locate the contact points for the two wires connecting the fuse terminals to the power block terminals. If a wire is loose or broken, repair the wire connection *(page 132)*. Set a multitester to test continuity *(page 128)*. Clip one probe to one contact point for a wire and touch the other probe to the contact point at the other end of the wire *(above)*. The multitester should register continuity. Repeat this step for the other wire. If the multitester does not register continuity for a wire, replace the wire *(page 132)*. If the multitester registers continuity for each wire, test the wires to the transformer *(step 3)*.

3 **Testing between the transformer and the fuse.** Locate the contact points for the two wires connecting the transformer to the fuse terminals. If a wire is loose or broken, repair the wire connection *(page 132)*. Set a multitester to test continuity *(page 128)*. Clip one probe to the fuse clip and touch the other probe to the transformer wire terminal *(above)*. The multitester should register continuity. Repeat this step for the other wire. If the multitester does not register continuity, suspect a faulty circuit board and take the receiver for professional service. If the multitester registers continuity, test the transformer *(step 4)*.

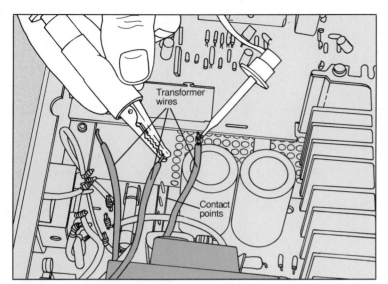

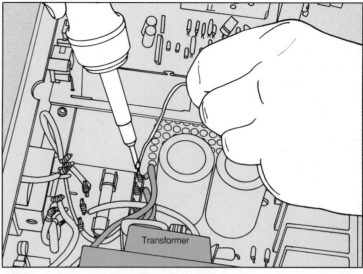

4 **Testing the transformer.** Locate the transformer-wire contact points on the circuit board. If the circuit board is not coded to the wire colors, note the wire positions. Desolder the wires *(page 130)* and isolate them. Set a multitester to test voltage *(page 129)*. Clip one probe to the odd-colored wire and hook the other probe to a matching-colored wire *(above)*; if there is no odd wire, clip the probes to a matching wire pair. Plug in the receiver and turn it on; the multitester should register voltage. Turn off the receiver and unplug it. Repeat this procedure with the odd wire and each other matching wire, or with each matching wire pair. If the multitester does not register voltage, replace the transformer *(step 5)*. If the multitester registers voltage, suspect a faulty circuit board and take the receiver for professional service.

5 **Replacing the transformer.** Tag and desolder *(page 130)* the two transformer wires connecting to fuse terminals, on/off switch terminals or power block terminals *(step 3)*. Unscrew the transformer and remove it from the receiver. Purchase an exact replacement transformer from the manufacturer, or buy a substitute at an electronics parts supplier. Screw in the transformer and solder the wires *(page 131)* to their terminals at the fuse, or the on/off switch, or the power block, and to the circuit board *(above)*. Then reinstall the top panel *(page 20)*.

SERVICING THE ELECTROLYTIC FILTER POWER CAPACITOR

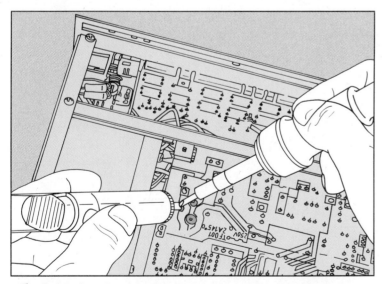

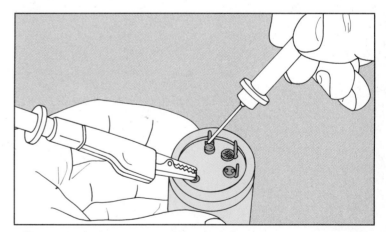

1 **Removing the capacitor.** Remove the top and bottom panels *(page 20)*. Wait 30 minutes for the capacitor to discharge completely any stored voltage. Find the capacitor near the power-supply components. Locate the capacitor contact pins on the circuit board, and carefully note their positions for reassembly. Desolder the pins *(page 130)* from the circuit board *(above)*, turn over the receiver and gently pull the capacitor off the circuit board.

2 **Testing and replacing the capacitor.** Set a multitester to test resistance *(page 129)*. Clip the negative probe to the negative pin and touch the positive probe to each positive pin in turn *(above)*; if there are negative-and-positive pin pairs, test each pair. For each pair, the multitester should register low ohms and then a rise in ohms. If the capacitor tests OK, suspect a faulty circuit board and take the receiver for professional service. If the capacitor is faulty, purchase an exact replacement capacitor at an electronics parts supplier and solder it to the circuit board *(page 131)*. Reinstall the bottom and top panels *(page 20)*.

AUDIOCASSETTE RECORDERS

The audiocassette recorder routes sound in two directions—out of the unit in the play mode and into the unit in the record mode. During the play mode, invisible magnetic tracks on the audiocassette tape are interpreted by the head as electrical current. The current is sent out of the recorder through cables, usually to the receiver and from there to the speakers. During the record mode, electrical current received from another audio unit is "written" by the head as magnetic tracks on the audiocassette tape for later play, when the head will route it back through the receiver and the speakers.

Many recorder problems can be remedied by adjusting cable hookups or by cleaning and demagnetizing the tape travel components. Consult the Troubleshooting Guide in Entertainment Systems *(page 14)* as well as in this chapter *(page 29)*.

Cleaning supplies and most replacement components are available at an electronics parts supplier; a specific motor, however, may have to be ordered from the manufacturer.

Refer to Tools & Techniques for the basic tool kit *(page 126)*, as well as instructions for disassembly and reassembly *(page 140)*, testing continuity and voltage *(pages 128-129)*, and desoldering and soldering *(pages 130-131)*.

Turn off and unplug the audiocassette recorder before any repair. Disconnect the cables hooked up to it and set it on a clean work table. Store fasteners and other small parts in labeled containers and write down the sequence of disassembly steps. Perform a cold check for leaking voltage *(page 141)* after reassembling the audiocassette recorder but before you plug it back in.

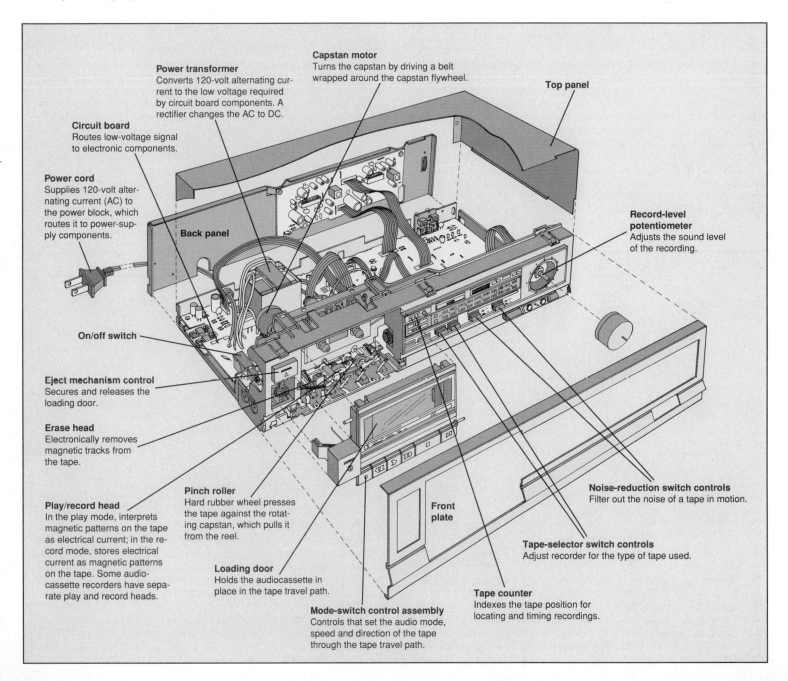

Capstan motor
Turns the capstan by driving a belt wrapped around the capstan flywheel.

Power transformer
Converts 120-volt alternating current to the low voltage required by circuit board components. A rectifier changes the AC to DC.

Top panel

Circuit board
Routes low-voltage signal to electronic components.

Power cord
Supplies 120-volt alternating current (AC) to the power block, which routes it to power-supply components.

Back panel

Record-level potentiometer
Adjusts the sound level of the recording.

On/off switch

Eject mechanism control
Secures and releases the loading door.

Erase head
Electronically removes magnetic tracks from the tape.

Play/record head
In the play mode, interprets magnetic patterns on the tape as electrical current; in the record mode, stores electrical current as magnetic patterns on the tape. Some audiocassette recorders have separate play and record heads.

Pinch roller
Hard rubber wheel presses the tape against the rotating capstan, which pulls it from the reel.

Loading door
Holds the audiocassette in place in the tape travel path.

Front plate

Mode-switch control assembly
Controls that set the audio mode, speed and direction of the tape through the tape travel path.

Noise-reduction switch controls
Filter out the noise of a tape in motion.

Tape-selector switch controls
Adjust recorder for the type of tape used.

Tape counter
Indexes the tape position for locating and timing recordings.

TROUBLESHOOTING GUIDE

SYMPTOM	POSSIBLE CAUSE	PROCEDURE
No display lights, no sound	Audiocassette recorder unplugged or off	Plug in and turn on audiocassette recorder
	No power to outlet or outlet faulty	Reset breaker or replace fuse (p. 10) □○; have outlet serviced
	Power fuse blown	Test and replace power fuse (p. 137) □○
	Power cord faulty	Test and replace power cord (p. 137) □○
	On/off switch faulty	Test and replace on/off switch (p. 40) □○
	Power supply faulty	Service power supply (p. 40) ■○
	Circuit board faulty	Take audiocassette recorder for professional service
Display lights, no sound	Controls set incorrectly	Adjust audiocassette recorder controls
	Audiocassette tape torn or jammed	Splice tape (p. 30) □○; remove jammed tape (p. 32) □○
	Receiver faulty	Troubleshoot entertainment system (p. 14) □○
	Drive belt loose or broken	Service drive belts (p. 33) □○
	Play/record head faulty	Test and replace head (p. 35) □○
	Play/record switch dirty or faulty	Clean play/record switch (p. 38) □○; replace switch (p. 38) ■◐
	Capstan motor faulty	Test and replace capstan motor (p. 41) ◧○
	Circuit board faulty	Take audiocassette recorder for professional service
Sound, no display lights	Display lights faulty	Replace display lights (p. 134) □○
Sound from only one channel	Controls set incorrectly	Adjust audiocassette recorder controls
	Receiver or speaker faulty	Troubleshoot entertainment system (p. 14) □○
	Play/record head faulty	Test and replace play/record head (p. 35) □○
	Record level potentiometer dirty or faulty	Clean potentiometer (p. 39) □○; test and replace (p. 39) ◧○
	Circuit board faulty	Take audiocassette recorder for professional service
Sound intermittent or distorted	Receiver or speaker faulty	Troubleshoot entertainment system (p. 14) □○
	Audiocassette tape damaged	Splice audiocassette tape (p. 30) □○; replace audiocassette
	Tape travel path dirty	Clean and demagnetize tape travel path (p. 30) □○▲
	Play/record head misaligned	Adjust play/record head (p. 33) □○
	Drive belt dirty or loose	Service drive belts (p. 33) □○
	Capstan motor runs too fast or too slow	Adjust capstan motor speed (p. 34) □○
	Pinch roller faulty	Replace pinch roller (p. 34) □○
	Play/record head faulty	Test and replace play/record head (p. 35) □○
	Tape transport assembly dirty	Service tape transport assembly (p. 36) ◧○
	Record level potentiometer dirty or faulty	Clean potentiometer (p. 39) □○; test and replace (p. 39) ◧○
	Tape selector or noise reduction switch dirty or faulty	Clean switch (p. 39) □○; test and replace switch (p. 39) ■◐
	Capstan motor faulty	Test and replace capstan motor (p. 41) ◧○
	Circuit board faulty	Take audiocassette recorder for professional service
Record level control abrupt, scratchy, or doesn't work	Record level potentiometer dirty or faulty	Clean potentiometer (p. 39) □○; test and replace (p. 39) ◧○
	Circuit board faulty	Take audiocassette recorder for professional service
Mode control can't be set or releases prematurely	Play/record switch dirty or faulty	Clean play/record switch (p. 38) □○; replace switch (p. 38) ■◐
	Circuit board faulty	Take audiocassette recorder for professional service
Noise in fast forward, rewind, pause or stop mode	Mute switch faulty	Service mute switch (p. 37) □○
	Circuit board faulty	Take audiocassette recorder for professional service
Audiocassette tape can't be erased or recorded over	Audiocassette safety tab removed	Service audiocassette safety tab (p. 30) □○
	Play/record head misaligned	Adjust play/record head (p. 33) □○
	Erase head faulty	Test and replace erase head (p. 35) □○
	Play/record switch dirty or faulty	Clean play/record switch (p. 38) □○; replace switch (p. 38) ■◐
Loading door doesn't open	Eject mechanism faulty	Service eject mechanism (p. 32) □○
	Audiocassette tape jammed	Remove jammed audiocassette (p. 32) □○

DEGREE OF DIFFICULTY: □ Easy ◧ Moderate ■ Complex
ESTIMATED TIME: ○ Less than 1 hour ◐ 1 to 3 hours ● Over 3 hours   ▲ Special tool required

SERVICING AUDIOCASSETTES

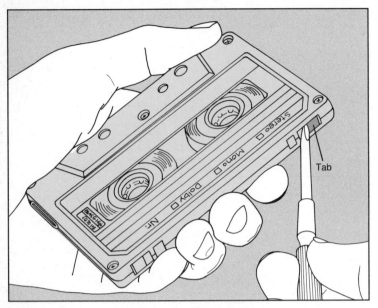

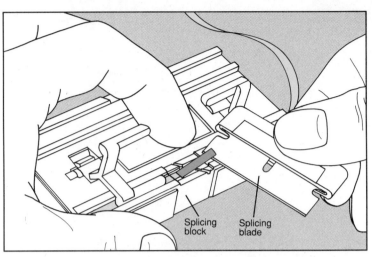

Tab

Splicing block Splicing blade

Removing and restoring the recording safety tabs. Locate the audiocassette safety tabs on the top edge of the housing, usually indicated by arrows on the side edges. To prevent the audiocassette tape from being erased or recorded over, break off each safety tab using a small, flat screwdriver *(above)*; if the safety tab falls into the audiocassette, remove it using long-nose pliers. To erase or record over the audiocassette tape, cover each safety tab opening with a small piece of plastic tape.

Splicing audiocassette tape. Touching the undamaged audiocassette tape as little as possible, snip off a length of rumpled tape with scissors. Slip the tape ends, shiny side up, into a splicing block, overlapping them slightly at the cutting groove. Push down the levers, cutting through the tape ends with the splicing blade, and blow away the tape scraps. Use the blade to slice off 1/2 inch of splicing tape, taking care not to touch the sticky side. Pick up the splicing tape with the blade and center it, sticky side down, across the cut ends of the audiocassette tape *(above)*. Run a foam swab over the splicing tape to press it firmly onto the audiocassette tape. Lift up the levers and remove the audiocassette tape from the splicing block. Turn the audiocassette takeup reel with a pencil to rewind the tape.

SERVICING THE TAPE TRAVEL PATH

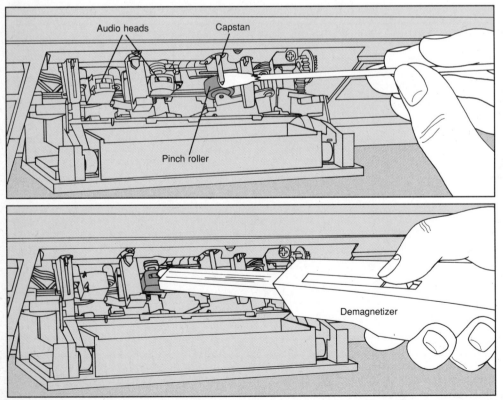

Audio heads   Capstan

Pinch roller

Demagnetizer

Cleaning and demagnetizing the tape travel path. Unload any audiocassette, turn off the audiocassette recorder and unplug it from the outlet. Using a foam swab dipped in denatured alcohol, wipe the audio heads, the capstan and the guides; for easier access to the heads, press the play or pause control. Use a foam swab dipped in rubber-cleaning compound to wipe the pinch roller *(left, top)*, turning it with a finger as you clean.

Purchase a demagnetizer at an electronics parts supplier. Plug the demagnetizer into a wall outlet and turn it on at least 2 feet away from the audiocassette recorder. Slowly bring the demagnetizer within 1/2 inch of an audio head *(left, bottom)*, draw it about 2 feet away and turn it off. Repeat this procedure for the other audio head as well as for the capstan, the guides and any other metal component that contacts an audiocassette. Plug in the audiocassette recorder.

ACCESS TO THE INTERNAL COMPONENTS

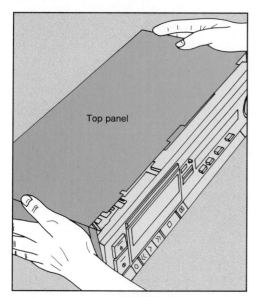

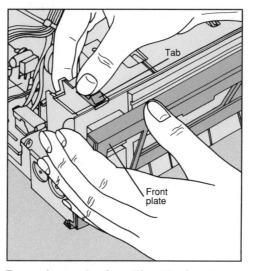

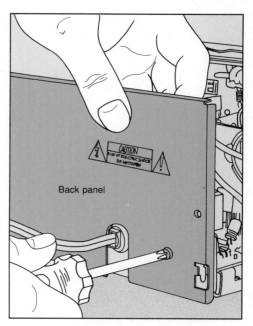

Removing and reinstalling the top panel. Unload any audiocassette, turn off and unplug the audiocassette recorder, and disconnect the cables hooked up to it *(page 12)*. Top panel screws may be located on the sides, back or bottom. Unscrew the top panel, slide it out from under any lip on the front panel and lift it off the frame *(above)*. To reinstall the top panel, slide it under the front panel lip and screw it to the frame. Cold check the audiocassette recorder for leaking voltage *(page 141)*. Reconnect the cables and plug in the audiocassette recorder.

Removing and reinstalling the front plate or panel. Remove the top panel *(left)*. If there is a front plate, check for tabs and screws securing it to the frame. Unscrew the front plate, press in the tabs and pull off the front plate *(above)*. If there is no front plate, unscrew the front panel. Pull off or unscrew any controls too large to fit through their openings, and pull the front panel off the frame. To reinstall the front plate, snap it onto the frame and put back any screws. To reinstall the front panel, screw it onto the frame and put back any controls removed. Reinstall the top panel *(left)*.

Removing and reinstalling the back panel. Remove the top panel *(far left)*. Unscrew the back panel, carefully pull it out from the frame *(above)* and turn it face down, exposing any interior wire connections, such as those leading to the power cord. To reinstall the back panel, set it against the frame and put back the screws. Reinstall the top panel *(far left)*.

ACCESS TO THE TAPE TRAVEL PATH COMPONENTS

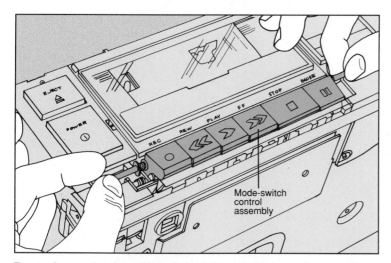

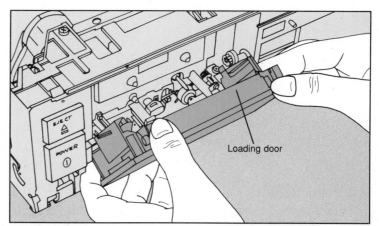

Removing and reinstalling the mode-switch control assembly. Remove the top panel and the front plate or panel *(steps above)*. Press the tabs at each end of the mode-switch control assembly toward each other and pull the assembly off the frame; for easier access, upend the audiocassette recorder *(above)*. Tape the ends of the mode-switch control assembly to prevent losing the washers and springs. Reverse the sequence to reinstall the mode-switch control assembly.

Removing and reinstalling the loading door. Push the eject mechanism control to open the loading door. Check for tabs securing a front plate on the loading door; press in the tabs and slide off the front plate. If there is no front plate, remove the mode-switch control assembly *(left)*. Press the tabs on each side of the loading door toward each other and pull off the loading door *(above)*. Reverse the sequence to reinstall the loading door.

SERVICING THE EJECT MECHANISM

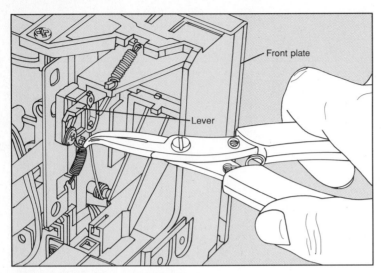

Front plate

Lever

1 **Checking the mechanism.** Remove the top panel *(page 31)* and locate the eject mechanism components. If the lever is broken, replace it *(step 2)*. If the lever slides poorly, use a foam swab to apply a little white grease to it. If the lever has worked loose, tighten its mounting screw. Reconnect an unhooked spring using long-nose pliers *(above)* or tweezers; if a spring is damaged, replace it *(page 135)*. Reinstall the top panel *(page 31)*.

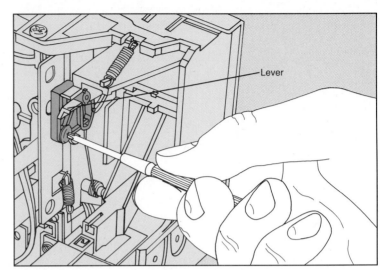

Lever

2 **Replacing the mechanism.** Unhook any springs connected to the lever using long-nose pliers or tweezers. Remove the lever mounting screw *(above)* and pull the lever free of any retaining clips. Order an exact replacement eject mechanism lever from the manufacturer or purchase a substitute at an electronics parts supplier. Press the lever into the retaining clips, put back the mounting screw and rehook the springs. Reinstall the top panel *(page 31)*.

REMOVING A JAMMED AUDIOCASSETTE

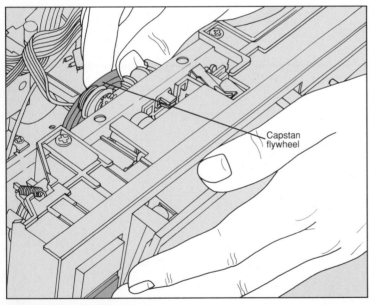

Capstan flywheel

1 **Releasing the audiocassette.** Turn off and unplug the audiocassette recorder. Press the eject control to open the loading door. If the loading door opens and the audiocassette can be lifted out easily, retrieve the jammed tape *(step 2)*. If the loading door does not open enough to reach the audiocassette, or if the audiocassette cannot be removed easily, take off the top panel *(page 31)* and the capstan plate *(page 36)*. Pull out the capstan flywheel to release the audiocassette from the capstan, then press the eject control *(above)*. Carefully lift out the audiocassette, push in the capstan flywheel and reinstall the capstan plate, reversing the sequence used to remove it *(page 36)*.

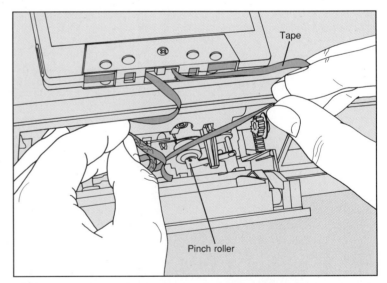

Tape

Pinch roller

2 **Retrieving jammed tape.** Resting the audiocassette on top of the audiocassette recorder, gently extract the tape from the tape travel path components *(above)*; avoid touching undamaged sections of tape with your fingers. If the tape is difficult to retrieve, cut it with scissors, making sure not to leave behind any stray pieces. Reinstall the top panel *(page 31)* if you removed it. If the tape has been cut or badly damaged, splice it *(page 30)*. If the tape is OK, turn the audiocassette takeup reel with a pencil to rewind the tape, being careful not to twist it.

ADJUSTING THE PLAY/RECORD HEAD

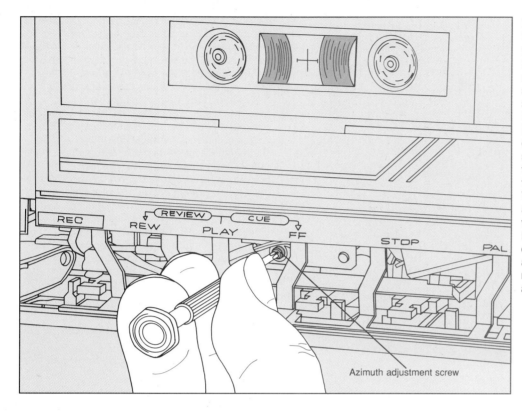

Azimuth adjustment screw

Resetting the azimuth adjustment screw. Without disconnecting the cables hooked up to the audiocassette recorder, unplug it and remove the mode-switch control assembly *(page 31)*. Locate the green or red azimuth adjustment screw on the play/record head and twist it slightly with a screwdriver to break any bond. Plug in and turn on the audiocassette recorder. Load a prerecorded audiocassette, preferably one with considerable high frequency or treble sound. Fast/forward or rewind the audiocassette tape to midposition. Turn down the bass control, turn up the treble control and play the tape. While listening closely, slowly turn the azimuth adjustment screw clockwise and counterclockwise until the sound quality is optimum *(left)*. Lock the screw in position by applying a small dab of nail polish. Remove the audiocassette and turn off and unplug the audiocassette recorder. Reinstall the mode-switch control assembly *(page 31)*.

SERVICING THE DRIVE BELTS

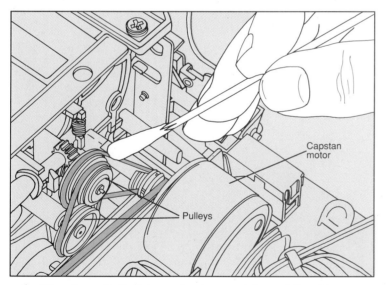

Capstan motor

Pulleys

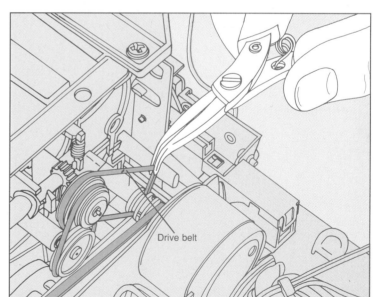

Drive belt

1 Cleaning a belt. Remove the top panel *(page 31)* and locate the drive belts on the tape transport assembly. If a belt is worn or broken, replace it *(step 2)*. If a belt is sticky or oily, clean it thoroughly on both sides using a foam swab dipped in rubber-cleaning compound *(above)*; never apply anything oily and avoid touching the belt with your fingers. Turn the belt pulleys or the capstan flywheel with a clean foam swab to reach the entire length of the belt. Reinstall the top panel *(page 31)*.

2 Replacing a belt. Use long-nose pliers or tweezers to slip off the belt and any other belt in its way *(above)*. Note the belt positions on the pulleys or the capstan flywheel; be careful not to pinch a belt. To reach the capstan drive belt, remove the capstan plate *(page 36)*. Purchase an exact replacement belt at an electronics parts supplier. Holding the belt loosely, wrap it around its pulleys or the capstan flywheel. Reinstall any other belts you removed. Put back the capstan plate by reversing the sequence used to remove it *(page 36)*. Reinstall the top panel *(page 31)*.

ADJUSTING THE CAPSTAN MOTOR SPEED

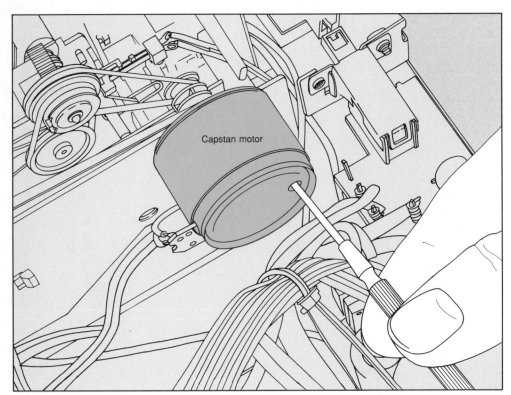

Capstan motor

Resetting the motor speed. Without disconnecting the cables hooked up to the audiocassette recorder, unplug it and remove the top panel *(page 31)*. Locate the motor-speed adjustment screw in the opening on the back of the motor. If there is no motor-speed adjustment screw, reinstall the top panel *(page 31)*; to have the motor speed adjusted, take the audiocassette recorder for professional service. If there is a motor-speed adjustment screw, plug in the audiocassette recorder, turn it on and load a prerecorded audiocassette, preferably one with considerable mid-range frequency or voice passages. Play the audiocassette tape for about five minutes to warm up the motor, then fast/forward or rewind it to midposition. While listening closely to the tape, slowly turn the motor-speed adjustment screw clockwise and counterclockwise until the sound quality is optimum *(left)*. Remove the audiocassette, turn off the audiocassette recorder, unplug it and reinstall the top panel *(page 31)*.

REPLACING THE PINCH ROLLER

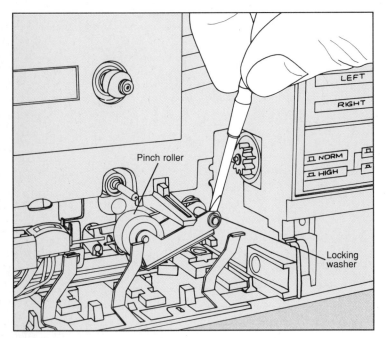

Pinch roller

Locking washer

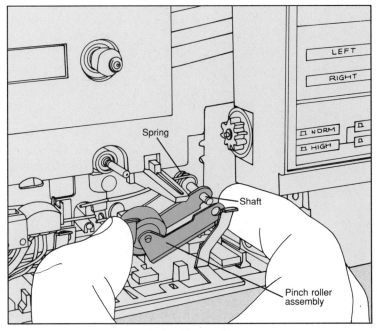

Spring

Shaft

Pinch roller assembly

1 **Removing the pinch roller assembly.** Remove the mode-switch control assembly and the loading door *(page 31)*. Locate the pinch roller assembly and note the pinch-roller spring position. Fit the tip of a small screwdriver under the locking washer and gently pry it off *(above)*; if required, use one hand to hold the pinch roller assembly stationary. Slide the pinch roller assembly off its shaft, noting its position.

2 **Installing a new pinch roller assembly.** If the pinch roller assembly spring is damaged, replace it *(page 135)*; if the spring is OK, leave it in place. Purchase an exact replacement pinch roller assembly at an electronics parts supplier and slip it onto the shaft *(above)*. Pressing the pinch roller assembly against the spring, push the locking washer onto the shaft. Reinstall the loading door and the mode-switch control assembly *(page 31)*.

TESTING AND REPLACING AN AUDIO HEAD

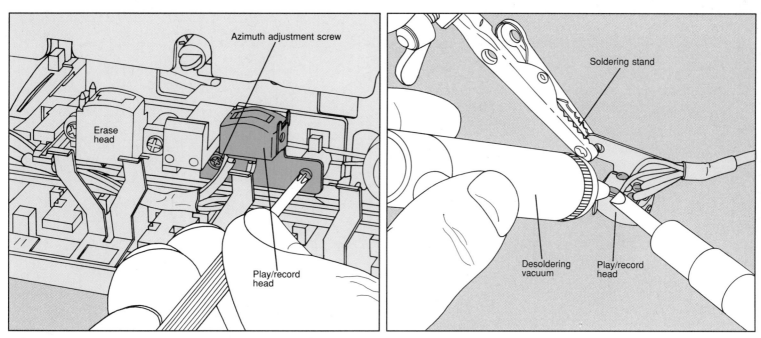

Azimuth adjustment screw

Erase head

Play/record head

Soldering stand

Desoldering vacuum

Play/record head

1 **Removing a head.** Remove the mode-switch control assembly and the loading door *(page 31)* and locate the play/record and erase heads; note the position of the green or red azimuth adjustment screw on the play/record head. Demagnetize a small screwdriver *(page 140)*, unscrew the head being serviced *(above, left)* and gently lift it out of the audio-cassette recorder. If a wire connection is loose or broken, repair it *(page 132)*. Put back the head; for the play/record head, reset the azimuth adjustment screw *(page 33)*. Reinstall the loading door and the mode-switch control assembly *(page 31)*. If the problem persists, test the head *(step 2)*. Access the head as above. Secure the head in a soldering stand and desolder *(page 130)* the wires *(above, right)*, noting their terminal positions.

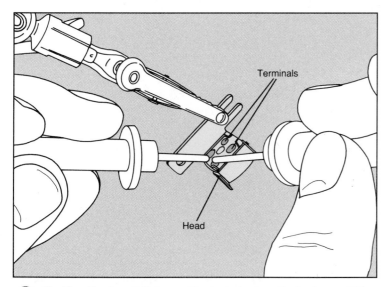

Terminals

Head

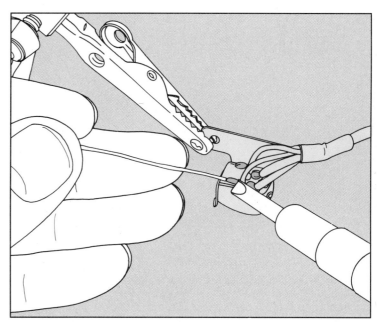

2 **Testing the head.** Set a multitester to test continuity *(page 128)*. If the head has three wires, touch one probe to the ground terminal and the second probe to each other terminal, in turn. The multitester should register continuity. If the head has four wires, there are two ground wires; touch the probes to each ground/non-ground pair of terminals. The multitester should register continuity for each pair. If the head tests faulty, replace it *(step 3)*. If the head tests OK, solder *(page 131)* the wires to the terminals and reinstall the head *(step 3)*.

3 **Replacing the head.** Order an exact replacement head from the manufacturer or purchase a substitute at an electronics parts supplier. Secure the head in the soldering stand, solder *(page 131)* the wires to the head terminals *(above)* and screw in the head. If you serviced the play/record head, reset the azimuth adjustment screw *(page 33)*. Reinstall the loading door and the mode-switch control assembly *(page 31)*.

SERVICING THE TAPE TRANSPORT ASSEMBLY

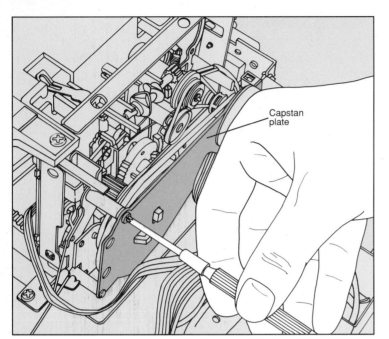

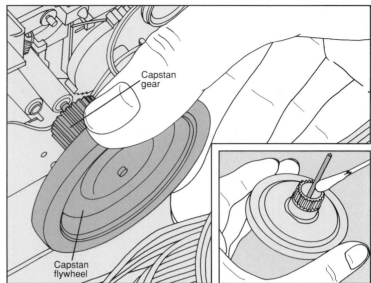

1 **Removing the capstan plate.** Remove the top panel *(page 31)* and unscrew the capstan plate *(above)*. Slip the drive belts off the motor pulley and the capstan flywheel using long-nose pliers or tweezers. Avoid touching or pinching any undamaged belt. Lift out the capstan plate and the motor along with the capstan drive belt, taking care not to damage the motor wires.

2 **Cleaning and lubricating the capstan.** Pull the capstan flywheel out of the tape transport assembly *(above)*, exposing the capstan. Clean the capstan flywheel and the capstan with a foam swab dipped in denatured alcohol *(inset)*. Use a toothpick to dislodge dirt from the capstan gear teeth. Lubricate the capstan base using a foam swab moistened with light machine oil, avoiding contact with the tip, which touches the audiocassette tape. Use a toothpick to apply a little white grease to the capstan gear teeth. Wipe off excess lubricant with a clean foam swab.

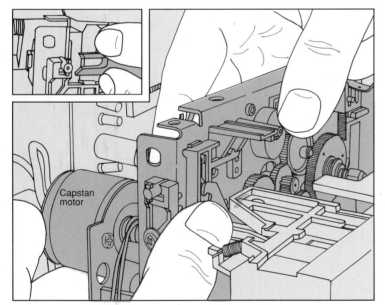

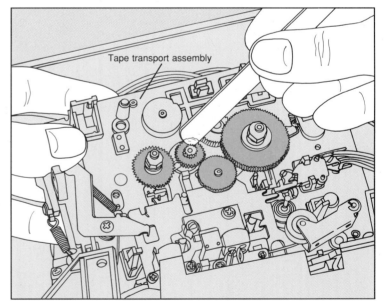

3 **Removing the tape transport assembly.** Unscrew the tape transport assembly from the frame. Using long-nose pliers or tweezers, remove from it the play/record switch lever, any eject mechanism springs and the tape-counter drive belt, noting their positions for reassembly. Unclip the tape transport assembly from tabs securing it to the front panel *(inset)* and carefully lift it out of the audiocassette recorder *(above)*.

4 **Cleaning and lubricating the gears.** Clean the tape transport assembly gears using a foam swab dipped in denatured alcohol. Use a toothpick to dislodge any dirt from the gear teeth. Lubricate the gear teeth by applying a little white grease with a clean stick *(above)*; use a clean foam swab to wipe off excess lubricant. If a gear is damaged, replace it *(page 135)*. To reinstall the tape transport assembly, clip it under the tabs on the front panel, screw it to the frame, and insert the capstan flywheel. Put back the play/record switch lever, any eject mechanism springs and the tape-counter drive belt. Reinstall the capstan plate, reversing the sequence in step 1, then reinstall the top panel *(page 31)*.

SERVICING THE MODE SWITCHES

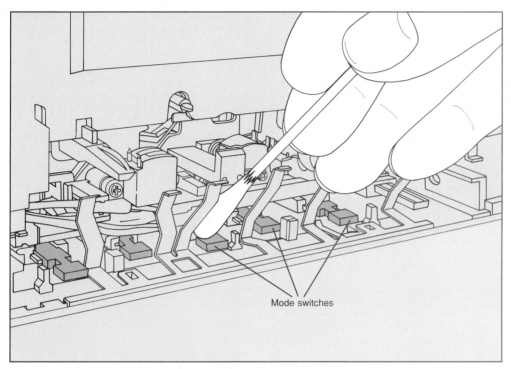

Mode switches

Cleaning and lubricating the switches.
Remove the mode-switch control assembly and the loading door *(page 31)*. Use a foam swab dipped in denatured alcohol to clean the entire surface of each switch *(left)*; for easier access, press in and release the switch lever so that it protrudes as far as possible. To lubricate the switch, use a toothpick to apply a little white grease where the switch lever enters the switch; press in and release the lever a number of times to work in the lubricant. Avoid applying lubricant to the control contact points. Wipe off excess lubricant with a clean foam swab. Reinstall the loading door and the mode-switch control assembly *(page 31)*.

SERVICING THE MUTE SWITCHES

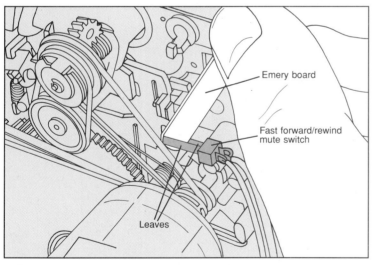

Emery board

Fast forward/rewind mute switch

Leaves

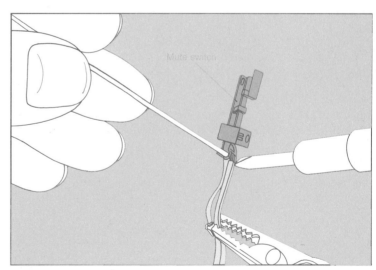

Mute switch

1 **Cleaning and testing the switch.** Remove the top panel *(page 31)*; to reach the pause/stop mute switch, also remove the capstan plate, the capstan flywheel and the tape transport assembly *(page 36)*. If a switch leaf is damaged, replace the switch *(step 2)*. If a switch wire is loose or broken, repair it *(page 132)*. Set a multitester to test continuity *(page 128)*. Touch one probe to a wire terminal on the switch and touch the other probe in turn to each wire terminal on the circuit board. The multitester should register continuity once—and only once. Repeat this procedure for each switch wire. If a wire tests faulty, replace it *(page 132)*. If each wire tests OK, gently run an emery board over each leaf *(above)*. Put back the tape transport assembly, if you removed it, reversing the sequence used *(page 36)*. Reinstall the top panel *(page 31)*. If the problem persists, suspect a faulty circuit board and take the audiocassette recorder for professional service.

2 **Removing and replacing the switch.** Unclip or unscrew the switch from the tape transport assembly. Tag the switch wires, noting their terminals, and desolder them from the switch *(page 130)*. Order an exact replacement switch from the manufacturer or purchase a substitute at an electronics parts supplier. Set the switch in a soldering stand and solder *(page 131)* the wires to the switch terminals *(above)*. Clip or screw the switch to the tape transport assembly. Put back the tape transport assembly, if you removed it, reversing the sequence used *(page 36)*. Reinstall the top panel *(page 31)*. If the problem persists, suspect a faulty circuit board and take the audiocassette recorder for professional service.

SERVICING THE PLAY/RECORD SWITCH

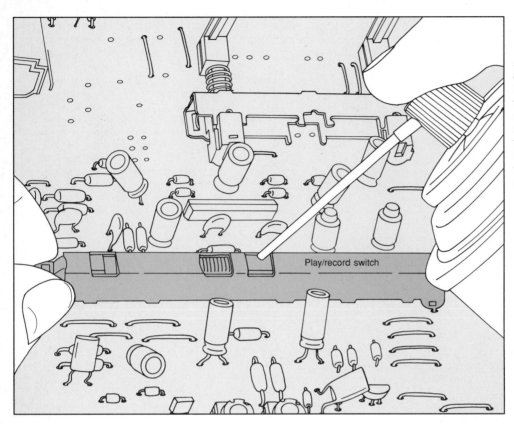

1 **Cleaning the switch:** Remove the top panel *(page 31)*. Locate the play/record switch on the circuit board. To clean the switch, spray short bursts of electronic contact cleaner through the opening in the switch casing. Press in and release the switch several times to work in the cleaner *(left)*, taking care not to damage the hook-like switch lever connected to the tape transport assembly. Reinstall the top panel *(page 31)*. If the problem persists, remove the top and back panels *(page 31)* and turn over the circuit board *(step 2)* to reach the play/record switch pins.

2 **Turning over the circuit board.** Carefully disengage the play/record switch lever connected to the tape transport assembly from the play/record switch; use long-nose pliers or tweezers, if required. Push the control levers off the tape selector and noise reduction switches *(above)*. To reach the switch pins, unscrew the circuit board, remove any components in the way and turn over the circuit board, avoiding damage to any wire connections.

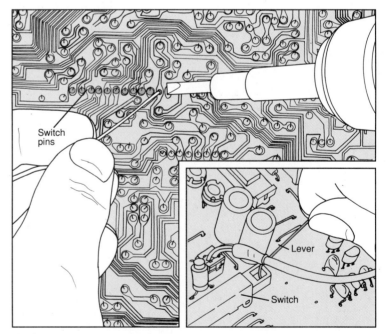

3 **Removing and replacing the switch.** Desolder the switch pins *(page 130)*. Turn over the circuit board and pull off the switch; wiggle it to help release the pins. Order an exact replacement play/record switch from the manufacturer or purchase a substitute at an electronics parts supplier. Fit the switch pins into the circuit board, turn over the circuit board and solder *(page 131)* the pins *(above)*. Put back the circuit board, reversing the sequence used to remove it *(step 2)*. Carefully reconnect the switch lever to the play/record switch *(inset)*. Reinstall the back and top panels *(page 31)*.

SERVICING THE RECORD LEVEL POTENTIOMETER

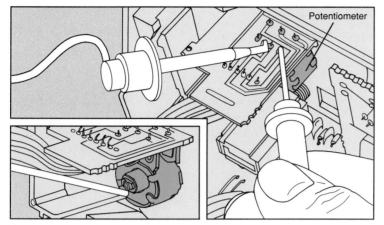

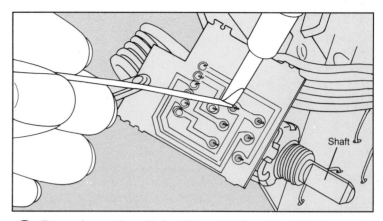

Potentiometer

Shaft

1 **Cleaning and testing the potentiometer.** Remove the top panel *(page 31)* and locate the potentiometer on the circuit board behind its control. Spray electronic contact cleaner into the potentiometer casing *(inset)* and rotate the control back and forth to work it in. If the problem persists, test the potentiometer. Set a multitester to test resistance *(page 129)*. Clip one probe to the center pin in one row on the circuit board and touch the other probe in turn to the other pins in the row *(above)*, turning the control back and forth. The multitester should register an ohms variation for each pin. Test the other row of pins the same way. If the potentiometer tests faulty, remove it *(step 2)*. If the potentiometer tests OK, suspect a faulty circuit board and take the audiocassette recorder for professional service.

2 **Removing and replacing the potentiometer.** Pull the control off the potentiometer and unscrew the shaft locknut. Lift out the potentiometer and circuit board, pulling the shaft through the opening in the front panel. Desolder the potentiometer pins *(page 130)*, and pull off the potentiometer; wiggle it to help release the pins. Test resistance again to confirm the potentiometer is faulty *(step 1)*. Purchase an exact replacement potentiometer at an electronics parts supplier. Fit the potentiometer pins into the circuit board, turn it over and solder *(page 131)* the pins *(above)*. Slide the shaft through the opening in the front panel, screw on the shaft locknut and put back the control. If the potentiometer now tests OK, but the problem persists, suspect a faulty circuit board and take the audiocassette recorder for professional service. Reinstall the top panel *(page 31)*.

SERVICING THE FEATURE SWITCHES

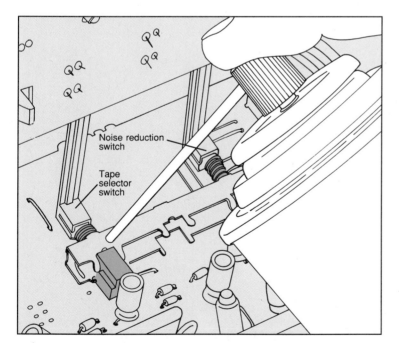

Noise reduction switch

Tape selector switch

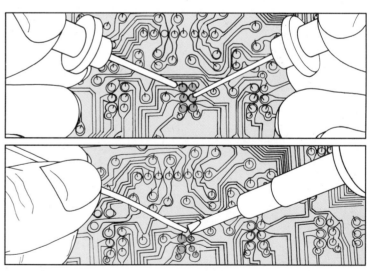

1 **Cleaning the switch.** Remove the top panel *(page 31)* and locate the switch on the circuit board behind the control. Spray short bursts of electronic contact cleaner through the opening in the switch casing *(above)*; press in and release the control several times to work in the cleaner. Reinstall the top panel *(page 31)*. If the problem persists, remove the top panel *(page 31)* and turn over the circuit board *(page 38)* to reach the switch pins.

2 **Testing and replacing the switch.** Set a multitester to test continuity *(page 128)*. Test as for a multi-pole switch *(page 138)*: Touch one probe to the center pin in one row and touch the other probe in turn to the other pins in the row *(above, top)*. For each switch setting, the multitester should register continuity with only one pair of pins. Test the other row of pins. If the switch tests faulty, desolder the pins *(page 130)* and pull off the switch. Purchase an exact replacement switch at an electronics parts supplier. Solder *(page 131)* the pins into the circuit board *(above, bottom)*. If the switch tests OK, suspect a faulty circuit board and take the audiocassette recorder for professional service. Put back the circuit board, reversing the sequence used to remove it *(page 38)*, and reinstall the panels *(page 31)*.

TESTING AND REPLACING THE ON/OFF SWITCH

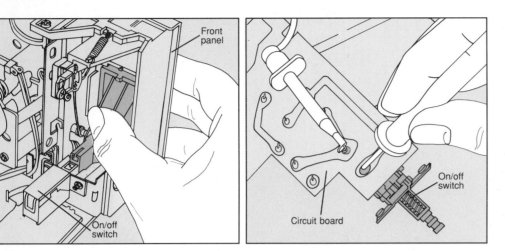

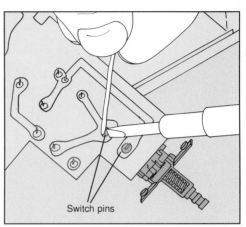

1 **Testing the switch.** Remove the top panel *(page 31)*. Disengage the control lever from the on/off switch *(above, left)*, unscrew the switch and the circuit board, and turn over the circuit board. Set a multitester to test continuity *(page 128)*. Hook one probe to one switch pin and touch the other probe to the other switch pin *(above, right)*. Set the switch to the ON position, then to the OFF position. The multitester should register continuity only in the ON position. If the switch tests faulty, replace it *(step 2)*. If the switch tests OK, screw in the circuit board and the switch, reconnect the control lever, and service the power supply *(below)*.

2 **Replacing the switch.** Desolder the pins *(page 130)*, turn over the circuit board and pull off the switch. Purchase an exact replacement switch at an electronics parts supplier. Fit the pins into the circuit board and solder *(page 131)* the pins *(above)*. Screw in the circuit board and the switch, put back the control lever, and reinstall the top panel *(page 31)*.

SERVICING THE POWER SUPPLY

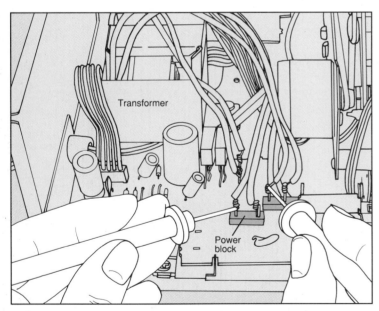

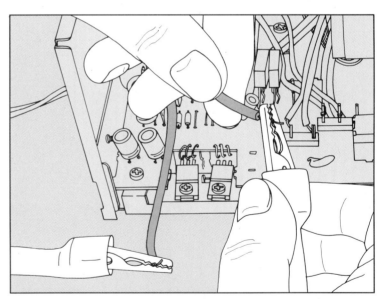

1 **Testing between the transformer and the power block or the on/off switch or the fuse.** Remove the top panel *(page 31)* and identify the power supply components *(page 138)*. Locate the contact points for the two transformer wires connecting to power block, on/off switch or fuse terminals. If a wire connection is loose or broken, repair it *(page 132)*. Set a multitester to test continuity *(page 128)*. Touch one probe to the terminal for one transformer wire and touch the other probe to each power block terminal, in turn *(above)*. The multitester should register continuity once — and only once. Test the other transformer wire. If the multitester registers continuity for each test, test the transformer *(step 2)*. If not, suspect a faulty circuit board and take the audiocassette recorder for professional service.

2 **Testing the transformer.** Locate the contact points for the transformer wires other than those tested in step 1. If the circuit board is not coded with the wire colors, note the wire positions and desolder them *(page 130)*. Set a multitester to test voltage *(page 129)*. If there are only matching-colored wire pairs, clip the probes to one matching pair *(above)*; if there is one odd-colored wire, clip one probe to it and clip the other probe to one of the matching wires. Plug in the audiocassette recorder and turn it on. The multitester should register voltage. Turn off the audiocassette recorder and unplug it. Repeat this procedure with each matching wire pair or with the odd wire and each matching wire. If the multitester does not register voltage, replace the transformer *(step 3)*. If the multitester registers voltage, suspect a faulty circuit board and take the recorder for professional service.

SERVICING THE POWER SUPPLY (continued)

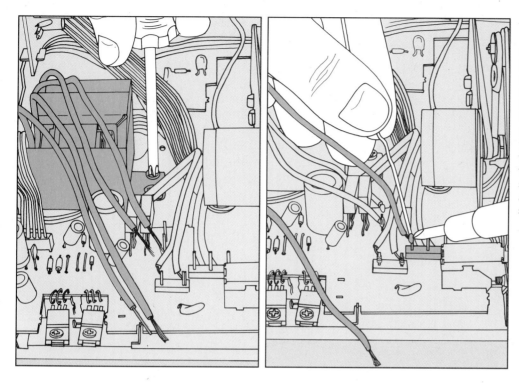

3 **Removing and replacing the transformer.** Desolder *(page 130)* the two transformer wires connected to power block, on/off switch or fuse terminals, noting the wire positions. Unscrew the transformer *(far left)* and remove it from the audiocassette recorder. Order an exact replacement transformer from the manufacturer or purchase a substitute at an electronics parts supplier. Install the transformer and solder *(page 131)* all the wires in their proper positions *(near left)*. Reinstall the top panel *(page 31)*. If the problem persists, suspect a faulty circuit board and take the audiocassette recorder for professional service.

SERVICING THE CAPSTAN MOTOR

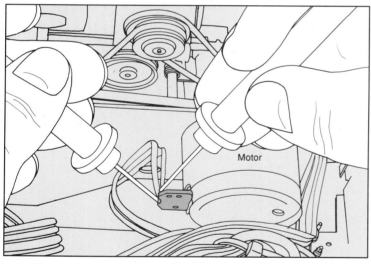

Motor

1 **Testing the motor.** Remove the top panel *(page 31)* and locate the two wires connecting the motor to the circuit board. If a wire is loose or broken, repair it *(page 132)*. Set a multitester to test voltage *(page 129)*. Plug in and turn on the audiocassette recorder. Press the play/mode control. Touch a probe to each wire contact point on the motor *(above)*, avoiding any contact with other components. The multitester should register voltage. Release the play/mode control, and turn off and unplug the audiocassette recorder. If the multitester registers voltage, replace the motor *(step 2)*. If the multitester does not register voltage, suspect a faulty circuit board; reinstall the top panel *(page 31)* and take the audiocassette recorder for professional service.

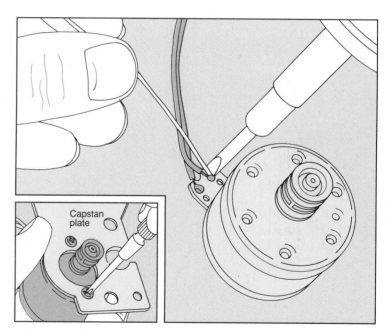

Capstan plate

2 **Replacing the motor.** Remove the capstan plate *(page 36)* and unscrew the motor from it *(inset)*. Tag the motor wires, noting their positions, and desolder the wires *(page 130)* from the motor. Order an exact replacement motor from the manufacturer or purchase a substitute at an electronics parts supplier. Solder the wires *(page 131)* to the motor *(above)*. Screw the motor onto the capstan plate and put back the capstan plate, reversing the sequence used to remove it *(page 36)*. Reinstall the top panel *(page 31)*. If the problem persists, suspect a faulty circuit board and take the audiocassette recorder for professional service.

TURNTABLES

The turntable *(below)*, whether belt drive or direct drive, automatic or manual, is the most mechanical unit of the audio system. The stylus tracks in the grooves of a record turning on the platter. The cartridge transforms this motion into an electrical signal, sending it through wires in the tone arm to cables leading to the receiver. There, the signal is amplified and sent through cables to the speakers.

To diagnose the turntable as the source of audio problems, consult the Troubleshooting Guide in Entertainment Systems *(page 14)* and in this chapter *(right)*. Most problems can be remedied by securing cable hookups, rebalancing the tone arm, realigning the cartridge or servicing the power supply. Replace-ment components are usually available at an electronics parts supplier; some, however, may have to be ordered from the turntable manufacturer.

A set of small screwdrivers, a multitester and a soldering iron make up the basic tool kit for turntable repairs *(page 126)*. Refer to Tools & Techniques for tips on disassembly and reassembly *(page 140)*, testing continuity and voltage *(pages 128-129)*, and desoldering and soldering *(pages 130-131)*.

Turn off and unplug the turntable before attempting any repair. Disconnect its cables and set it on a clean work table. Cold check for leaking voltage *(page 141)* after reassembling the turntable but before plugging it in.

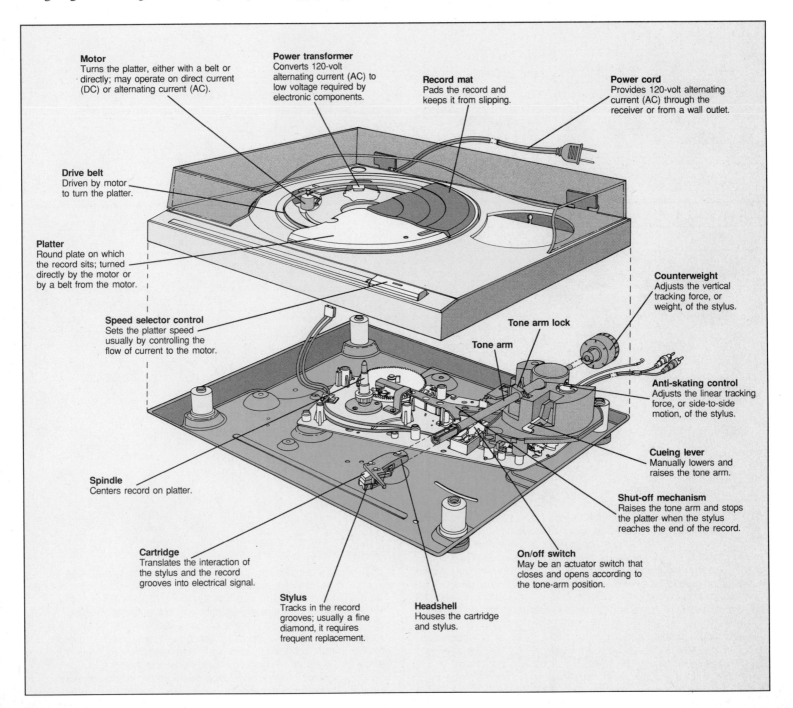

Motor
Turns the platter, either with a belt or directly; may operate on direct current (DC) or alternating current (AC).

Power transformer
Converts 120-volt alternating current (AC) to low voltage required by electronic components.

Record mat
Pads the record and keeps it from slipping.

Power cord
Provides 120-volt alternating current (AC) through the receiver or from a wall outlet.

Drive belt
Driven by motor to turn the platter.

Platter
Round plate on which the record sits; turned directly by the motor or by a belt from the motor.

Counterweight
Adjusts the vertical tracking force, or weight, of the stylus.

Speed selector control
Sets the platter speed usually by controlling the flow of current to the motor.

Tone arm lock

Tone arm

Anti-skating control
Adjusts the linear tracking force, or side-to-side motion, of the stylus.

Cueing lever
Manually lowers and raises the tone arm.

Spindle
Centers record on platter.

Shut-off mechanism
Raises the tone arm and stops the platter when the stylus reaches the end of the record.

Cartridge
Translates the interaction of the stylus and the record grooves into electrical signal.

On/off switch
May be an actuator switch that closes and opens according to the tone-arm position.

Stylus
Tracks in the record grooves; usually a fine diamond, it requires frequent replacement.

Headshell
Houses the cartridge and stylus.

TROUBLESHOOTING GUIDE

SYMPTOM	POSSIBLE CAUSE	PROCEDURE
Platter does not turn	Turntable unplugged or turned off	Plug in and turn on turntable
	No power to outlet, or outlet faulty	Reset breaker or replace fuse (p. 10) □○; have outlet serviced
	Receiver faulty	Troubleshoot entertainment system (p. 14) □○
	Power cord faulty	Test and replace power cord (p. 137) □○
	Drive belt loose or broken	Service drive belt (p. 45) □○
	Shut-off mechanism jammed	Clean and lubricate shut-off mechanism (p. 49) □○
	On/off switch faulty	Test and replace on/off switch (p. 50) □○
	Power supply faulty	Service power supply (p. 50) ◨○
	Motor faulty	Test and replace motor (p. 51) ◨○
	Circuit board faulty	Take turntable for professional service
Platter turns at wrong speed or at only one speed	Drive belt dirty or loose	Service drive belt (p. 45) □○
	Motor running too fast or too slow	Adjust motor speed (p. 46) □○
	Shut-off mechanism dirty	Clean and lubricate shut-off mechanism (p. 49) □○
	Speed selector switch faulty	Test and replace speed selector switch (p. 49) □○
	Power supply faulty	Service power supply (p. 50) ◨○
	Motor faulty	Test and replace motor (p. 51) ◨○
	Circuit board faulty	Take turntable for professional service
Platter does not stop turning or stops before end of record	Shut-off mechanism dirty or jammed	Clean and lubricate shut-off mechanism (p. 49) □○
	Shut-off mechanism faulty	Take turntable for professional service
No sound	Receiver faulty	Troubleshoot entertainment system (p. 14) □○
	Cartridge faulty	Test and replace cartridge (p. 47) □○
	Tone arm wires loose or broken	Service tone arm (p. 48) □○
	Circuit board faulty	Take turntable for professional service
Sound from only one channel or intermittent sound	Record or stylus dusty	Clean record and stylus (p. 44) □○
	Receiver or speaker faulty	Troubleshoot entertainment system (p. 14) □○
	Tone arm unbalanced	Balance tone arm (p. 44) □○
	Cartridge misaligned	Adjust cartridge (p. 45) □○▲
	Stylus worn or broken	Replace stylus assembly (p. 46) □○
	Cartridge faulty	Test and replace cartridge (p. 47) □○
	Tone arm wire loose or broken	Service tone arm (p. 48) □○
	Circuit board faulty	Take turntable for professional service
Sound distorted; scratching or hissing noise	Record or stylus dusty	Clean record and stylus (p. 44) □○
	Receiver or speaker faulty	Troubleshoot entertainment system (p. 14) □○
	Tone arm unbalanced	Balance tone arm (p. 44) □○
	Cartridge misaligned	Adjust cartridge (p. 45) □○▲
	Stylus worn or broken	Replace stylus assembly (p. 46) □○
	Cartridge faulty	Test and replace cartridge (p. 47) □○
	Circuit board faulty	Take turntable for professional service
Humming, buzzing or rumbling noise	Ground wire loose	Check ground wire connection (p. 17) □○
	Receiver or speaker faulty	Troubleshoot entertainment system (p. 14) □○
	Cartridge faulty	Test and replace cartridge (p. 47) □○
	Circuit board faulty	Take turntable for professional service
Burning odor	Power supply faulty	Service power supply (p. 50) ◨○
	Motor faulty	Test and replace motor (p. 51) ◨○
	Circuit board faulty	Take turntable for professional service

DEGREE OF DIFFICULTY: □ Easy ◨ Moderate ◼ Complex
ESTIMATED TIME: ○ Less than 1 hour ◑ 1 to 3 hours ● Over 3 hours   ▲ Special tool required

CLEANING RECORDS AND THE STYLUS

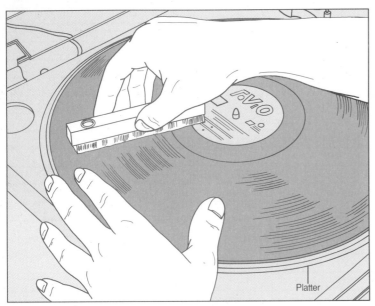

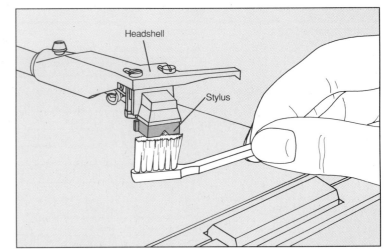

1 Dusting records. Turn off the turntable, leaving the record in place on the spindle. Position a nylon record brush across the record and lightly touch the bristles to the grooves. Applying steady, gentle pressure on the brush with one hand, slowly rotate the platter with the other hand *(above)*. Wipe off the brush on a clean, lint-free cloth. Turn over the record and repeat this step. Turn on the turntable. To prevent record damage, perform this procedure before each play. If the record sound quality is still poor, clean the stylus *(step 2)*.

2 Brushing the stylus. Turn off the turntable. With the tone arm at rest on its stand, position a nylon stylus brush behind the stylus, just below the headshell. Pull the brush slowly forward from under the headshell, lightly touching the bristles to the stylus *(above)*; avoid any side-to-side or front-to-back motion. Wipe off the brush on a clean, lint-free cloth. Turn on the turntable. To prevent damage to the stylus or records, perform this procedure before each record-playing session.

BALANCING THE TONE ARM

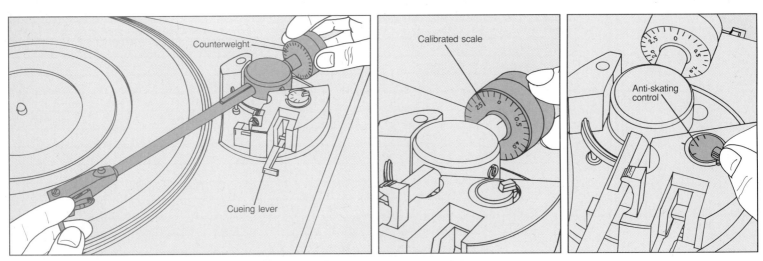

Adjusting the counterweight and the anti-skating control. Turn off the turntable and remove any record from the platter. With the tone arm at rest on its stand, flip down the stylus guard, if any, and set the anti-skating control to 0. With the cueing lever lowered, lift the tone arm and position it over the platter. Supporting the tone arm with one hand, rotate the counterweight with the other hand until the tone arm floats perpendicular above the platter; then turn the calibrated scale control until the 0 on the scale is aligned with the mark on the tone arm *(above, left)*. Place the tone arm back on its stand. Set the counterweight and calibrated scale to the midpoint of the range specified by the cartridge manufacturer *(above, center)*; adjust the anti-skating control to the identical setting *(above, right)*. Flip up the stylus guard, if any.

ADJUSTING THE CARTRIDGE

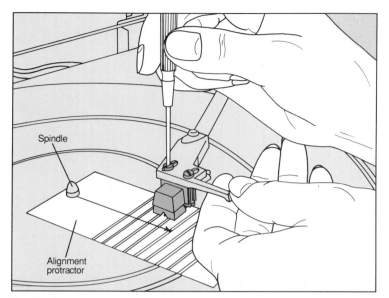

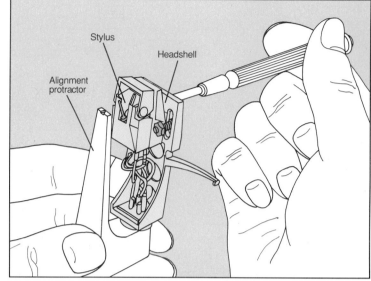

Stylus

Headshell

Alignment protractor

Spindle

Alignment protractor

Realigning a straight tone-arm cartridge. Turn off the turntable and remove any record from the platter. If the tone arm starts and stops the platter, unplug the turntable from the receiver *(page 12)* or wall outlet. Use a straight tone-arm alignment protractor supplied by the turntable manufacturer or purchased at an electronics parts supplier. Position the protractor on the spindle and gently lower the tone arm to seat the stylus in the stylus opening on the protractor. Check the cartridge alignment by looking straight down from above the tone arm. If the cartridge is not exactly parallel to the grid lines, lift the tone arm and loosen the cartridge screws *(above)*. Lower the tone arm to reseat the stylus and adjust the cartridge so it is exactly parallel to the grid lines. Lift the tone arm and tighten the headshell screws. Place the tone arm back on its stand and remove the protractor.

Realigning a J- or S-shaped tone-arm cartridge. Turn off the turntable and remove the headshell *(page 47)*. Depending on the shape of the tone arm, use a J- or S-shaped tone-arm alignment protractor supplied by the turntable manufacturer or purchased at an electronics parts supplier. Position the headshell in the protractor and check the cartridge alignment by looking straight down at the cartridge from the front of the headshell. If the stylus is not exactly centered over the stylus mark on the protractor, loosen the cartridge screws *(above)*. Adjust the cartridge so the stylus is exactly centered over the stylus mark and tighten the headshell screws. Reinstall the headshell *(page 47)*.

SERVICING THE DRIVE BELT

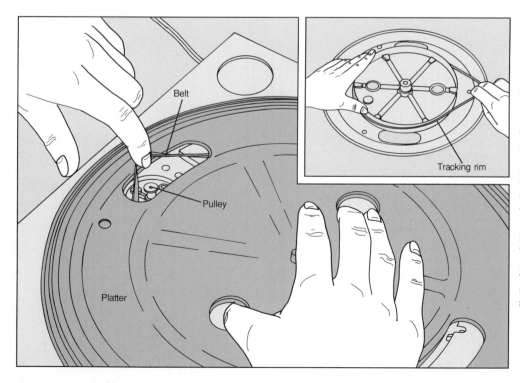

Belt

Pulley

Platter

Tracking rim

Cleaning and replacing the drive belt.
Turn off the turntable, remove any record from the platter and lock the tone arm. Lift off the record mat and locate the drive belt through the opening in the platter. Pull the belt away from the pulley *(left)*, lift off the platter and remove the belt. If the belt is worn or broken, order an exact replacement belt from the turntable manufacturer or purchase a substitute belt at an electronics parts supplier. If the belt is sticky or greasy, wipe it thoroughly using a clean, lint-free cloth sprinkled with a little rubber cleaning compound; never apply anything oily. To replace the belt, turn the platter face down and wrap the belt around the tracking rim *(inset)*, pulling it to the opening in the platter. Lift the platter enough to reach the belt through the opening from the other side and turn the platter upright without twisting the belt. Still holding the belt, reseat the platter and pull the belt around the pulley. Put back the record mat and unlock the tone arm. Adjust the motor speed *(page 46)* if necessary.

ADJUSTING THE MOTOR SPEED

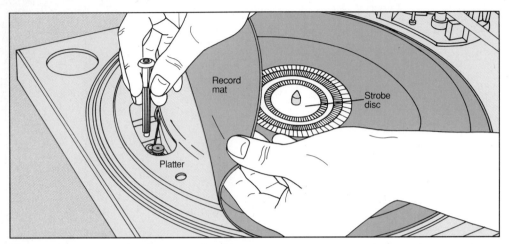

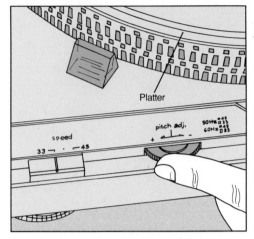

Fine-tuning the speed using a strobe disc. Turn off the turntable and remove any record from the platter. If the turntable is not equipped with a built-in stroboscope, use a strobe disc supplied by the turntable manufacturer or purchased at an electronics parts supplier. Locate the pitch adjustment screws, either on the top panel or reached through openings in the platter beneath the record mat, as shown. Position the strobe disc on the spindle and turn on the turntable. Shine a fluorescent light on the turntable and observe the strobe disc markings that correspond to the speed-selector switch setting. Adjust the screw corresponding to the switch setting to the exact point at which the markings appear as a solid, motionless band. If the screw is under the platter, you must turn off the turntable, lift up the record mat and adjust the screw *(above)*; then, put back the record mat, turn on the turntable and again observe the strobe disc markings. Repeat this procedure, if required, for each speed selector switch setting.

Fine-tuning the speed using a built-in stroboscope. Turn on the turntable and observe the stroboscope markings on the outer edge of the platter that correspond to the speed-selector switch setting. Adjust the pitch adjustment control dial on the front, top or side of the turntable to the exact point at which the markings appear as a solid, motionless band *(above)*. Repeat this procedure, if required, for each speed-selector switch setting.

REPLACING THE STYLUS ASSEMBLY

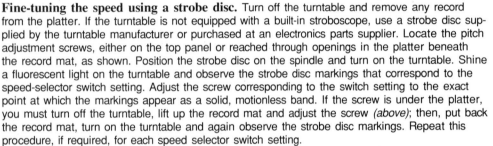

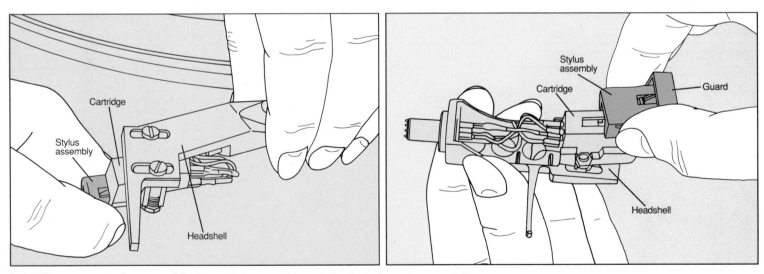

Installing a new stylus assembly. Turn off the turntable and flip down the stylus guard, if any. Lift up the tone arm to check how the stylus assembly fits into the cartridge; if you cannot determine how to take out the stylus assembly, remove the headshell *(page 47)* and take it to an electronics parts supplier. In many cases, the stylus assembly slides out from tracks under the cartridge. Grip the headshell in one hand and gently pull the stylus assembly straight out from under the cartridge using a thumb and forefinger *(above, left)*. In other cases, the stylus assembly is pulled straight off the cartridge. For better access to this type, remove the headshell *(page 47)* and turn it over. Grip the headshell in one hand and pull straight up on the stylus assembly with the other *(above, right)*. Purchase an identical replacement stylus assembly from an electronics parts supplier. Slide the stylus assembly along the tracks of the cartridge until it fits snugly, or press the stylus assembly into the cartridge and reinstall the headshell *(page 47)*. Flip up the stylus guard, if any. If necessary, adjust the cartridge *(page 45)* and balance the tone arm *(page 44)*.

TESTING AND REPLACING THE CARTRIDGE

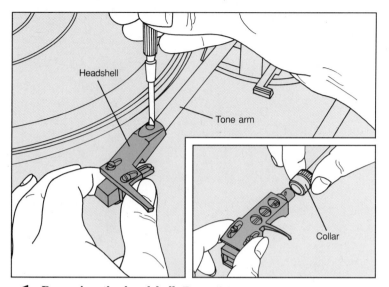

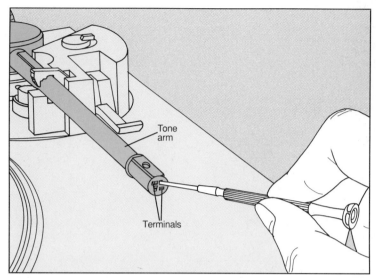

1 **Removing the headshell.** Turn off the turntable and lock the tone arm. Flip down the stylus guard, if any, or remove the stylus assembly if it slides out easily from under the cartridge *(page 46)*. Supporting the headshell with one hand, loosen the screw *(above)* or the collar *(inset)* securing it to the tone arm and gently slide it off. If the headshell cannot be detached, test the cartridge wires *(step 3)*. Turn over the headshell and check the cartridge wire connections. If the wire connections are secure, check for signal through the tone arm *(step 2)*. If a wire is loose, carefully reconnect it to its terminal using tweezers. Reinstall the headshell and, if required, put back the stylus assembly or flip up the stylus guard. Unlock the tone arm.

2 **Checking for signal through the tone arm.** To check the wire connections beyond the headshell, turn on the turntable and receiver, set the receiver selector control to PHONO and adjust the receiver volume control to slightly above its lowest setting. Using a small metal screwdriver or holding a larger screwdriver by its blade, lightly touch the screwdriver tip to each terminal at the end of the tone arm *(above)*. If there is an audible hum from the speakers at more or less than two tone-arm terminals, test the tone arm wires *(page 48)*. If there is an audible hum from the speakers at only two tone-arm terminals, turn off the turntable and test the cartridge wires *(step 3)*.

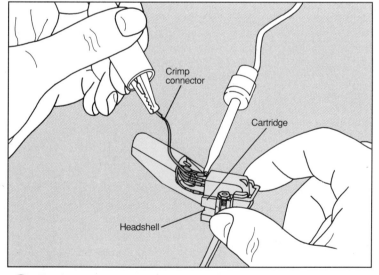

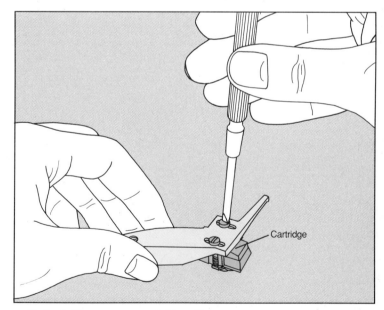

3 **Testing the cartridge wires.** Set a multitester to test continuity *(page 128)*. Hook one probe to the crimp connector at the end of one wire and touch the other probe to the crimp connector at the other end of the wire; for easier access, pull the wire off its terminal *(above)*. Test each wire. If each wire registers continuity, install a new cartridge *(step 4)*. If each wire does not register continuity, purchase an identical replacement set of cartridge wires from an electronics parts supplier. If the cartridge wire terminals are not coded to the cartridge wire colors, note the terminal positions for the wires or remove and replace the wires one at a time. Reinstall the headshell *(step 1)*.

4 **Installing a new cartridge.** To remove the cartridge, disconnect the cartridge wires from the cartridge terminals and unscrew the cartridge from the headshell. If required, remove the stylus assembly *(page 46)*. Purchase a replacement cartridge at an electronics parts supplier. Reinstall the stylus assembly, screw the cartridge to the headshell *(above)* and connect the cartridge wires to the terminals using tweezers. If the cartridge terminals are not coded to the wire colors, connect the wires in the identical sequence as at the headshell terminals. Reinstall the headshell *(step 1)*. If necessary, adjust the cartridge *(page 45)* and balance the tone arm *(page 44)*.

ACCESS TO THE INTERNAL COMPONENTS

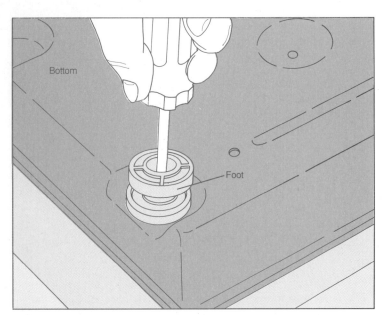

1 **Unscrewing the bottom panel.** Turn off the turntable and unplug it from the receiver or wall outlet. Remove any record from the platter and lock the tone arm. Disconnect the turntable cables and ground wire hooked up to the receiver *(page 12)*. Secure any transit screws, remove the record mat and lift off the platter; if required, first remove the drive belt *(page 46)*. Turn over the turntable and unscrew the bottom panel, checking for hidden screws in the turntable feet *(above)*. Lift off the bottom panel if the tone arm assembly is mounted on the top panel. If the tone arm assembly is mounted through an opening in the top panel, remove the top panel *(step 2)*.

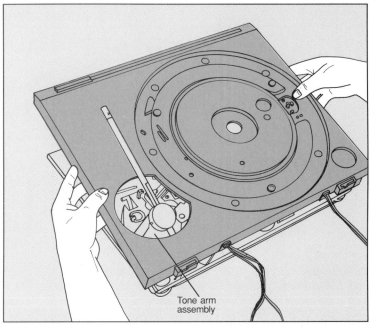

2 **Lifting off the top panel.** Carefully turn the turntable upright, pull off the dust cover, and remove the headshell *(page 47)*. Screw off the counterweight, remove the counterweight shaft and unlock the tone arm. Lift up the top panel, slide the tone arm through the opening for the tone arm assembly *(above)* and relock the tone arm. Gently turn the top panel face down beside the bottom panel. To reinstall the top panel, reverse this step and step 1 *(left)*, and reconnect the cables *(page 16)* and ground wire *(page 17)*. Rebalance the tone arm *(page 44)*.

SERVICING THE TONE ARM

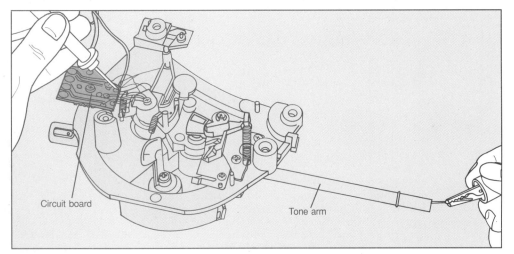

1 **Testing the tone arm wires.** Remove the top or bottom panel *(step above)*. If the tone arm assembly is mounted on the bottom panel, unscrew it and carefully turn it over, as shown, to reach the tone-arm wire contact points on the circuit board. If a wire is loose or broken, repair it *(page 132)*. Set a multitester to test continuity *(page 128)*. Touch one probe to a wire terminal on the tone arm and touch the other probe in turn to each wire contact point on the circuit board *(above)*. The multitester should register continuity once—and only once. Test each wire; if one is faulty, replace the tone arm *(step 2)*. If each wire tests OK, screw the tone arm assembly in place, if required, and reinstall the top or bottom panel *(step above)*. If the problem persists, suspect a faulty circuit board and take the turntable for professional service.

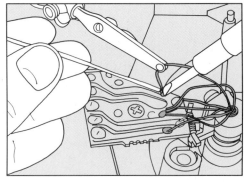

2 **Replacing the tone arm.** Note the wire positions and desolder the wires *(page 130)*. Remove the headshell *(page 47)*, unlock the tone arm and unscrew it from the tone arm assembly. Order an exact replacement from the manufacturer or purchase a substitute at an electronics parts supplier. Thread the tone arm wires through the opening in the tone arm assembly, screw in the tone arm and lock it. Solder the wires to the circuit board *(page 131)*, turning over the turntable, if required. Reinstall the top or bottom panel *(step above)* and the headshell *(page 47)*.

SERVICING THE SHUT-OFF MECHANISM

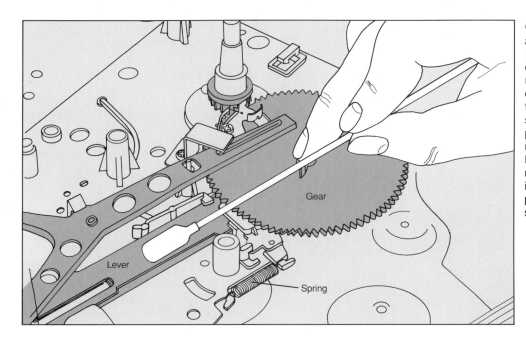

Cleaning and lubricating the gears and levers. Remove the top or bottom panel *(page 48)* and check the shut-off mechanism components. If a spring or gear is damaged, replace it *(page 135)*. Using a foam swab dipped in denatured alcohol, clean dirt or dust from the gears and levers *(left)*. To dislodge stubborn particles, spray short bursts of compressed air. If required, use a toothpick to remove particles from between the gear teeth. Lubricate the levers and any other mechanical metal parts using a little light machine oil. Reinstall the top or bottom panel. If the problem persists, take the turntable for professional service.

SERVICING THE SPEED SELECTOR SWITCH

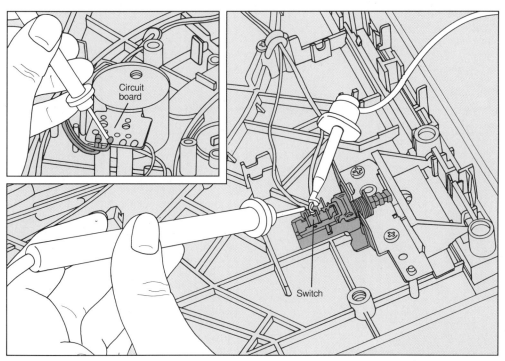

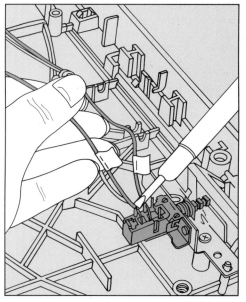

1 Testing the switch. Remove the top or bottom panel *(page 48)* and locate the speed-selector switch terminals. If a wire is loose or broken, repair it *(page 132)*. Set a multitester to test continuity *(page 128)*. If the switch has two wires, hook one probe to one switch wire terminal and touch the other probe to the other switch wire terminal *(above)*. Set the switch to one position, then the other. The multitester should register continuity in only one position. If the switch has three wires, hook one probe to the center terminal and touch the other probe, in turn, to each of the other two terminals. In each switch position, the multitester should register continuity between only one pair of wires. If the switch tests faulty, replace it *(step 2)*. If the switch tests OK, locate the contact points for the switch wires on the circuit board. Hook one probe to a wire terminal at the switch and touch the other probe to the wire's contact point on the circuit board *(inset)*. Repeat this test for the other switch wire. If a wire does not have continuity, replace it *(page 132)*. If each wire has continuity, test the motor *(page 51)*.

2 Replacing the switch. Tag each switch wire, noting its terminal, and desolder the wires *(page 130)*. Unscrew the switch from its mounting. Buy an exact replacement switch at an electronics parts supplier. Screw in the switch and solder *(page 131)* the wires to the terminals *(above)*. Reinstall the top or bottom panel *(page 48)*. If the problem persists, test the motor *(page 51)*.

SERVICING THE ON/OFF SWITCH

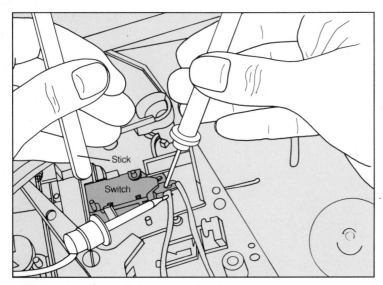

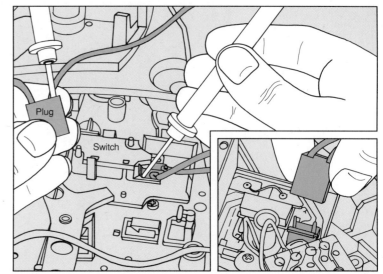

1 **Testing the switch.** Remove the top or bottom panel *(page 48)* and locate the on/off switch terminals. If a wire is loose or broken, repair it *(page 132)*. Set a multitester to test continuity *(page 128)*. Hook one probe to one switch terminal and touch the other probe to the other switch terminal. Set the switch to the ON position and then to the OFF position; for an actuator switch, use a small stick to press in and release the side button *(above)*. The switch should have continuity only in the ON position. If the switch tests OK, test the switch wires *(step 2)*. If the switch tests faulty, desolder the wires *(page 130)* from the switch terminals. Remove the switch and purchase an exact replacement at an electronics parts supplier. Install the switch and solder the wires *(page 131)*. Reinstall the top or bottom panel *(page 48)*.

2 **Testing the wires.** Locate the contact points on the circuit board for the wires connected to the switch terminals; if the wires are connected to contact pins in a plug, remove the plug from the circuit board *(inset)*. Touch one probe to a wire terminal on the switch and touch the other probe to the wire's contact point in the plug *(above)* or on the circuit board. Repeat this procedure for the other switch wire. If a wire does not have continuity, replace it *(page 132)*. If each wire has continuity, service the power supply *(below)*.

SERVICING THE POWER SUPPLY

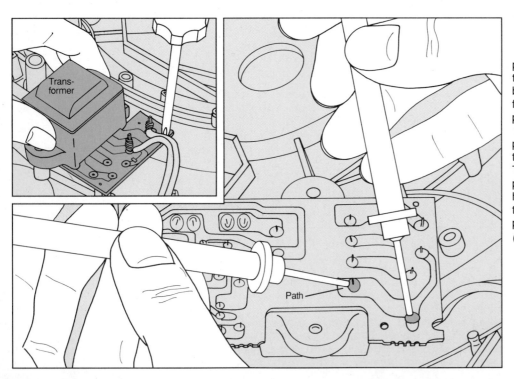

1 **Testing between the transformer and the power block.** Remove the top or bottom panel *(page 48)* and identify the power supply components *(page 138)*. Unscrew the circuit board *(inset)* and turn over the circuit board to reach the two paths connecting transformer contact points to power-block contact points. Set a multitester to test continuity *(page 128)*. Touch one probe to a transformer contact point in one path and touch the other probe to the power block contact point in the path *(left)*. The path should have continuity. Repeat this procedure for the other path. If a path does not have continuity, suspect a faulty circuit board and take the turntable for professional service. If each path registers continuity, test the transformer *(step 2)*.

SERVICING THE POWER SUPPLY (continued)

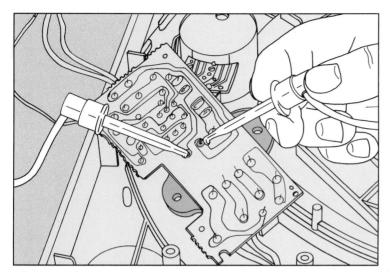

2 **Testing the transformer.** Locate the two transformer contact points in paths other than to the power block. Set a multitester to test voltage *(page 129)*. Carefully hook the probes to the transformer contact points, avoiding any contact with other components *(above)*. Plug the turntable into a wall outlet and turn it on; for an actuator on/off switch, use a small stick to press in and hold the side button *(page 50)*. The multitester should register voltage. Turn off the turntable and unplug it. If the transformer tests faulty, replace the transformer *(step 3)*. If the transformer tests OK, test the motor *(below)*.

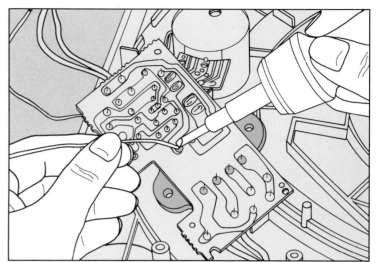

3 **Replacing the transformer.** Desolder the transformer contact points *(page 130)*, noting the transformer pin positions and checking for any orientation pins not in a circuit board path. Carefully turn over the circuit board and pull off the transformer, wiggling the pins if required. Order an exact replacement transformer from the turntable manufacturer or purchase a substitute transformer at an electronics parts supplier. Fit the transformer into the circuit board, turn over the circuit board and solder *(page 131)* the pins in place *(above)*. Screw in the circuit board. Reinstall the top or bottom panel *(page 48)*.

TESTING AND REPLACING THE MOTOR

Circuit board

Motor

1 **Testing the motor.** Remove the top or bottom panel *(page 48)*. If a wire connecting the motor circuit board to the power supply is loose or broken, repair it *(page 132)*. Set a multitester to test voltage *(page 129)*. Plug the turntable into a wall outlet and turn on the turntable; for an actuator on/off switch, use a small stick to press in and hold the side button *(page 50)*. Carefully touch a probe to each motor contact point, avoiding any contact with other components *(above)*. Record the multitester result, turn off the turntable and unplug it. If the multitester registers voltage, replace the motor *(step 2)*. If the multitester does not register voltage, suspect a faulty circuit board and take the turntable for professional service.

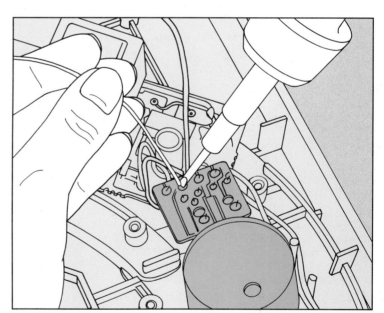

2 **Replacing the motor.** Desolder the wires *(page 130)* from the motor's circuit board that connect to the power supply, noting their positions. Unplug the speed-selector switch wires and unscrew the motor. Order an exact replacement motor and circuit board from the turntable manufacturer or purchase a substitute motor and circuit board at an electronics parts supplier. Screw in the motor, plug in the speed-selector switch wires and solder the power supply wires *(page 131)*. Reinstall the top or bottom panel *(page 48)*. If the problem persists, suspect a faulty circuit board and take the turntable for professional service.

COMPACT DISC PLAYERS

The compact disc player is the most intricate unit of the audio system, performing complex optical functions. The objective lens focuses the laser onto digitally-encoded tracks stamped in the rotating compact disc. The optical pickup assembly transforms the patterns of reflected light into electrical signal. After further electronic modification, this signal is sent out by cables to the receiver, which amplifies it.

To diagnose problems, consult the Troubleshooting Guide in Entertainment Systems *(page 14)* and in this chapter *(page 53)*. Many problems can be remedied by adjusting cable hookups, cleaning the compact disc or the objective lens, or servicing a drive belt or a wire. Cleaning supplies and replacement components are available at an electronics parts supplier; specific parts may have to be ordered from the manufacturer.

A set of small screwdrivers, a multitester and a soldering iron compose the basic tool kit for compact-disc player repairs *(page 126)*. Refer to Tools & Techniques for instructions on disassembly and reassembly *(page 140)*, testing continuity and voltage *(pages 128-129)*, and desoldering and soldering *(pages 130-131)*. While working, store fasteners and other small parts in labeled containers and write down the sequence of disassembly steps. Never look directly at the laser with the power on. Cold check for leaking voltage *(page 141)* after reassembling the compact disc player.

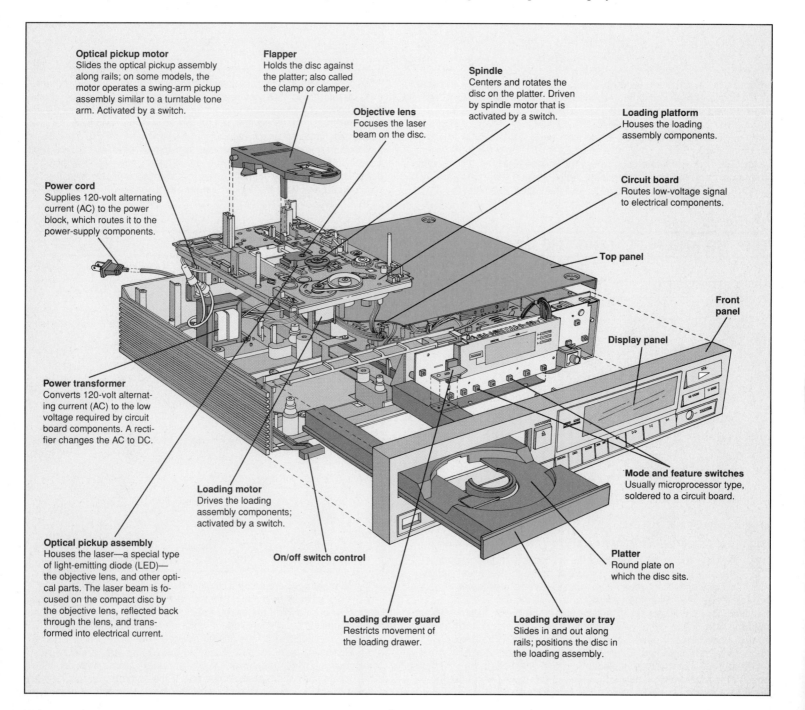

Optical pickup motor
Slides the optical pickup assembly along rails; on some models, the motor operates a swing-arm pickup assembly similar to a turntable tone arm. Activated by a switch.

Flapper
Holds the disc against the platter; also called the clamp or clamper.

Objective lens
Focuses the laser beam on the disc.

Spindle
Centers and rotates the disc on the platter. Driven by spindle motor that is activated by a switch.

Loading platform
Houses the loading assembly components.

Power cord
Supplies 120-volt alternating current (AC) to the power block, which routes it to the power-supply components.

Circuit board
Routes low-voltage signal to electrical components.

Top panel

Power transformer
Converts 120-volt alternating current (AC) to the low voltage required by circuit board components. A rectifier changes the AC to DC.

Front panel

Display panel

Loading motor
Drives the loading assembly components; activated by a switch.

On/off switch control

Mode and feature switches
Usually microprocessor type, soldered to a circuit board.

Optical pickup assembly
Houses the laser—a special type of light-emitting diode (LED)— the objective lens, and other optical parts. The laser beam is focused on the compact disc by the objective lens, reflected back through the lens, and transformed into electrical current.

Platter
Round plate on which the disc sits.

Loading drawer guard
Restricts movement of the loading drawer.

Loading drawer or tray
Slides in and out along rails; positions the disc in the loading assembly.

TROUBLESHOOTING GUIDE

SYMPTOM	POSSIBLE CAUSE	PROCEDURE
No display lights, no sound	Compact disc player unplugged or off	Plug in and turn on compact disc player
	Remote control faulty	Service remote control (p. 136) □○
	No power to outlet or outlet faulty	Reset breaker or replace fuse (p. 10) □○; have outlet serviced
	Power cord faulty	Test and replace power cord (p. 137) □○
	Power fuse faulty	Test and replace power fuse (p. 137) □○
	On/off switch faulty	Test and replace on/off switch (p. 57) ■◒
	Power supply faulty	Service power supply (p. 58) ▣○
	Laser or circuit board faulty	Take compact disc player for professional service
Display lights, no sound	Controls set incorrectly	Adjust compact disc player controls
	Transit screws secured	Loosen transit screws
	Receiver faulty	Troubleshoot entertainment system (p. 14) □○
	Objective lens dirty	Clean objective lens (p. 54) □○
	Drive belt loose or broken	Service drive belts (p. 56) □○
	Optical pickup/spindle motor switch faulty	Clean, test and replace motor switch (p. 56) □○
	Mode or feature switch dirty or faulty	Clean switch (p. 57) □○; test and replace switch (p. 57) ▣○
	Optical pickup motor faulty	Test and replace optical pickup motor (p. 59) ■◒
	Spindle motor faulty	Test and replace spindle motor (p. 59) ■◒
	Laser or circuit board faulty	Take compact disc player for professional service
Sound, no display lights	Display lights faulty	Replace display lights (p. 134) □○
Sound from only one channel	Controls set incorrectly	Adjust compact disc player controls
	Receiver or speaker faulty	Troubleshoot entertainment system (p. 14) □○
	Circuit board faulty	Take compact disc player for professional service
Sound intermittent or distorted	Receiver or speaker faulty	Troubleshoot entertainment system (p. 14) □○
	Compact disc dirty or faulty	Clean compact disc (p. 54) □○; replace compact disc
	Objective lens dirty	Clean objective lens (p. 55) □○
	Drive belt dirty or loose	Service drive belts (p. 56) □○
	Optical pickup/spindle motor switch faulty	Clean, test and replace motor switch (p. 56) □○
	Mode or feature switch dirty or faulty	Clean switch (p. 57) □○; test and replace switch (p. 57) ▣○
	Optical pickup motor faulty	Test and replace optical pickup motor (p. 59) ■◒
	Spindle motor faulty	Test and replace spindle motor (p. 59) ■◒
	Circuit board faulty	Take compact disc player for professional service
Mode or feature control doesn't work	Mode or feature switch dirty or faulty	Clean switch (p. 57) □○; test and replace switch (p. 57) ▣○
	Laser or circuit board faulty	Take compact disc player for professional service
Compact disc loads, plays, then stops prematurely	Transit screws secured	Loosen transit screws
	Compact disc dirty or faulty	Clean compact disc (p. 54) □○; replace compact disc
	Objective lens dirty	Clean objective lens (p. 55) □○
	Drive belt loose or broken	Service drive belts (p. 56) □○
	Optical pickup/spindle motor switch faulty	Clean, test and replace motor switch (p. 56) □○
	Optical pickup motor faulty	Test and replace optical pickup motor (p. 59) ■◒
	Spindle motor faulty	Test and replace spindle motor (p. 59) ■◒
	Laser or circuit board faulty	Take compact disc player for professional service
Loading drawer doesn't open or doesn't close	Drive belt loose or broken	Service drive belts (p. 56) □○
	Loading motor switch faulty	Clean, test and replace loading motor switch (p. 56) □○
	On/off switch faulty	Test and replace on/off switch (p. 57) ■◒
	Loading motor faulty	Test and replace loading motor (p. 58) ■◒

DEGREE OF DIFFICULTY: □ Easy ▣ Moderate ■ Complex
ESTIMATED TIME: ○ Less than 1 hour ◒ 1 to 3 hours ● Over 3 hours

SERVICING COMPACT DISCS

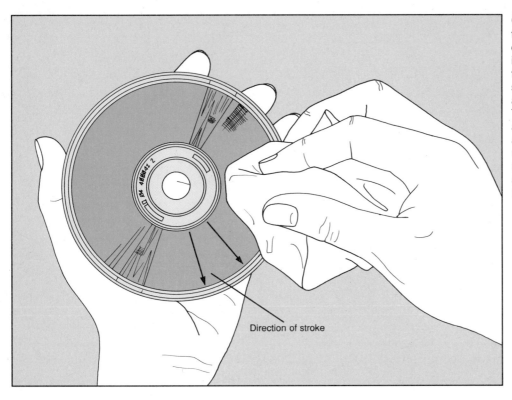

Direction of stroke

Cleaning a disc. Unload the compact disc from the compact disc player. Using a clean, dry, lint-free cloth, wipe dust off the disc. Holding the disc by its outside edge, gently wipe from the center toward the edge in smooth, straight strokes *(left)*; avoid any circular motion and never wipe around the disc circumference. To clean sticky fingerprints or dirt from the disc, apply a commercial compact-disc cleaner, available at an electronics parts supplier. Or, use a clean, lint-free cloth moistened with denatured alcohol. A disc may be washed with a solution of mild detergent and warm water; rinse well and dry with a lint-free cloth.

ACCESS TO THE INTERNAL COMPONENTS

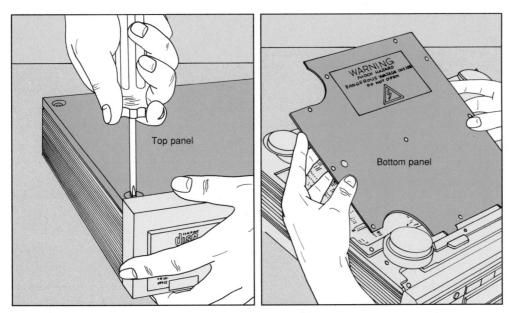

Top panel

Bottom panel

WARNING
SHOCK HAZARD
DANGEROUS VOLTAGE INSIDE
DO NOT OPEN

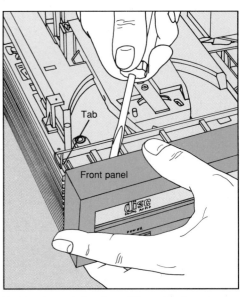

Tab

Front panel

disc

Removing and reinstalling the top and bottom panels. To reach components beneath the loading assembly, first open the loading door *(page 55)*. Unload any compact disc, turn off and unplug the compact disc player, and disconnect the cables hooked up to it *(page 12)*. Secure any transit screws. To remove the top panel, check for screws on the top, sides, back or bottom. Unscrew the top panel *(above, left)*, slide it out from under any lip on the front panel, and lift it off the frame. To remove the bottom panel, check for hidden screws in the feet; unscrew the panel and lift it off the frame *(above, right)*. Reverse this sequence to reinstall the panels. Cold check the compact disc player for leaking voltage *(page 141)*. Reconnect the cables *(page 16)* and plug in the compact disc player.

Removing and reinstalling the front panel or plate. Remove the top panel *(left)*. Check the top, sides and bottom for tabs and screws securing the front panel or plate to the frame. Unscrew the front panel or plate, press in the tabs *(above)* and pull it off. To reinstall the front panel or plate, push it onto the frame to lock the tabs and put back the screws. Reinstall the top panel *(left)*.

ACCESS TO THE INTERNAL COMPONENTS (continued)

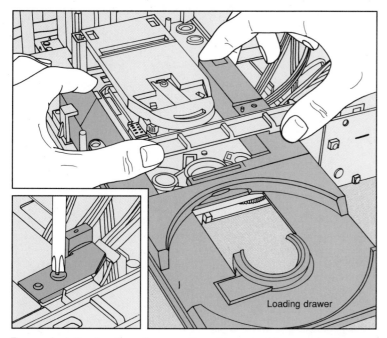

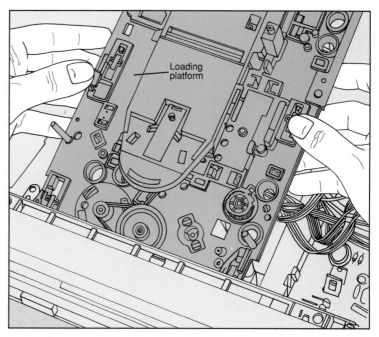

Loading platform

Loading drawer

Removing the loading drawer. Press the open/close control to open the loading drawer, then remove the top panel *(page 54)*. Unscrew the loading drawer guard *(inset)* and set it aside. Gently slide out the loading drawer through the front panel *(above)*. To reach components beneath the loading assembly, remove the loading platform *(right)*. To reinstall the loading drawer, slide it in through the front panel and screw on the guard. Reinstall the top panel *(page 54)* and press the open/close control to close the loading drawer.

Removing the loading platform. Press the open/close control to open the loading drawer. Remove the top panel *(page 54)* and the loading drawer *(left)*. Unscrew the loading platform and disconnect any ground wire connected to it. Lift out the loading platform, sliding it toward the back panel *(above)*. Turn it face down inside the compact disc player, taking care not to damage wire connections. Reverse this sequence to reinstall the loading platform. Reinstall the loading drawer *(left)* and the top panel *(page 54)*.

SERVICING THE OBJECTIVE LENS

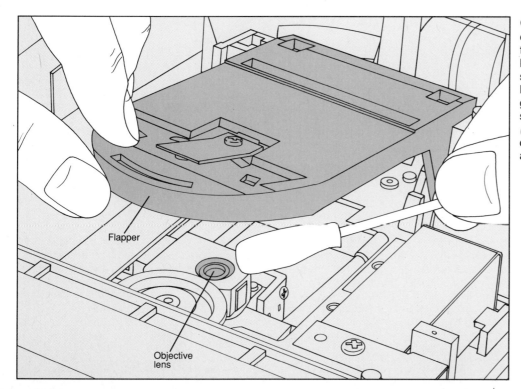

Flapper

Objective lens

Cleaning the objective lens. Press the open/close control to open the loading drawer, and then remove the top panel *(page 54)*. Carefully lift up the flapper and blow dust off the lens with short bursts of compressed air. To clean the lens, use a foam swab moistened with photographic lens cleaner, available at a photographic supplier. Gently wipe the swab across the lens *(left)*; use a fresh, dry swab to wipe off excess cleaner. Reposition the flapper over the lens and reinstall the top panel *(page 54)*.

SERVICING THE DRIVE BELTS

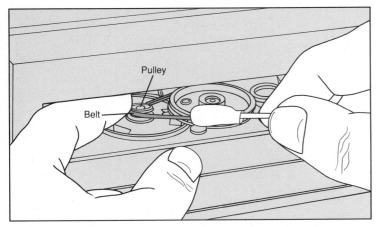

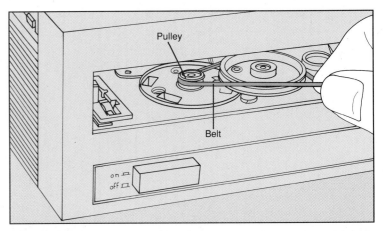

1 **Cleaning a belt.** Remove the top panel *(page 54)* and then the loading drawer *(page 55)*; to reach a belt on the bottom of the loading platform, also remove the loading platform *(page 55)*. If a belt is loose or broken, replace it *(step 2)*. If a belt is sticky or greasy, clean it using a foam swab dipped in rubber-cleaning compound *(above)*; never apply anything oily and avoid touching the belt with your fingers. Turn the belt pulleys to reach the entire length of the belt. Put back the loading platform *(page 55)* if you removed it. Reinstall the loading drawer *(page 55)* and the top panel *(page 54)*.

2 **Replacing a belt.** Slip the damaged belt off the pulleys *(above)*, noting its position. First use long-nose pliers or tweezers to remove any other belt in the way; be careful not to pinch a belt. Purchase an exact replacement belt at an electronics parts supplier. Holding the belt loosely with long-nose pliers or tweezers, wrap it around the pulleys; then reinstall any other belt removed. Put back the loading platform, if you removed it, and the loading drawer *(page 55)*. Reinstall the top panel *(page 54)*.

SERVICING THE MOTOR SWITCHES

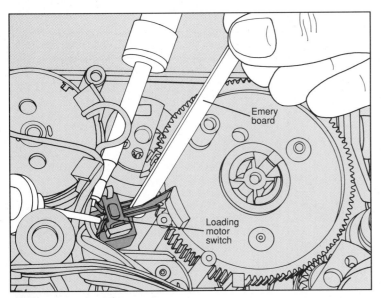

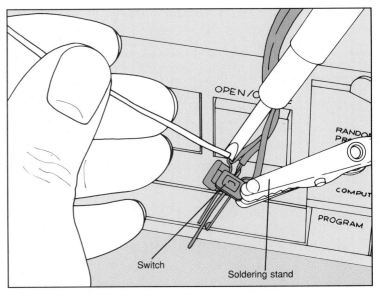

1 **Cleaning and testing a switch.** Remove the top panel *(page 54)* and the loading platform *(page 55)*. The loading motor switch is near the loading gears and lever, as shown; the optical pickup/spindle motor switch is next to the optical pickup assembly rail. If a switch leaf is damaged, replace the switch *(step 2)*. If a switch wire is loose or broken, repair it *(page 132)*. Set a multitester to test continuity *(page 128)*. Touch one probe to a wire terminal on the switch and touch the other probe in turn to each switch-wire terminal on the circuit board. The multitester should register continuity once — and only once. Test each switch wire. If a wire tests faulty, replace it *(page 132)*. If each wire tests OK, gently run an emery board over each leaf to clean the contacts *(above)*. Reinstall the loading platform *(page 55)* and the top panel *(page 54)*.

2 **Removing and replacing a switch.** Unclip or unscrew the switch from the loading platform. Tag the switch wires, noting their terminals, and desolder *(page 130)* the wires from the switch terminals. Order an exact replacement switch from the manufacturer or purchase one at an electronics parts supplier. Set the switch in a soldering stand and solder the wires *(page 131)* to the switch terminals *(above)*. Clip or screw the switch to the loading platform. Reinstall the loading platform *(page 55)* and the top panel *(page 54)*.

SERVICING THE MODE AND FEATURE SWITCHES

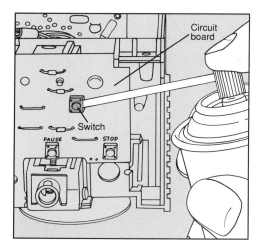

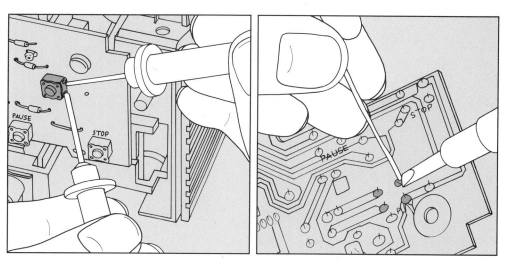

1 **Cleaning a switch.** Remove the top panel and the front panel or plate *(page 54)*. Locate the switch on the circuit board, behind its control. Clean the switch with electronic contact cleaner, directing a short burst into the switch opening *(above)*. Press the switch several times to work in the cleaner. Reinstall the front panel or plate and the top panel *(page 54)*. If the problem persists, remove the panels again to test the switch *(step 2)*.

2 **Testing and replacing a switch.** Set a multitester to test continuity *(page 128)*. Set the switch to one position and touch a probe to each pin on one side of the switch *(above, left)*; repeat this step with the switch set in the other position. The switch should register continuity in only one position. Repeat the procedure at the pins on the other side of the switch. If the switch tests faulty, unscrew and turn over the circuit board. Desolder the switch pins *(page 130)* and wiggle off the switch. Test continuity again to confirm the switch is faulty. Order an exact replacement switch from the manufacturer or purchase one at an electronics parts supplier. Fit the switch pins onto the circuit board and solder *(page 131)* the pins *(above)*. If the switch tests OK, suspect a faulty circuit board and take the compact disc player for professional service. Put back the circuit board and reinstall the panels *(page 54)*.

SERVICING THE ON/OFF SWITCH

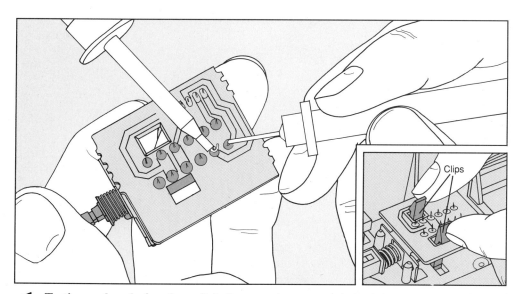

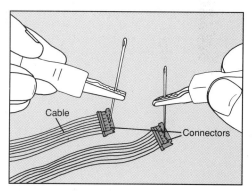

1 **Testing and replacing the switch.** Remove the top panel, the front panel or plate *(page 54)* and the loading platform *(page 55)*. Push off the switch control lever, unclip the switch circuit board *(inset)* and lift it out. Unplug or desolder *(page 130)* the wires from the switch circuit board. Set a multitester to test continuity *(page 128)* and test as for a multi-pole switch *(page 136)*. Hook one probe to a switch contact point and touch the other probe in turn to the other switch contact points, pressing in and releasing the switch for each test *(above)*. Test each contact point with each other contact point, checking for a continuity pattern. If there is a pattern, test the switch wires *(step 2)*. If not, desolder the switch pins *(page 130)* and pull off the switch. Order an exact replacement switch from the manufacturer or purchase one at an electronics parts supplier. Solder the switch pins onto the circuit board *(page 131)*. Put back the switch circuit board, and reinstall the loading platform *(page 55)* and the panels *(page 54)*.

2 **Testing and replacing the switch wires.** If the wires are housed in a cable with connectors at the ends, unplug it. Set a multitester to test continuity *(page 128)*. Clip a needle to each probe. Touch one needle to a contact point at one end of a wire and touch the other needle to each contact point at the other end of the cable *(above)*. The multitester should register continuity once—and only once. Repeat the procedure for each wire. If a wire tests faulty, replace it *(page 132)*. If each wire tests OK, plug in the cable or solder the wires *(page 131)* to the switch circuit board. Put back the circuit board, reversing the sequence used to remove it *(step 1)*. Reinstall the loading platform *(page 55)* and the panels *(page 54)*.

SERVICING THE POWER SUPPLY TRANSFORMER

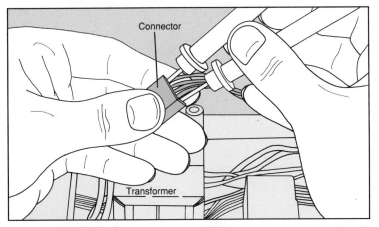

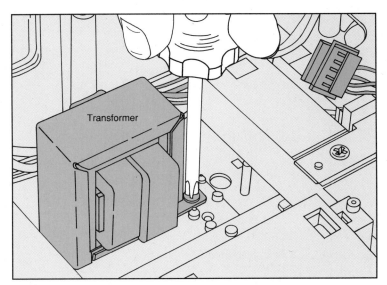

1 **Testing the transformer.** Remove the top panel *(page 54)* and identify the power supply components *(page 138)*. Locate the transformer wires connected to the circuit board and unplug or desolder the wires *(page 130)*. Set a multitester to test voltage *(page 129)*. Clip one probe to the odd-colored wire and clip the other probe to each matching wire, in turn *(above)*; if there is no odd wire, clip the probes to each matching wire pair, in turn. Plug in and turn on the compact disc player; do not look at the laser. The multitester should register voltage for each test. If not, replace the transformer *(step 2)*. If the transformer tests OK, suspect a faulty circuit board and take the compact disc player for professional service. Reinstall the top panel *(page 54)*.

2 **Replacing the transformer.** Disconnect the transformer wires connected to the power cord. Unscrew and remove the transformer from the frame *(above)*. Order an exact replacement transformer from the manufacturer or purchase a substitute at an electronics parts supplier. Install the transformer and reconnect the wires to the power cord. Plug in or solder *(page 131)* the wires to the circuit board. Reinstall the top panel *(page 54)*.

TESTING AND REPLACING THE LOADING MOTOR

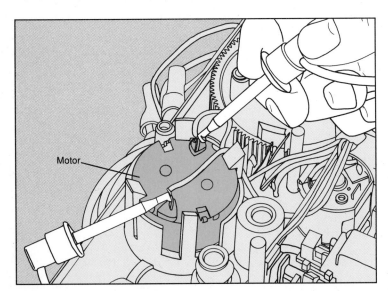

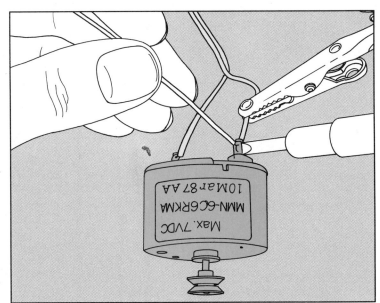

1 **Testing the motor.** Remove the top panel *(page 54)* and the loading platform *(page 55)*. Set a multitester to test voltage *(page 129)*. Hook a probe to each motor wire, avoiding any contact with other components *(above)*. Plug in and turn on the compact disc player; do not look at the laser. Press the loading drawer open/close control and note the multitester reading. Turn off and unplug the compact disc player. If the multitester registers voltage, replace the motor *(step 2)*. If not, suspect a faulty circuit board and take the compact disc player for professional service. Reinstall the loading platform *(page 55)* and the top panel *(page 54)*.

2 **Replacing the motor.** Using long-nose pliers or tweezers, carefully slip the belt off the motor pulley. Unclip the motor and lift it from its housing. Desolder the wires from the motor terminals *(page 130)*. Order an exact replacement motor from the manufacturer. Solder *(page 131)* the wires to the motor terminals *(above)* and clip the motor into the housing. Reinstall the drive belt using long-nose pliers or tweezers. Reinstall the loading platform *(page 55)* and the top panel *(page 54)*. If the problem persists, suspect a faulty circuit board and take the compact disc player for professional service.

TESTING AND REPLACING THE OPTICAL PICKUP MOTOR

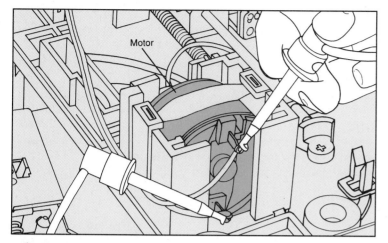

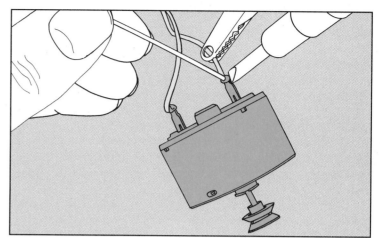

1 Testing the motor. Remove the top panel *(page 54)* and the loading platform *(page 55)*. Set a multitester to test voltage *(page 129)*. Hook a probe to each optical-pickup motor wire *(above)*. Reinstall the loading drawer in the platform *(page 55)*. Plug in and turn on the compact disc player; do not look at the laser. Load a compact disc and press the play mode control. Note the multitester reading. Unload the compact disc, and turn off and unplug the compact disc player. If the multitester registers voltage, replace the motor *(step 2)*. If not, suspect a faulty circuit board and take the compact disc player for professional service. Remove the loading drawer, put back the loading platform *(page 55)* and reinstall the top panel *(page 54)*.

2 Replacing the motor. Using long-nose pliers or tweezers, carefully slip the drive belt off the optical-pickup motor pulley. Unclip the motor and lift it from its housing. Desolder the wires *(page 130)* from the motor terminals. Order an exact replacement motor from the manufacturer. Solder the wires *(page 131)* to the motor terminals *(above)* and clip the motor into the housing. Slip the drive belt around the motor pulley. Remove the loading drawer, put back the loading platform *(page 55)* and reinstall the top panel *(page 54)*. If the problem persists, suspect a faulty circuit board and take the compact disc player for professional service.

TESTING AND REPLACING THE SPINDLE DRIVE MOTOR

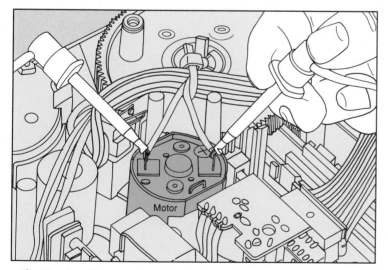

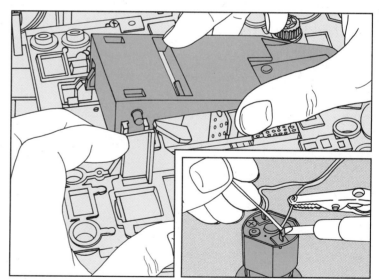

1 Testing the motor. Remove the top panel *(page 54)* and the loading platform *(page 55)*. Set a multitester to test voltage *(page 129)*. Hook a probe to each spindle motor wire *(above)*. Reinstall the loading drawer in the platform *(page 55)*. Plug in and turn on the compact disc player; do not look at the laser. Load a compact disc and press the play mode control. Note the multitester reading. Unload the compact disc, and turn off and unplug the compact disc player. If the multitester registers voltage, replace the motor *(step 2)*. If not, suspect a faulty circuit board and take the compact disc player for professional service. Remove the loading drawer, put back the loading platform *(page 55)* and reinstall the top panel *(page 54)*.

2 Replacing the motor. Use long-nose pliers or tweezers to slip the belt off the motor pulley and remove the flapper spring. Unclip the flapper *(above)*. Unscrew the motor; turn the optical-pickup motor pulley to move the laser assembly out of the way. Desolder the wires *(page 130)* from the motor terminals. Order an exact replacement motor from the manufacturer. Solder the wires *(page 131)* to the terminals *(inset)* and screw in the motor. Slip the belt around the pulley, clip on the flapper and rehook the spring. Remove the loading drawer, put back the loading platform *(page 55)* and reinstall the top panel *(page 54)*. If the problem persists, suspect a faulty circuit board and take the compact disc player for professional service.

SPEAKERS AND HEADPHONES

The final step in sound transmission by an audio system is performed by your speakers or headphones *(below)*. In the speaker, incoming electrical signals are routed to the crossover network, where they are divided into frequency ranges and directed to the drivers, which reproduce the signals as various sound frequencies. In headphones, incoming signals are sent directly to the drivers.

Many audio problems are experienced through the speakers or headphones; often these units are not the cause, but can be a valuable tool in troubleshooting other units in the audio system. Consult the Troubleshooting Guide in Entertainment Systems *(page 14)* and in this chapter *(page 61)*.

Often, problems can be remedied by adjusting cable hook-ups. A wire may be loose or broken, or a component may test faulty. Replacement components are usually available from an electronics parts supplier. A special driver or crossover network may have to be ordered from the manufacturer.

A set of small screwdrivers, a multitester and a soldering iron complete the basic tool kit required for speaker and headphone repairs *(page 126)*. Refer to Tools & Techniques for instructions on testing continuity and resistance *(pages 128-129)* and for directions on desoldering and soldering *(pages 130-131)*.

When disconnecting a speaker cable, tag the positive wire to maintain the polarity of the electrical connection.

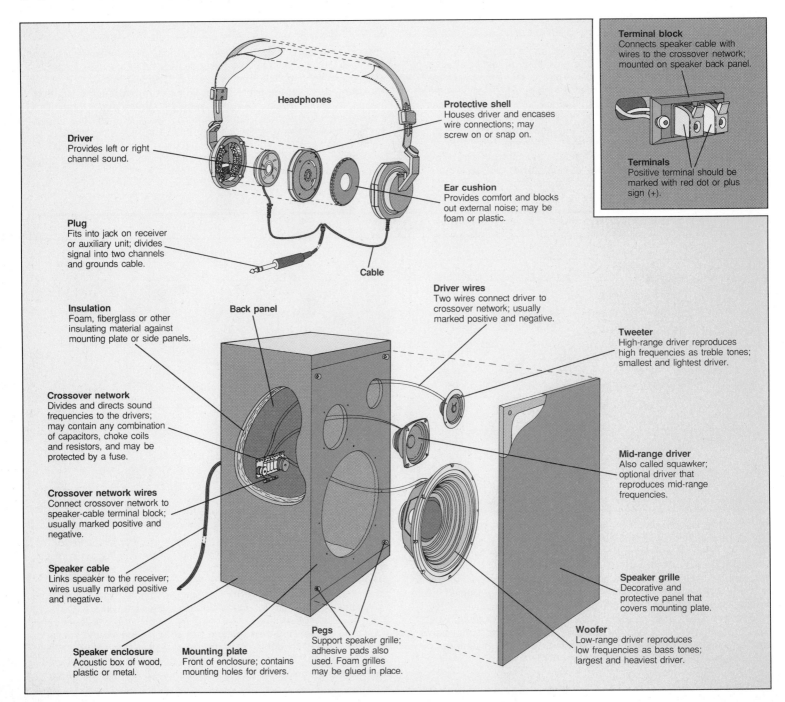

Terminal block
Connects speaker cable with wires to the crossover network; mounted on speaker back panel.

Terminals
Positive terminal should be marked with red dot or plus sign (+).

Headphones

Driver
Provides left or right channel sound.

Protective shell
Houses driver and encases wire connections; may screw on or snap on.

Ear cushion
Provides comfort and blocks out external noise; may be foam or plastic.

Plug
Fits into jack on receiver or auxiliary unit; divides signal into two channels and grounds cable.

Cable

Insulation
Foam, fiberglass or other insulating material against mounting plate or side panels.

Back panel

Driver wires
Two wires connect driver to crossover network; usually marked positive and negative.

Tweeter
High-range driver reproduces high frequencies as treble tones; smallest and lightest driver.

Crossover network
Divides and directs sound frequencies to the drivers; may contain any combination of capacitors, choke coils and resistors, and may be protected by a fuse.

Crossover network wires
Connect crossover network to speaker-cable terminal block; usually marked positive and negative.

Speaker cable
Links speaker to the receiver; wires usually marked positive and negative.

Mid-range driver
Also called squawker; optional driver that reproduces mid-range frequencies.

Speaker enclosure
Acoustic box of wood, plastic or metal.

Mounting plate
Front of enclosure; contains mounting holes for drivers.

Pegs
Support speaker grille; adhesive pads also used. Foam grilles may be glued in place.

Speaker grille
Decorative and protective panel that covers mounting plate.

Woofer
Low-range driver reproduces low frequencies as bass tones; largest and heaviest driver.

TROUBLESHOOTING GUIDE

SYMPTOM	POSSIBLE CAUSE	PROCEDURE
No sound	Receiver or auxiliary unit faulty	Troubleshoot entertainment system (p. 14) □○
No sound from speakers; sound from headphones	Receiver or auxiliary unit faulty	Troubleshoot entertainment system (p. 14) □○
	Speaker fuses blown	Test and replace fuses (p. 137) □○
Sound from only one speaker	Receiver or auxiliary unit faulty	Troubleshoot entertainment system (p. 14) □○
	Speaker fuse blown	Test and replace fuses (p. 137) □○
	Crossover network faulty	Service crossover network (p. 64) □○
Intermittent sound from speaker	Receiver or auxiliary unit faulty	Troubleshoot entertainment system (p. 14) □○
	Driver faulty	Test and replace drivers (p. 63) □○
	Crossover network faulty	Service crossover network (p. 64) □○
Distorted sound from speaker	Receiver or auxiliary unit faulty	Troubleshoot entertainment system (p. 14) □○
	Cone loose or punctured	Repair speaker cone (p. 63) □○
	Driver faulty	Test and replace drivers (p. 63) □○
	Crossover network faulty	Service crossover network (p. 64) □○
Humming, buzzing or rumbling noise from speaker	Receiver or auxiliary unit faulty	Troubleshoot entertainment system (p. 14) □○
	Speaker vibrating or too close to turntable	Reposition speakers
	Cone loose or punctured	Repair speaker cone (p. 63) □○
	Insulation loose	Apply rubber cement to corners of insulation
	Driver faulty	Test and replace drivers (p. 63) □○
	Crossover network faulty	Service crossover network (p. 64) □○
No low-range (bass) sound from speaker	Receiver or auxiliary unit faulty	Troubleshoot entertainment system (p. 14) □○
	Woofer faulty	Test and replace drivers (p. 63) □○
	Crossover network faulty	Service crossover network (p. 64) □○
No high-range (treble) sound from speaker	Receiver or auxiliary unit faulty	Troubleshoot entertainment system (p. 14) □○
	Tweeter faulty	Test and replace drivers (p. 63) □○
	Crossover network faulty	Service crossover network (p. 64) □○
No mid-range (voice) sound from speaker	Receiver or auxiliary unit faulty	Troubleshoot entertainment system (p. 14) □○
	Mid-range driver faulty	Test and replace drivers (p. 63) □○
	Crossover network faulty	Service crossover network (p. 64) □○
Speaker grille damaged	Wear and tear	Replace speaker grille (p. 62) □○
No sound from headphones; sound from speakers	Headphones unplugged	Plug in headphones
	Receiver or auxiliary unit faulty	Troubleshoot entertainment system (p. 14) □○
	Plug faulty	Test and replace headphone plug (p. 67) □○
	Cable faulty	Test and replace headphone cable (p. 67) □○
	Jack faulty	Take unit for professional service
Sound from only one headphone	Receiver or auxiliary unit faulty	Troubleshoot entertainment system (p. 14) □○
	Driver faulty	Test and replace headphone drivers (p. 66) □○
	Plug faulty	Test and replace headphone plug (p. 67) □○
	Cable faulty	Test and replace headphone cable (p. 67) □○
Intermittent sound from headphones	Receiver or auxiliary unit faulty	Troubleshoot entertainment system (p. 14) □○
	Plug faulty	Test and replace headphone plug (p. 67) □○
	Cable faulty	Test and replace headphone cable (p. 67) □○
	Jack faulty	Take unit for professional service
Distorted sound from headphones	Receiver or auxiliary unit faulty	Troubleshoot entertainment system (p. 14) □○
	Driver faulty	Test and replace headphone drivers (p. 66) □○

DEGREE OF DIFFICULTY: □ Easy ◪ Moderate ■ Complex
ESTIMATED TIME: ○ Less than 1 hour ◖ 1 to 3 hours ● Over 3 hours

ACCESS TO THE COMPONENTS

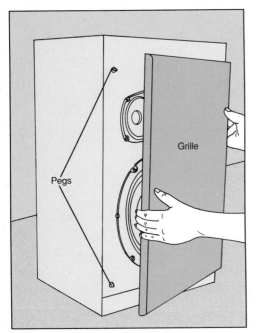

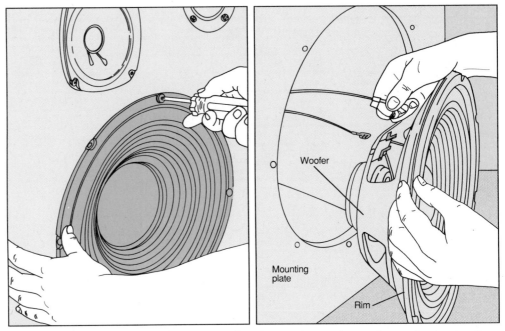

1 **Removing and reinstalling the speaker grille.** Remove any screws securing the front grille and gently pull it off the pegs or adhesive tabs *(above)*. If the grille does not come off easily, run a small putty knife under each corner to break any glue bond. To reach internal components, remove the woofer *(step 2)*. To reinstall the speaker grille, press it onto the pegs or adhesive tabs and put back any screws; if required, apply a small dab of cement to the corners.

2 **Removing and reinstalling the woofer.** Turn off the receiver and any other input unit and disconnect the cable from the speaker terminals *(page 12)*, tagging the positive terminal wire. Unscrew the woofer from the mounting plate *(above, left)*. Hold the woofer securely by the rim and gently pull it free of the mounting plate. Supporting the woofer on its rim or turning it face down, tag the positive wire and disconnect or desolder *(page 130)* the wires from the woofer terminals *(above, right)*. Carefully set the woofer aside. If required, repeat this procedure to remove the tweeter or the mid-range driver. To reinstall a driver, reconnect or solder *(page 131)* the wires to the driver terminals, screw the driver to the mounting plate, and put back the grille *(step 1)*. Reconnect the cable to the speaker terminals *(page 16)*.

REPLACING THE GRILLE

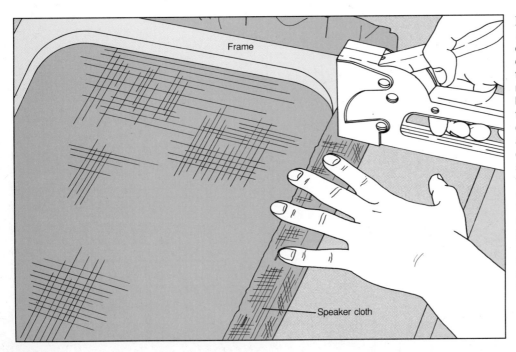

Recovering the grille. Remove the grille *(above)*. If the grille is foam, purchase an identical replacement grille. If the speaker grille is cloth-covered, pry off any staples or tacks holding the cloth to the frame using a small screwdriver; run a utility knife around the edges, if required, to break any glue bond. Remove old glue from the frame with medium-grit sandpaper. Measure the old grille cloth and purchase replacement cloth at an electronics parts supplier. If the replacement cloth is too large, trim it almost to size using scissors. Set the new cloth face down on a clean work table and lay the frame on it. Staple the cloth smoothly along one side of the frame. Pull the cloth snugly across the frame and staple it along the opposite frame edge *(left)*. Repeat this procedure on the other two sides of the frame. If the cloth wrinkles, pull out the nearest staples, stretch the cloth and restaple it. Cut off any excess cloth, especially at the corners, to avoid bulky pleats.

REPAIRING DRIVER CONES

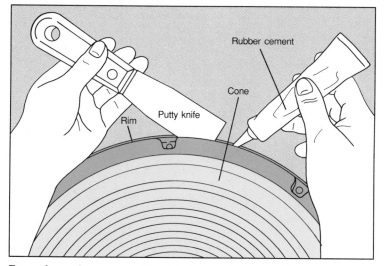

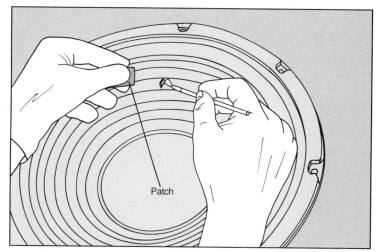

Reseating a loose cone. Remove the speaker grille *(page 62)*. If the woofer, tweeter or mid-range driver cone is damaged, remove the driver *(page 62)*. If the driver cone is badly torn or separated from the spider, or frame, replace the driver *(page 64)*. If there is a small hole in the driver cone, seal the puncture *(right)*. If a small section of the driver cone is separated from the rim, gently raise the cone away from the rim with a small putty knife and spread a small amount of rubber cement along the edges of the cone and rim *(above)*. Allow the cement to dry, then lightly press the cone against the rim until the rubber cement adheres. Reinstall the driver and the speaker grille *(page 62)*.

Sealing a punctured cone. Remove the speaker grille *(page 62)*. If the woofer, tweeter or mid-range driver cone is damaged, remove the driver *(page 62)*. If the driver cone is badly torn or separated from the spider, or frame, replace the driver *(page 64)*. If a small section of the driver cone is separated from the rim, reseat the cone *(left)*. If there is a small hole in the driver cone, cut a patch slightly larger than the puncture from paper about the same thickness as the cone. Wearing a rubber glove, saturate the patch with rubber cement and use a small brush to apply a light coat of rubber cement around the cone puncture *(above)*. Allow the cement to dry, then set the patch over the puncture and gently press it until the cement adheres. Reinstall the driver and the speaker grille *(page 62)*.

SERVICING THE DRIVERS

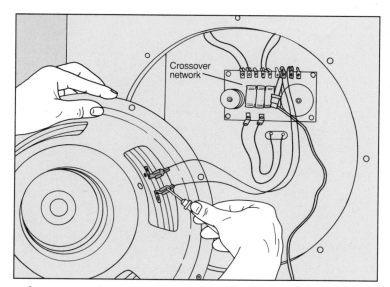

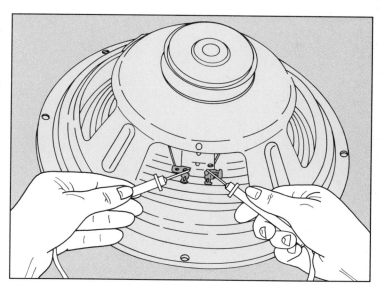

1 Testing between the driver and the crossover network. Remove the speaker grille and the woofer *(page 62)*. To test from the woofer, the tweeter or the mid-range driver, remove the driver *(page 62)* but leave the wires connected to the terminals. If a wire connecting to the crossover network is loose or broken, tighten or replace it *(page 132)*. Set a multitester to test continuity *(page 128)*. Hook one probe to a wire terminal on the crossover network and touch the other probe to that wire's terminal on the driver *(above)*. Repeat this step for the other wire. If a wire does not have continuity, replace it *(page 132)*. If each wire has continuity, test the driver *(step 2)*.

2 Testing the driver. Tag the positive terminal wire and disconnect or desolder *(page 130)* the wires from the driver terminals. Place the driver face down on a work table and set a multitester to test resistance *(page 129)*. Touch the positive probe to the positive driver terminal and touch the negative probe to the negative driver terminal *(above)*. The multitester should register close to the ohms rating indicated on the driver or specified by the speaker manufacturer. If the driver does not register what it should, replace it *(step 3)*. If the driver registers what it should, service the crossover network *(page 64)*.

SERVICING THE DRIVERS (continued)

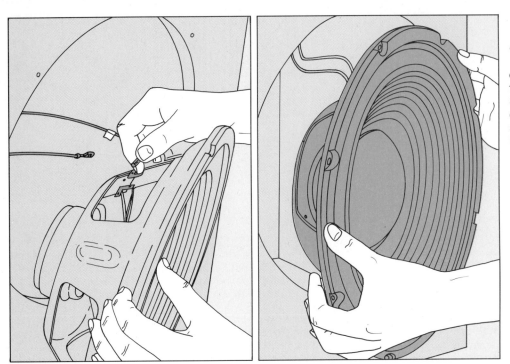

3 **Replacing the driver.** Purchase an exact replacement driver at an electronics parts suppliers. Connect or solder *(page 131)* the tagged positive wire to the positive driver terminal *(far left)* and connect or solder the other wire to the negative driver terminal. Supporting the driver by its rim, set it into the opening in the mounting plate *(near left)* and screw it securely in place. Reinstall the woofer, if required, and the speaker grille *(page 62)*.

SERVICING THE CROSSOVER NETWORK

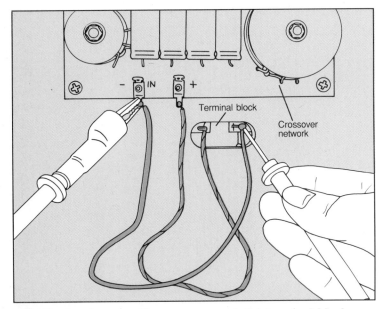

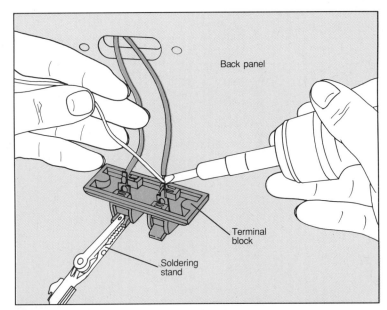

Back panel

Terminal block

Soldering stand

1 **Testing between the crossover and the terminal block.** Remove the speaker grille and the woofer *(page 62)*. Locate the two wires connecting the crossover network to the terminal block. If a wire is loose or broken, tighten or replace it *(page 132)*; if required, remove the terminal block *(step 2)*. Set a multitester to test continuity *(page 128)*. Clip one probe to a wire terminal on the crossover network and touch the other probe to that wire's terminal on the terminal block. Repeat this step for the other wire. If a wire does not have continuity, replace it *(step 2)*. If each wire has continuity, test the crossover network *(step 3)*.

2 **Repairing the wire connections.** Disconnect or desolder *(page 130)* the wire from the crossover network terminal. To gain access to the wire terminal on the terminal block, remove the exterior terminal block screws and pull the terminal block off the back panel. Secure the terminal block in a soldering stand and desolder the wire. Purchase a length of replacement wire the identical gauge at an electronics parts supplier; if required, also purchase a set of crimp connectors. Cut the wire to length and crimp on a connector at one end *(page 132)*. Connect the end with the crimp connector to the terminal on the crossover network and solder *(page 131)* the other wire end to the terminal on the terminal block *(above)*. Screw in the terminal block and reinstall the woofer and the speaker grille *(page 62)*.

SERVICING THE CROSSOVER NETWORK (continued)

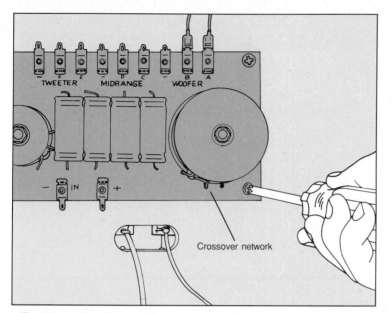

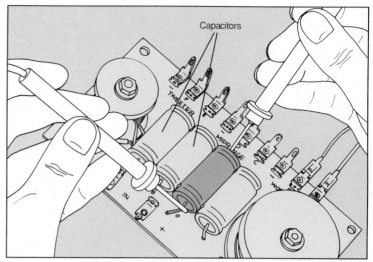

Capacitors

3 **Removing the crossover network.** Tag the wires connecting the crossover network to the tweeter, any mid-range driver and the terminal block, noting the terminal positions. Disconnect or desolder *(page 130)* the wires from the crossover network, leaving the woofer wires connected. Unscrew the crossover network from the back panel *(above)* and lift it out. Test the crossover network capacitors *(step 4)* and choke coils *(step 5)*; or, tag and disconnect the wires to the woofer, noting the terminal positions, and install an exact replacement crossover network purchased at an electronics parts supplier *(step 6)*.

Crossover network

4 **Testing and replacing the capacitors.** Desolder one capacitor wire *(page 130)* and pull it off the circuit board with long-nose pliers. Set a multitester to test resistance *(page 129)* and touch the positive probe to the positive wire and the negative probe to the negative wire *(above)*. The multitester should register a sharp drop and then a rise in ohms. Repeat this procedure for each capacitor. If each capacitor registers what it should, resolder the capacitor wires *(page 131)* and test the choke coils *(step 5)*. If a capacitor does not register what it should, desolder its other wire *(page 130)* and remove the capacitor. Purchase an exact replacement capacitor at an electronics parts supplier. Position the capacitor on the circuit board, thread the wires through the openings and solder them *(page 131)*. Reinstall the crossover network *(step 6)*.

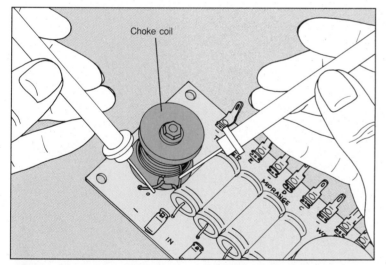

Choke coil

5 **Testing and replacing the choke coils.** Desolder one choke coil wire *(page 130)* and pull it off the circuit board with long-nose pliers. Set a multitester to test resistance *(page 129)*. Touch one probe to the middle choke coil wire and touch the other probe in turn to each other choke coil wire *(above)*. The multitester should register low, steady ohms for both tests. Repeat this test for the other choke coil. If each choke coil registers what it should, resolder the choke coil wires *(page 131)* and reinstall the crossover network *(step 6)*. If a choke coil does not register what it should, desolder the other choke coil wires *(page 130)*, noting their positions, and remove the choke coil. Purchase an exact replacement choke coil at an electronics parts supplier. Position it on the circuit board, thread the wires through the openings and solder them *(page 131)*. Reinstall the crossover network *(step 6)*.

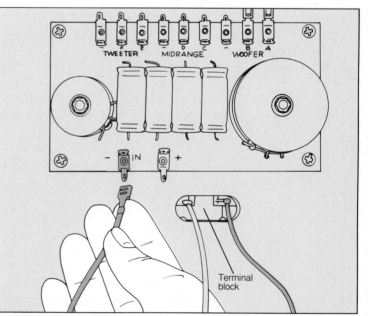

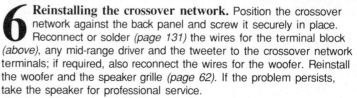

Terminal block

6 **Reinstalling the crossover network.** Position the crossover network against the back panel and screw it securely in place. Reconnect or solder *(page 131)* the wires for the terminal block *(above)*, any mid-range driver and the tweeter to the crossover network terminals; if required, also reconnect the wires for the woofer. Reinstall the woofer and the speaker grille *(page 62)*. If the problem persists, take the speaker for professional service.

SERVICING THE HEADPHONE DRIVERS

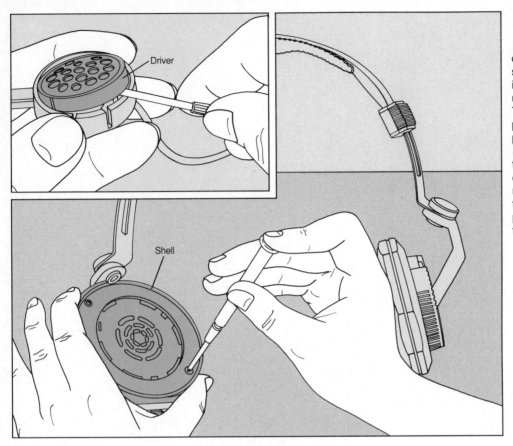

1 Removing the shell. Unplug the headphones from the receiver or other auxiliary unit jack. To reach the driver wire terminals on large headphones, pull the ear cushion off the shell and remove any screws from the shell casings *(left)*. If the casings do not separate easily, use a small putty knife to pry them gently apart. To reach the driver wire terminals on small headphones, remove the outer foam cap and carefully pry out the driver using a small screwdriver *(inset)*. If the wire connections look secure, test the driver *(step 2)*. If a wire is loose or broken, either repair the wire connection *(page 132)* or replace the entire cable *(page 67)*. To reinstall the shell, reverse the procedure above. If the problem persists, remove the shell again and test the driver *(step 2)*.

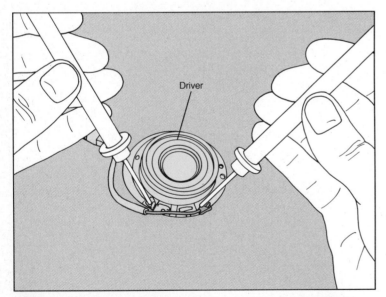

2 Testing the driver. Lift the driver out of the shell and desolder the wire *(page 130)* from the positive driver terminal. Place the driver face down on a clean work table and set a multitester to test resistance *(page 129)*. Touch the positive probe to the positive driver terminal and touch the negative probe to the negative driver terminal *(above)*. The multitester should register close to the ohms rating indicated on the driver or specified by the headphone manufacturer. If the driver registers 0 or infinite ohms, replace it *(step 3)*. If the driver registers what it should, solder the wire to the positive driver terminal *(page 131)*, fit the driver into the shell, reinstall the shell *(step 1)* and service the headphone plug *(page 67)*.

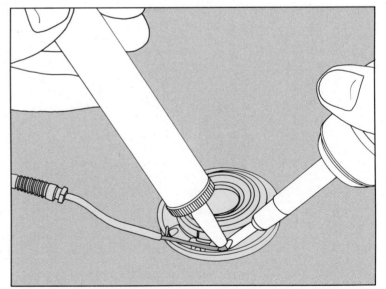

3 Replacing the driver. Desolder *(page 130)* the other wire from the driver terminal *(above)*. Order an exact replacement driver from the headphone manufacturer or purchase a substitute driver at an electronics parts supplier. Solder *(page 131)* the insulated wire to the positive driver terminal and solder the uninsulated wire to the negative terminal. Position the driver in the shell and reinstall the shell *(step 1)*.

SERVICING THE HEADPHONE PLUG

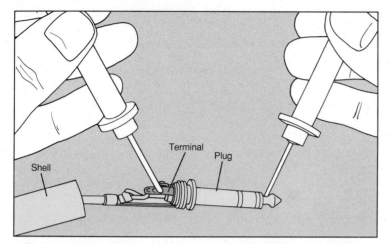

1 **Testing the plug.** Unplug the headphone cable and unscrew the plug shell to expose the wire terminals. If a wire is loose or broken, repair it *(page 132)* or replace the cable *(below)*. Set a multitester to test continuity *(page 128)*. Touch one probe to one wire terminal and touch the other probe in turn to each of the three plug sections *(above)*. The multitester should register continuity once—and only once. Repeat this procedure at each wire terminal. If the plug tests faulty, replace it *(step 2)* or the cable *(below)*. If the plug is molded to the cable, put on the headphones and set a multitester to test resistance *(page 129)*. Touch one probe to the plug tip and touch the other probe in turn to the other two plug sections; then, touch both probes to the two sections farthest from the tip. There should be an audible click for each test. If the plug tests faulty, replace the cable. If the plug tests OK, have the receiver or auxiliary unit jack serviced.

2 **Replacing the plug.** Snip off the plug using wire cutters or a utility knife and remove the shell and insulating sleeve from the cable. Purchase an exact replacement plug at an electronics parts supplier. Unscrew the shell and slide it and any insulating sleeve onto the cable. Using a soldering stand to support the plug, repair the wire connections *(page 132)*, matching their positions in the old plug. Solder *(page 131)* the uninsulated wire to the terminal farthest from the plug tip and the insulated wires to the other plug terminals *(above)*. Squeeze the plug clips together with pliers to secure the cable. Slide any insulating sleeve and the shell over the plug wire terminals and screw on the shell.

SERVICING THE HEADPHONE CABLE

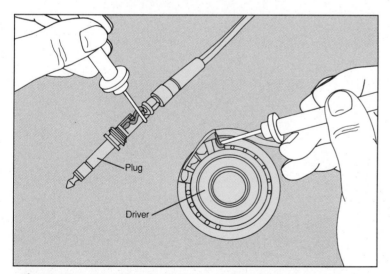

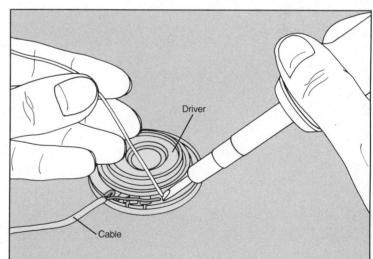

1 **Testing the wires.** Remove the shell *(page 66)* and lift out the driver. Desolder the wire *(page 130)* from the positive driver terminal. Set a multitester to test continuity *(page 128)*. Touch one probe to a driver wire terminal and touch the other probe in turn to each wire terminal on the plug *(above)*. The multitester should register continuity once—and only once. Repeat this step for the other driver terminal wire. If a wire tests faulty, replace the cable *(step 2)*. If each wire tests OK, solder the wire *(page 131)* to the positive driver terminal, fit the driver into the shell and reinstall the shell *(page 66)*; have the receiver or auxiliary unit jack serviced.

2 **Replacing the cable.** Remove the other headphone shell and desolder the wires *(page 130)* from the terminals of each driver *(above)*. Purchase a replacement headphone cable-and-plug set at an electronics parts supplier. Connect one side of the cable to each driver, soldering *(page 131)* the insulated wires to the positive driver terminals and the uninsulated wires to the negative driver terminals *(above)*. Position the drivers in the shells and put back any screws in the casings; if required, apply a little cement around the casing edges. Press in the ear cushions or reinstall the foam caps. If the problem persists, have the receiver or auxiliary unit jack serviced.

TELEVISIONS

Through cables from the antenna or cable system, the television tuner receives a broadcast signal and changes it into electrical video and audio signals. The video signal is sent to the picture tube. A cathode ray tube, it projects visual images by beaming electrons through a vacuum against the phosphorescent inside face of the screen. The audio signal is routed to one or more drivers inside the television, or possibly through cables to the receiver and then to the speakers.

Thanks to its solid-state circuitry, little goes wrong with a modern television (below). To diagnose problems, consult the Troubleshooting Guide in Entertainment Systems (page 14) and in this chapter (page 69). Often, problems can be reme-

died by adjusting cable hookups; on an older television, the mechanical tuner may need cleaning. Cleaning supplies and most replacement components are available at an electronics parts supplier.

Refer to Tools & Techniques for instructions on disassembly and reassembly (page 140), testing continuity and resistance (pages 128-129), and desoldering and soldering (pages 130-131). Turn off and unplug the television before any repair. Perform a cold check for leaking voltage (page 141) both before disassembling and after reassembling the television. Stay away from the picture tube when working; there may be high voltage stored in it, even after 24 hours.

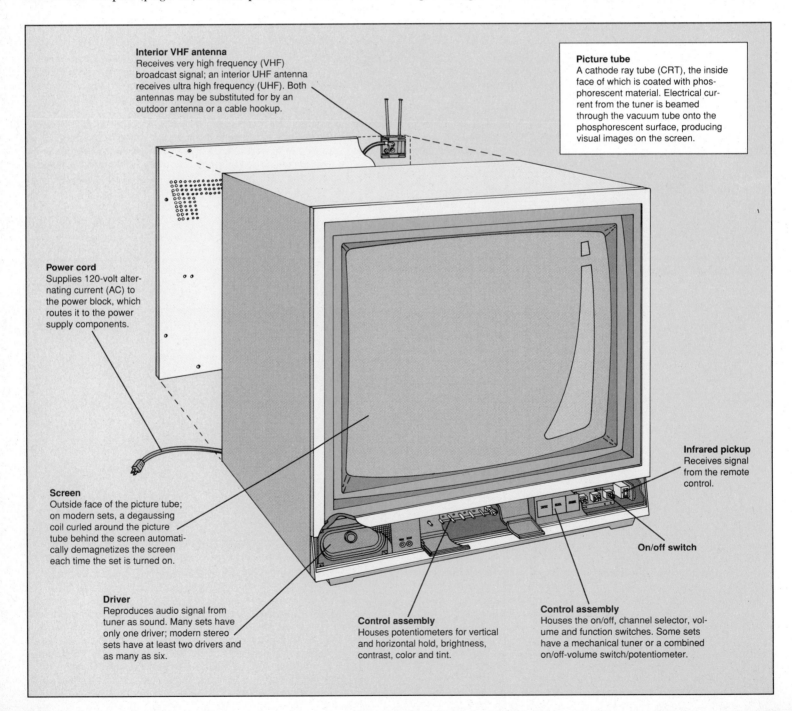

Interior VHF antenna
Receives very high frequency (VHF) broadcast signal; an interior UHF antenna receives ultra high frequency (UHF). Both antennas may be substituted for by an outdoor antenna or a cable hookup.

Picture tube
A cathode ray tube (CRT), the inside face of which is coated with phosphorescent material. Electrical current from the tuner is beamed through the vacuum tube onto the phosphorescent surface, producing visual images on the screen.

Power cord
Supplies 120-volt alternating current (AC) to the power block, which routes it to the power supply components.

Infrared pickup
Receives signal from the remote control.

Screen
Outside face of the picture tube; on modern sets, a degaussing coil curled around the picture tube behind the screen automatically demagnetizes the screen each time the set is turned on.

On/off switch

Driver
Reproduces audio signal from tuner as sound. Many sets have only one driver; modern stereo sets have at least two drivers and as many as six.

Control assembly
Houses potentiometers for vertical and horizontal hold, brightness, contrast, color and tint.

Control assembly
Houses the on/off, channel selector, volume and function switches. Some sets have a mechanical tuner or a combined on/off-volume switch/potentiometer.

TROUBLESHOOTING GUIDE

SYMPTOM	POSSIBLE CAUSE	PROCEDURE
No display lights, no picture and no sound	Television unplugged or turned off	Plug in and turn on television
	Remote control dirty or faulty	Service remote control *(p. 136)* □○
	No power to outlet or outlet faulty	Reset breaker or replace fuse *(p. 10)* □○; have outlet serviced
	Power cord faulty	Test and replace power cord *(p. 137)* □○
	Power fuse blown	Test and replace power fuse *(p. 72)* □○
	On/off switch faulty	Test and replace combined switch/potentiometer *(p. 73)* □○ or test and replace mode switch *(p. 74)* □○
	Power supply or circuit board faulty	Take television for professional service
Display lights, but no picture and no sound	Videocassette recorder faulty	Troubleshoot entertainment system *(p. 14)* □○
	Circuit board faulty	Take television for professional service
Picture, but no sound	Controls set incorrectly	Adjust television controls
	Videocassette recorder or receiver faulty	Troubleshoot entertainment system *(p. 14)* □○
	Driver faulty	Test and replace driver *(p. 72)* □○
	Volume switch or potentiometer dirty or faulty	Clean, test and replace combined switch/potentiometer *(p. 73)* □○, or switch *(p. 74)* □○ or potentiometer *(p. 75)* □○
	Circuit board faulty	Take television for professional service
Sound, but no picture	Controls set incorrectly	Adjust television controls
	Videocassette recorder faulty	Troubleshoot entertainment system *(p. 14)* □○
	Potentiometer dirty or faulty	Clean, test and replace potentiometer *(p. 75)* □○
	Picture tube or circuit board faulty	Take television for professional service
Sound from only one channel	Videocassette recorder, receiver or speaker faulty	Troubleshoot entertainment system *(p. 14)* □○
	Driver faulty	Test and replace driver *(p. 72)* □○
	Circuit board faulty	Take television for professional service
Picture or sound intermittent or distorted	Antenna or cable system, videocassette recorder, receiver or speaker faulty	Troubleshoot entertainment system *(p. 14)* □○
	Screen static	Service screen *(p. 70)* □○▲
	Interior antenna broken	Replace antenna *(p. 71)* □○
	Mechanical tuner dirty	Service mechanical tuner *(p. 71)* □○
	Driver faulty	Test and replace driver *(p. 72)* □○
	Circuit board faulty	Take television for professional service
Mode or feature control doesn't work	Mode or feature switch or potentiometer dirty or faulty	Clean, test and replace combined switch/potentiometer *(p. 73)* □○, or mode or feature switch *(p. 74)* □○ or potentiometer *(p. 75)* □○
	Circuit board faulty	Take television for professional service
Feature control abrupt or scratchy	Feature potentiometer dirty or faulty	Clean, test and replace potentiometer *(p. 75)* □○
	Circuit board faulty	Take television for professional service
Mechanical tuner abrupt, scratchy or doesn't work	Mechanical tuner dirty	Service mechanical tuner *(p. 71)* □○
	Mechanical tuner or circuit board faulty	Take television for professional service
Color tones wrong	Controls set incorrectly	Adjust television controls
	Antenna or cable system or videocassette recorder faulty	Troubleshoot entertainment system *(p. 14)* □○
	Screen static	Service screen *(p. 70)* □○
	Interior antenna broken	Replace antenna *(p. 71)* □○
	Potentiometer dirty or faulty	Clean, test and replace potentiometer *(p. 75)* □○
	Tuner or circuit board faulty	Take television for professional service
Burning odor	Air vents blocked or dirty	Reposition television or clean air vents
	Power fuse blown	Test and replace power fuse *(p. 72)* □○
	Internal component faulty	Take television for professional service

DEGREE OF DIFFICULTY: □ **Easy** ◨ **Moderate** ■ **Complex**
ESTIMATED TIME: ○ **Less than 1 hour** ◗ **1 to 3 hours** ● **Over 3 hours**　　　　　　▲ **Special tool required**

SERVICING THE SCREEN

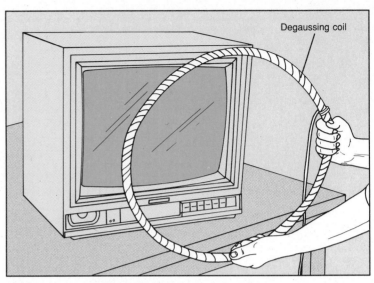

Degaussing coil

1 Cleaning the screen. Turn off the television. Wipe dust and fingerprints off the television screen using a clean, lint-free cloth moistened with window cleaner or a solution of mild detergent and warm water *(above)*. Rinse detergent off the screen, then dry it using a fresh cloth. Wash the screen at least once a month. If your television has a built-in degaussing coil, it is demagnetized automatically; turn on the television. If your television has no degaussing coil, or if the coil no longer functions, demagnetize the screen *(step 2)*.

2 Demagnetizing the screen. Purchase a degaussing coil at an electronics parts supplier. Unplug the television from the wall outlet and plug in the degaussing coil. Turn on the degaussing coil about 6 feet away from the television and bring it within an inch of the screen. Slowly circle the coil several times around the front of the screen without touching it *(above)*. Gradually draw the coil 6 feet away and turn it off. Unplug the degaussing coil and plug in and turn on the television. Demagnetize after each cleaning.

ACCESS TO THE INTERNAL COMPONENTS

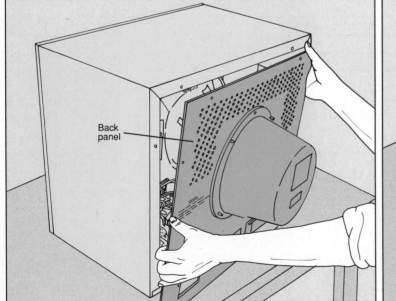

Back panel

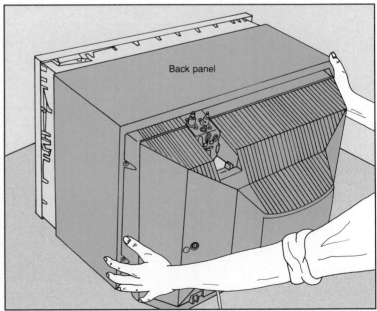

Back panel

Removing and reinstalling the back panel. Turn off the television, unplug it from the wall outlet and disconnect the cables hooked up to it *(page 12)*. Wait at least 24 hours for the picture tube to discharge stored voltage. Cold check the television for leaking voltage *(page 141)*. If there is an interior antenna mounted on the back panel, unscrew and remove the mounting plate; if the wires interfere with removing the back panel, note their terminal positions and disconnect them *(page 12)*. On some models, the back panel is flat *(above, left)*; on other models, the

panel is a molded casing with a top, sides and bottom *(above, right)*. Check the back panel for screws or clips. Unscrew or unclip the back panel and slide it out from under any lip on the top panel. Slide the power cord and any interior antenna through their openings and pull the back panel off the frame. On some models, the power cord may unplug from terminals inside the television and come off with the back panel. Reverse the sequence to reinstall the back panel, then cold check the television again for leaking voltage *(page 141)*.

REPLACING THE ANTENNA

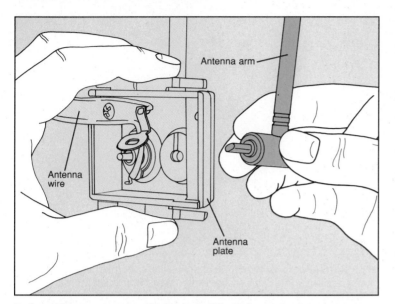

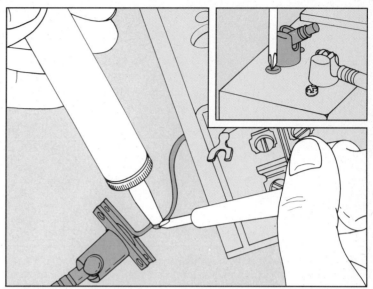

Reinstalling an externally-mounted interior antenna. Turn off and unplug the television. Unscrew the antenna plate from the back panel. Remove the locknut securing the antenna arm to the back of the antenna plate, disconnect the antenna wire and pull out the antenna arm. Order an exact replacement antenna arm from the manufacturer or purchase a substitute at an electronics parts supplier. Fit the antenna arm into the antenna plate *(above)*, connect the antenna wire and install the locknut. Screw the antenna plate to the back panel. Plug in the television.

Reinstalling an internally-mounted interior antenna. Remove the back panel *(page 70)*. Disconnect the antenna wire from the antenna housing terminal. Unscrew the antenna arm *(inset)* and slip it down through the opening in the antenna housing. Desolder *(page 130)* the antenna wire from the antenna arm *(above)*. Order an exact replacement antenna arm from the manufacturer or purchase a substitute at an electronics parts supplier. Slide the antenna arm through the opening in the antenna housing and solder the antenna wire to it *(page 131)*. Screw in the antenna arm and reconnect the wire to the antenna housing terminal. Reinstall the back panel *(page 70)*.

SERVICING A MECHANICAL TUNER

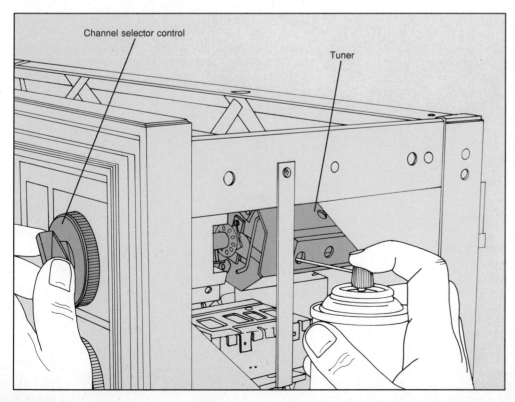

Cleaning a mechanical tuner. Remove the back panel *(page 70)* and locate the tuner behind the channel selector control on the front panel. Using tuner cleaner, direct the nozzle through an opening in the tuner casing and spray short bursts of cleaner; gently rotate the channel selector control back and forth several times to work in the cleaner *(left)*. Repeat this procedure at each opening in the tuner casing. Reinstall the back panel *(page 70)*. If the problem persists, suspect a faulty tuner and take the television for professional service.

SERVICING THE DRIVERS

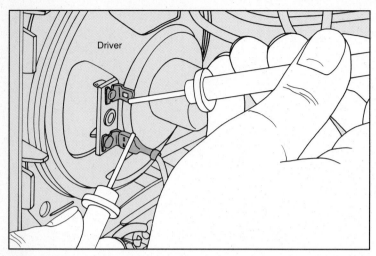

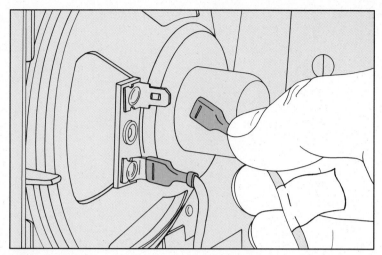

1 **Testing a driver.** Remove the back panel *(page 70)* and locate the driver wire terminals. If a wire connection is loose or broken, repair it *(page 132)*. Reinstall the back panel; remove it again if the problem persists. Tag the positive wire and disconnect or desolder it *(page 130)* from the terminal. Set a multitester to test resistance *(page 129)*. Touch one probe to the positive terminal and touch the other probe to the negative terminal *(above)*. The multitester should register close to the ohms rating indicated on the driver or specified by the manufacturer. If the driver tests faulty, replace it *(step 2)*. If it tests OK, suspect a faulty circuit board; reinstall the back panel *(page 70)* and take the television for professional service.

2 **Replacing a driver.** Disconnect or desolder *(page 130)* the negative wire. Unscrew the driver from the frame and remove it from the television. Order an exact replacement driver from the manufacturer or purchase a substitute at an electronics parts supplier. Position the driver in the television and screw it to the frame. Connect or solder *(page 131)* the tagged wire to the positive driver terminal *(above)* and the other wire to the negative driver terminal. Reinstall the back panel *(page 70)*. If the problem persists, suspect a faulty circuit board and take the television for professional service.

REPLACING THE POWER FUSE

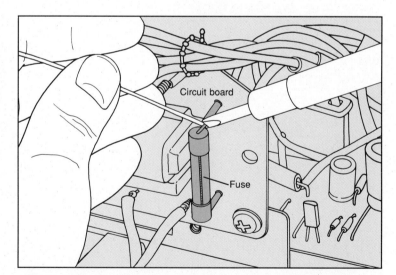

1 **Testing the fuse.** Remove the back panel *(page 70)* and locate the power fuse on the power-supply circuit board. If the fuse is held by retaining clips, use a fuse puller to remove it. If the fuse is soldered to posts, leave it in place. Set a multitester to test continuity *(page 128)*. Touch a probe to the cap at each end of the fuse *(above)*. If a soldered fuse does not register continuity, desolder it *(page 131)* and test again. If the fuse does not register continuity out of circuit, re-place it *(step 2)*. If the fuse registers continuity out of circuit, put it back and reinstall the back panel *(page 70)*. If the problem persists, suspect a faulty circuit board and take the television for professional service.

2 **Installing a new fuse.** Purchase an exact replacement fuse at an electronics parts supplier. Gently push the fuse into the retaining clips on the circuit board; if the old fuse was soldered to posts on the circuit board, carefully solder *(page 131)* the new fuse in place *(above)*. Reinstall the back panel *(page 70)*. If the fuse blows repeatedly, suspect a faulty power supply and take the television for professional service.

SERVICING A COMBINED SWITCH/POTENTIOMETER

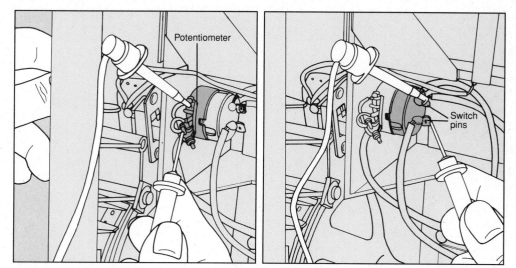

1 Cleaning the potentiometer. Remove the back panel *(page 70)* and locate the switch/potentiometer behind its control on the front panel; the switch has two pins and the potentiometer has three pins. To clean the potentiometer, spray electronic contact cleaner into the openings in the casing and rotate the control back and forth several times to work in the cleaner *(above)*. Never apply cleaner to the on/off switch. Reinstall the back panel *(page 70)*. If the problem persists, test the switch/potentiometer *(step 2)*.

2 Testing the switch/potentiometer. Remove the back panel *(page 70)*. To test the switch, set a multitester to test continuity *(page 128)*. Hook one probe to one switch pin and touch the other probe to the other switch pin *(above, left)*. Set the switch in the ON position, then in the OFF position. The switch should register continuity only in the ON position. If the switch tests faulty, remove the switch/potentiometer *(step 3)*. If the switch tests OK, test the potentiometer. Set the multitester to test resistance *(page 129)*. Hook one probe to the center potentiometer pin and touch the other probe in turn to the outer potentiometer pins, rotating the control back and forth *(above, right)*. The multitester should register a variation in ohms. If there is no ohms variation, remove the switch/potentiometer *(step 3)*. If there is an ohms variation, suspect a faulty circuit board; reinstall the back panel *(page 70)* and take the television for professional service.

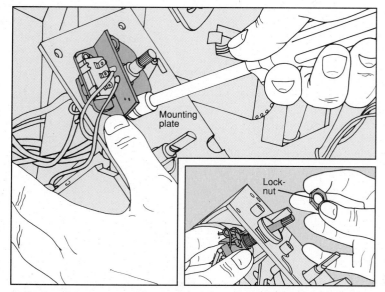

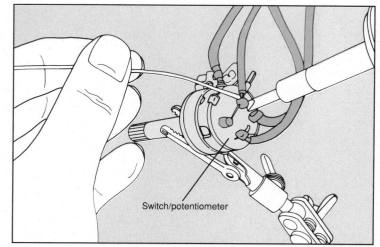

3 Removing the switch/potentiometer. Unscrew and lift out the switch/potentiometer mounting plate and unscrew the switch/potentiometer from it *(above)*. Remove the locknut from the potentiometer shaft and slide the shaft through the opening in the mounting plate *(inset)*. Tag the switch/potentiometer wires, noting their terminal positions, and desolder them *(page 130)*. To confirm the switch/potentiometer is faulty, test it again *(step 2)*. If the switch/potentiometer once more tests faulty, replace it *(step 4)*. If it now tests OK, suspect a faulty circuit board; put back the switch/potentiometer, reinstall the back panel *(page 70)* and take the television for professional service.

4 Replacing the switch/potentiometer. Purchase an exact replacement switch/potentiometer at an electronics parts supplier. Solder *(page 130)* the wires to the switch/potentiometer terminals *(above)*. Slide the potentiometer shaft through the opening in the mounting plate and twist on the locknut. Screw the switch/potentiometer to the mounting plate and screw the mounting plate to the frame. Reinstall the back panel *(page 70)*. If the problem persists, suspect a faulty circuit board and take the television for professional service.

SERVICING MODE AND FEATURE SWITCHES

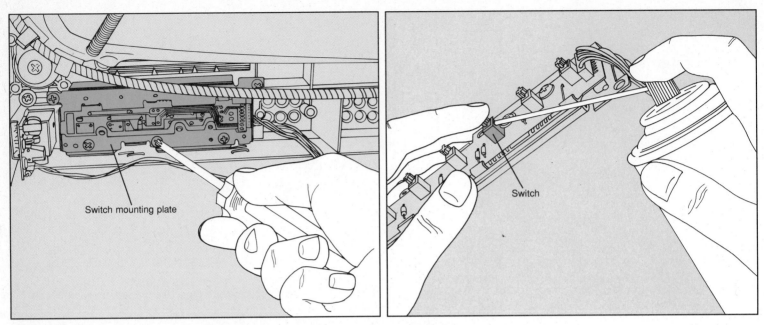

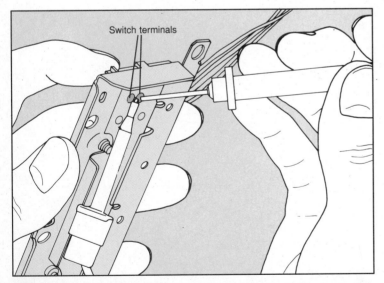

1 **Cleaning a mode or feature switch.** Remove the back panel *(page 70)* and locate the switch mounting plate behind its control on the front panel. Unscrew the mounting plate from the frame *(above, left)* and carefully pull it out of the television. To clean a switch other than the on/off control, use electronic contact cleaner; never apply cleaner to an on/off switch. Spray short bursts of cleaner through the opening in the switch casing; press in and release the switch several times to work in the cleaner *(above, right)*. Screw in the mounting plate and reinstall the back panel *(page 70)*. If the problem persists, test the switch *(step 2)*.

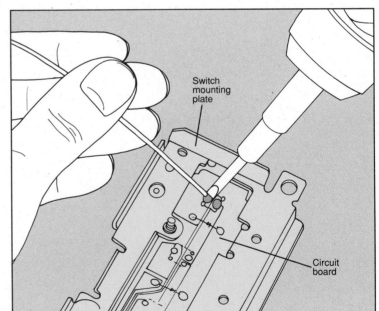

2 **Testing a mode or feature switch.** Remove the back panel *(page 70)*. Unscrew and lift out the switch mounting plate. Set a multitester to test continuity *(page 128)*. Hook one probe to one switch terminal and touch the other probe to the other switch terminal. Set the switch in the ON position, then in the OFF position *(above)*. The switch should register continuity only in the ON position. If the switch tests faulty, replace it *(step 3)*. If the switch tests OK, suspect a faulty circuit board; put back the mounting plate, reinstall the back panel *(page 70)* and take the television for professional service.

3 **Replacing a mode or feature switch.** Desolder the switch pins *(page 130)* and pull the switch off the circuit board; wiggle the switch to help release the pins. To confirm the switch is faulty, test it again *(step 3)*. If the switch once more tests faulty, purchase an exact replacement switch at an electronics parts supplier. Fit the switch into the circuit board and solder *(page 131)* the pins *(above)*. Test the new switch. If the switch now tests OK, suspect a faulty circuit board and take the television for professional service. Put back the mounting plate and reinstall the back panel *(page 70)*.

SERVICING POTENTIOMETERS

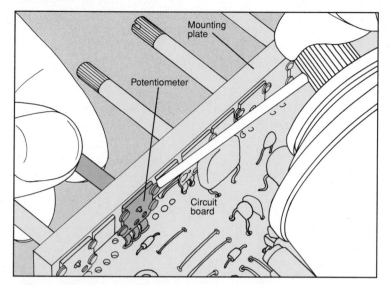

Mounting plate

Potentiometer

Circuit board

1 **Cleaning a potentiometer.** Remove the back panel *(page 70)* and locate the potentiometer on the circuit board behind its control. Unscrew the potentiometer mounting plate from the frame and carefully pull it out of the television; remove any obstructing controls or locknuts. Spray short bursts of electronic contact cleaner into the opening in the potentiometer casing; rotate the potentiometer shaft back and forth several times to work in the cleaner *(above)*. Screw in the mounting plate, put back any locknuts or controls you removed and reinstall the back panel *(page 70)*. If the problem persists, test the potentiometer *(step 2)*.

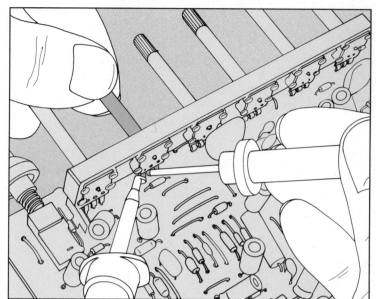

2 **Testing a potentiometer.** Remove the back panel *(page 70)* and access the potentiometer as in step 1. Set a multitester to test resistance *(page 129)*. Hook one probe to the center potentiometer pin and touch the other probe in turn to the outer potentiometer pins, rotating the control back and forth for each position *(above)*. The multitester should register a variation in ohms. If there is no ohms variation, remove the potentiometer *(step 3)*. If there is an ohms variation, suspect a faulty circuit board; put back the mounting plate and any controls or locknuts removed, reinstall the back panel *(page 70)* and take the television for professional service.

3 **Replacing a potentiometer.** To replace one potentiometer or the entire mounting plate/potentiometer assembly, you must desolder *(page 130)* all the potentiometer pins from the circuit board. Pull the mounting plate off the circuit board; wiggle it to help release the pins. Order an exact replacement mounting plate/potentiometer assembly from the manufacturer, if necessary. Otherwise, remove and replace only the faulty potentiometer: Drill out or snap off the rivets securing its backing and slide the potentiometer out of the mounting plate. Slide in the new potentiometer and secure the backing with screws or glue. Fit the mounting plate onto the circuit board *(left)* and solder *(page 131)* the pins for each potentiometer. Screw the mounting plate to the frame, put back any locknuts or controls removed, and reinstall the back panel *(page 70)*. If the problem persists, suspect a faulty circuit board and take the television for professional service.

ANTENNA AND CABLE SYSTEMS

A rooftop antenna system can greatly improve the picture and sound received by a television, as well as increase the range of channels available. The antenna picks up the broadcast signal and transmits it through a cable to the television, the videocassette recorder or, for FM reception, to the receiver. An optional rotor, controlled from inside the house, turns the antenna for better reception of a selected broadcast signal. A cable system works in a similar way. The cable company sends the broadcast signal received by their own antenna to your television or videocassette recorder via cable. A converter tunes in the channels and changes them to frequencies usable by the television; a cable-ready television has a built-in converter. Call the cable company for service to a rented converter or to the cable itself.

Most antenna and cable malfunctions are experienced through the television or videocassette recorder. Consult the

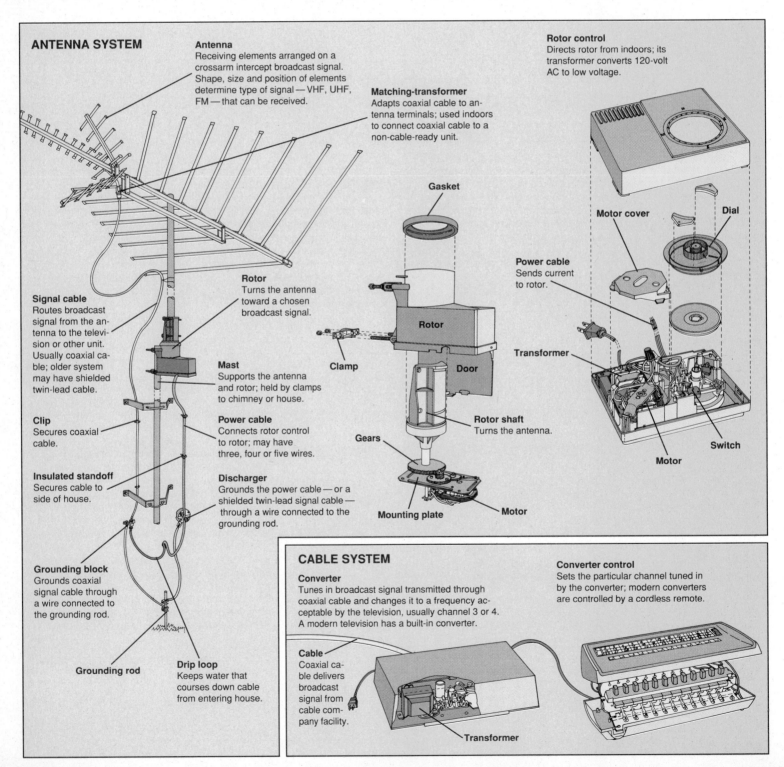

ANTENNA SYSTEM

Antenna
Receiving elements arranged on a crossarm intercept broadcast signal. Shape, size and position of elements determine type of signal — VHF, UHF, FM — that can be received.

Matching-transformer
Adapts coaxial cable to antenna terminals; used indoors to connect coaxial cable to a non-cable-ready unit.

Rotor control
Directs rotor from indoors; its transformer converts 120-volt AC to low voltage.

Gasket

Motor cover

Dial

Power cable
Sends current to rotor.

Rotor
Turns the antenna toward a chosen broadcast signal.

Signal cable
Routes broadcast signal from the antenna to the television or other unit. Usually coaxial cable; older system may have shielded twin-lead cable.

Mast
Supports the antenna and rotor; held by clamps to chimney or house.

Clamp

Rotor

Door

Transformer

Clip
Secures coaxial cable.

Power cable
Connects rotor control to rotor; may have three, four or five wires.

Rotor shaft
Turns the antenna.

Switch

Motor

Insulated standoff
Secures cable to side of house.

Discharger
Grounds the power cable — or a shielded twin-lead signal cable — through a wire connected to the grounding rod.

Gears

Mounting plate

Motor

Grounding block
Grounds coaxial signal cable through a wire connected to the grounding rod.

Grounding rod

Drip loop
Keeps water that courses down cable from entering house.

CABLE SYSTEM

Converter
Tunes in broadcast signal transmitted through coaxial cable and changes it to a frequency acceptable by the television, usually channel 3 or 4. A modern television has a built-in converter.

Converter control
Sets the particular channel tuned in by the converter; modern converters are controlled by a cordless remote.

Cable
Coaxial cable delivers broadcast signal from cable company facility.

Transformer

Troubleshooting Guide in Entertainment Systems *(page 14)* and in this chapter *(below)*. Most problems can be remedied by adjusting cable hookups. Refer to Tools & Techniques for instructions on disassembly and reassembly *(page 140)*, testing continuity and voltage *(pages 128-129)*, desoldering and soldering *(pages 130-131)*, and cold checking for leaking voltage *(page 141)*. Check the antenna ground-wire connections at least once a year *(page 17)*.

Keep safety in mind when working on the roof. Work only in dry weather with low winds, and have a helper nearby. Use a wooden ladder and set it well away from power lines. Avoid carrying tools in your hands or pockets; place them in a bucket and hoist it up with a rope slung over a ladder rung. If the antenna contacts a power line, immediately call the utility company or the fire department, and warn others to stay away. Do not use any unit connected to the antenna.

TROUBLESHOOTING GUIDE

SYMPTOM	POSSIBLE CAUSE	PROCEDURE
ANTENNA SYSTEM		
No picture and no sound	Television or videocassette recorder faulty	Troubleshoot entertainment system *(p. 14)* □●
	Remote control dirty or faulty	Service remote control *(p. 136)* □○
Picture and/or sound intermittent or distorted	Antenna positioned incorrectly	Adjust rotor control
	Television or other unit faulty	Troubleshoot entertainment system *(p. 14)* □○
	Antenna down or broken	Replace antenna *(p. 83)* □●
	Signal cable loose	Reconnect loose cable *(p. 83)* □○
	Signal cable faulty	Test and replace signal cable *(p. 84)* □●
Rotor control doesn't work	Rotor control unplugged	Plug in rotor control
	No power to outlet or outlet faulty	Reset breaker or replace fuse *(p. 10)* □○; have outlet serviced
	Power cord faulty	Test and replace power cord *(p. 137)* □○
	Rotor-control gear assembly dirty or faulty	Service rotor-control gear assembly *(p. 78)* □○
	Switches dirty or faulty	Clean, test and replace switches *(p. 79)* □○
	Power supply or motor faulty	Test rotor-control voltage output *(p. 80)* □○
	Power cable faulty	Test and replace power cable *(p. 81)* □●
	Rotor motor faulty	Replace rotor motor *(p. 82)* ▬●
	Rotor gear assembly dirty or faulty	Service rotor gear assembly *(p. 82)* ▮●
Rotor control works intermittently or only in one direction	Rotor-control gear assembly dirty or faulty	Service rotor-control gear assembly *(p. 78)* □○
	Rotor control switches dirty or faulty	Clean, test and replace rotor control switches *(p. 79)* □○
	Rotor gear assembly dirty or faulty	Service rotor gear assembly *(p. 82)* ▮●
CABLE SYSTEM		
No picture and no sound	Television or videocassette recorder faulty	Troubleshoot entertainment system *(p. 14)* □○
	Converter unplugged	Plug in converter
	Remote control dirty or faulty	Service remote control *(p. 136)* □○
	No power to outlet or outlet faulty	Reset breaker or replace fuse *(p. 10)* □○; have outlet serviced
	Converter power cord faulty	Test and replace power cord *(p. 137)* □○
	Converter power supply faulty	Service power supply *(p. 87)* ▬○
	Converter circuit board or tuner faulty	Take converter for professional service
Picture and/or sound intermittent or distorted	Television or other unit faulty	Troubleshoot entertainment system *(p. 14)* □○
	Fine tuning potentiometer dirty or faulty	Clean, test and replace potentiometer *(p. 86)* □○
	Converter control cable faulty	Test and replace converter control cable *(p. 87)* □○
	Converter circuit board or tuner faulty	Take converter for professional service
Converter doesn't change channels	Remote control, or converter-control switch assembly, dirty or faulty	Service remote control *(p. 136)* □○; service converter-control switch assembly *(p. 85)* □○
	Converter control cable faulty	Test and replace converter control cable *(p. 87)* □○
	Circuit board or tuner faulty	Take system for professional service

DEGREE OF DIFFICULTY: □ Easy ▬ Moderate ▮ Complex
ESTIMATED TIME: ○ Less than 1 hour ◗ 1 to 3 hours ● Over 3 hours

ACCESS TO THE ROTOR-CONTROL INTERNAL COMPONENTS

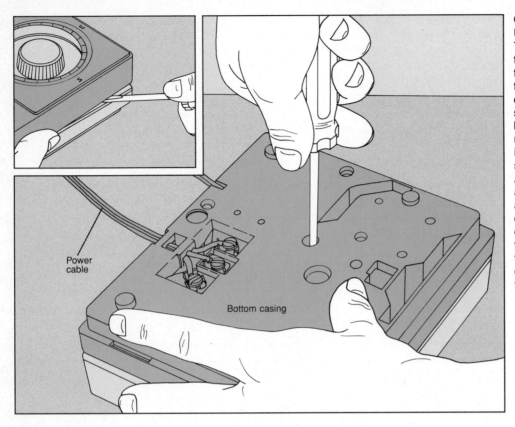

Power cable

Bottom casing

Opening and closing the rotor control.
Unplug the rotor control from the wall outlet. Tag the rotor power-cable wires, noting their terminal positions, and disconnect them from the rotor control. Check the bottom casing for hidden screws holding the top and bottom casings together; there may be only one screw, recessed in the center. Unscrew the bottom casing *(left)*, turn the rotor control upright and snap off the top casing. If the casings do not separate easily, use a broad, flat screwdriver to pry them gently apart *(inset)*. After working on the rotor control, fit the top and bottom casings together and put back any screws removed. Cold check the rotor control for leaking voltage *(page 141)*. Reconnect the rotor power-cable wires and plug the rotor control into the wall outlet. To reset the rotor control, turn the dial fully in one direction, wait for the antenna to adjust, and then turn it in the other direction.

SERVICING THE ROTOR CONTROL GEARS

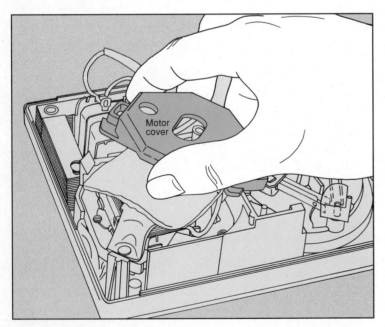

Motor cover

1 **Reaching the gear assembly.** Unplug and open the rotor control *(step above)*. Unclip the cover from the motor *(above)* and lift out the motor. If the gears are dirty, clean and lubricate them *(step 2)*. If a gear is damaged, note its position and remove it. Order an exact replacement gear from the manufacturer or purchase a substitute at an electronics parts supplier. Slide the gear into place, put back the motor and clip on the cover.

2 **Cleaning and lubricating the gears.** To clean the rotor control gears, wipe them using a foam swab moistened with denatured alcohol. Use a toothpick to dislodge any dirt from between the gear teeth *(above)*. Lubricate the gear teeth by applying a little white grease with a small stick or a clean toothpick. Wipe off excess lubricant using a clean foam swab. Put back the motor, clip on the cover and close the rotor control *(step above)*.

SERVICING THE ROTOR CONTROL SWITCHES

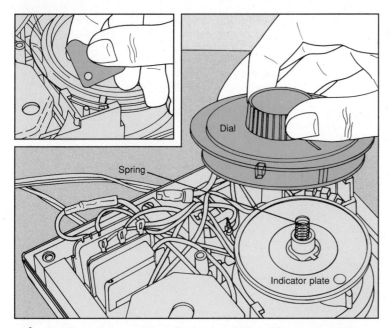

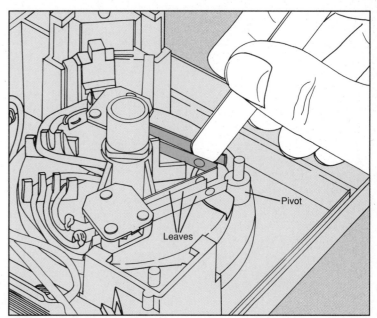

1 **Gaining access to the switch assembly.** Unplug and open the rotor control *(page 78)*. Pry out the clips holding the dial and indicator plate in place *(inset)*. Lift off the dial *(above)* and the indicator plate to expose the switches. If the spring on the switch assembly is damaged, replace it *(page 135)*. If a leaf on a switch is damaged, replace the switch *(step 4)*. If the spring on the switch assembly and the leaves on both switches look OK, test and clean each switch *(step 2)*.

2 **Cleaning the switches.** To test the switches, turn the pivot arm *(pictured below)* by hand fully in one direction and then the other. The leaves on the two-leaf switch should make contact in each direction, and two leaves on the three-leaf switch should make contact. If not, replace the switch *(step 4)*. If each switch tests OK, lift off the pivot arm and gently run an emery board over each leaf to polish the contacts *(above)*. Reinstall the pivot arm, indicator plate and dial, and close the rotor control *(page 78)*. If the problem persists, test the switch wires *(step 3)*.

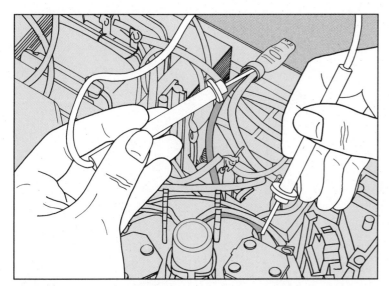

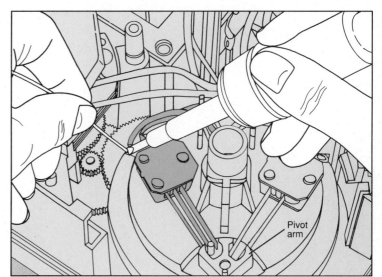

3 **Testing the wiring.** Open the rotor control *(page 78)* and gain access to the switch assembly *(step 1)*. Locate the wires connected to the terminals for each switch. If a wire connection is loose or broken, repair it *(page 132)*. Set a multitester to test continuity *(page 128)*. Touch one probe to one wire terminal on a switch and touch the other probe to the other end of the wire *(above)*. The multitester should register continuity. Test each wire on both switches. If a wire tests faulty, replace it *(page 132)*. If the wires test OK, clip on the indicator plate and dial, and close the rotor control *(page 78)*. If the problem persists, test its voltage output *(page 80)*.

4 **Replacing a switch.** Lift off the pivot arm. Tag the switch wires, noting their terminal positions, and desolder them from the switch *(page 130)*. Drill out or snap off any rivets securing the switch casing, pry off the casing and lift out the switch. Order an exact replacement switch from the manufacturer or purchase a substitute at an electronics parts supplier. Position the switch precisely and secure the casing with screws or glue. Solder the wires *(page 131)* to the switch terminals *(above)*. Install the pivot, clip on the indicator plate and dial, and close the rotor control *(page 78)*. If the problem persists, test the rotor-control voltage output *(page 80)*.

TESTING THE ROTOR-CONTROL VOLTAGE OUTPUT

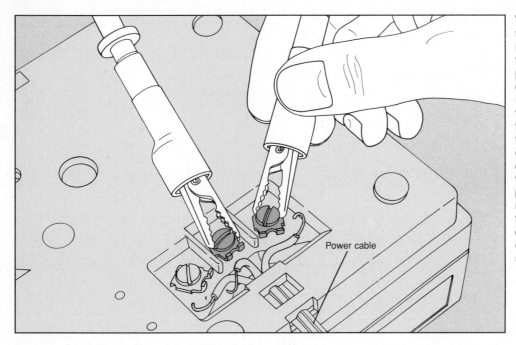

Testing for voltage. Unplug the rotor control from the wall outlet, turn it over and disconnect the rotor power-cable wires. Set a multitester to test voltage *(page 129)*. Clip one probe to the center terminal and clip the second probe to one of the outer terminals *(left)*. Plug in the rotor control. Taking care not to touch the terminals or the multitester, turn the rotor control dial in one direction and then the other; there should be voltage in only one direction. Unplug the rotor control, clip the second probe to the other outer terminal, plug in the control and repeat the procedure. If the rotor control tests OK, reconnect the rotor power-cable wires and test the power cable *(page 81)*. If the rotor control tests faulty, suspect the transformer or motor; take the rotor control for professional service.

ACCESS TO THE ROTOR AND THE ANTENNA

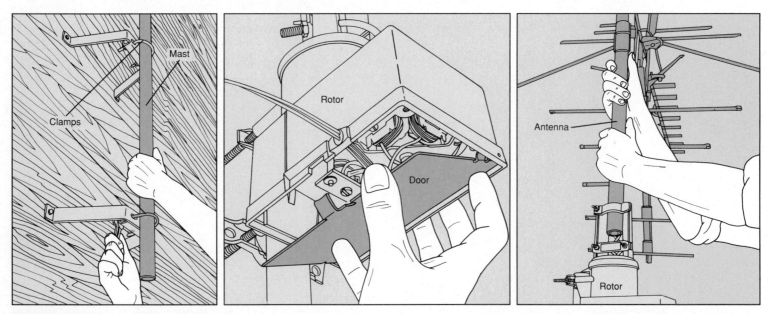

Reaching the rotor and the antenna safely. Inside the house, unplug the rotor control from the wall outlet. In some outside installations, the rotor and the antenna can be reached only if the mast is lowered; in other installations, the rotor and the antenna are easily reached from the roof. To remove the rotor from either type, however, the antenna must first be taken down.

When working on the roof, observe standard safety precautions. Work only in good weather and always with a helper. Use a wooden ladder and position it well away from power lines. Avoid carrying tools in your hands or pockets; place them in a bucket and hoist it up with a rope looped over a ladder rung.

If the mast must be lowered, mark the mast along one clamp to guide you when repositioning it. Disconnect any grounding strap that interferes with moving the mast. If the mast can only be lowered

from a ladder, have a helper firmly support the mast from the roof. Using a wrench, loosen the bolts securing the clamps around the mast, have your helper slowly lower the mast, then retighten the clamp bolts *(above, left)*.

To open the rotor, check for a door on the bottom or a mounting plate on the side. If there is a door, press in the tab or remove the screw holding it in place and open it *(above, center)*. If there is a mounting plate, unscrew and remove it, and pull out the mounting plate gasket. To take down the antenna, first mark the relative positions of the antenna, rotor and mast for repositioning. With a helper supporting the antenna, use a wrench to loosen the bolts on the clamps securing the antenna to the rotor. Lift out the antenna *(above, right)* and lay it carefully on the roof. Reverse these steps to reinstall the antenna or close the rotor.

TESTING AND REPLACING THE ROTOR POWER CABLE

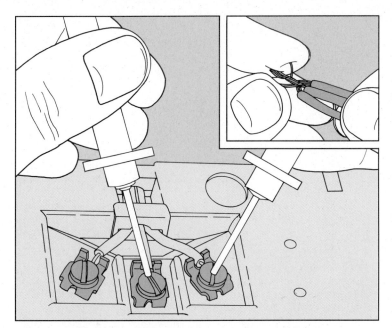

1 **Testing the power cable.** Open the rotor *(page 80)* and locate the power-cable terminal block. If a wire connection is loose or broken, repair it *(page 132)*. Tag the power cable wires and disconnect them from the rotor. Set a multitester to test continuity *(page 128)*. Touch a probe to one wire and touch the other probe in turn to each other wire. There should be no continuity. Test each wire with each other wire. If there is continuity, connect a new cable *(step 2)*. If there is no continuity, twist the wire ends together *(inset)*. Indoors, test the wires at the rotor control the same way *(above)*. This time there should be continuity for each test. If the wires test faulty, connect a new cable *(step 2)*.

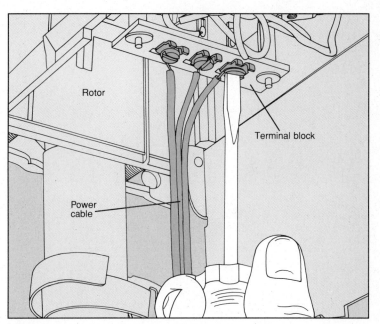

2 **Connecting a new power cable to the rotor.** Pry out any grommet securing the power cable at the rotor, open the grommet and remove the cable. Purchase the required length of replacement cable of the same gauge at an electronics parts supplier. Strip the wires and tin the leads *(page 132)*. Fit the cable into the grommet and reinstall it. Connect the wires to the terminal block in the same positions as the old cable *(above)*; check the new cable for a ridged or odd-colored wire to use as a reference. Remove the old cable from any standoffs on the mast and replace it with the new cable *(page 83)*. Close the rotor *(page 80)*, but leave the rotor control unplugged.

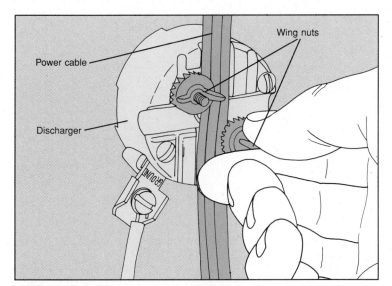

3 **Running the power cable through the discharger.** Following the route of the old cable, run the new cable to the discharger: Open each standoff, remove the old cable, insert the new cable, and close the standoff *(page 83)*. At the discharger, loosen the wing nuts, slide out the old cable, position the new cable and tighten the wing nuts *(above)*. At the entry point to the house, dig out the caulk around the old cable and have a helper pull it into the house. Leaving a foot-long drip loop below the discharger, feed the new cable into the opening and seal around it with caulk.

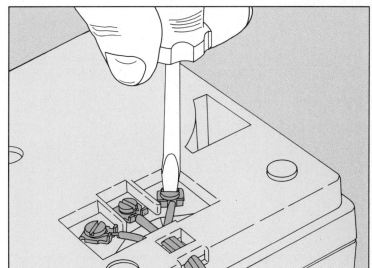

4 **Connecting the power cable to the rotor control.** Run the new cable as unobtrusively as possible to the rotor control. Turn over the rotor control, tag the wires of the old cable, noting their terminals, and disconnect them. Pull out the old cable. Cut off any excess from the new cable. Strip the wires and tin the leads *(page 132)*. Connect the wires to the terminals in the same positions as the old cable *(above)*. Plug in the rotor control and reset it by turning the dial fully in one direction, waiting for the antenna to adjust, and then in the other direction.

REPLACING THE ROTOR MOTOR

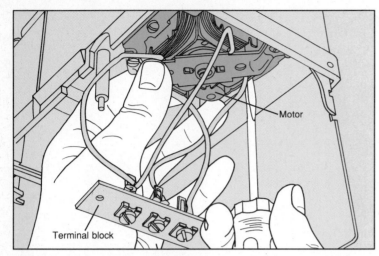

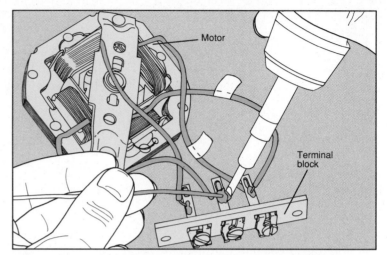

1 **Removing the rotor motor.** Open the rotor *(page 80)*. Tag the power cable wires, noting their terminals, and disconnect them. If the motor cannot be reached through a door on the rotor, take down the antenna *(page 80)*, remove the rotor from the mast and disassemble it *(step below)*. If the motor can be reached through a door on the rotor, unscrew the terminal block and pull it away from the rotor. Then, for either type of rotor installation, unscrew the motor *(above)* and pull it out of the rotor. Tag the motor wires, noting their terminal positions, and desolder them *(page 130)* from the terminal block.

2 **Installing a new rotor motor.** Order an exact replacement motor from the manufacturer. Solder the motor wires to the terminal block *(page 131)* in the same positions as the old motor wires *(above)* and screw the motor in place. If the rotor was not disassembled, screw in the terminal block. If the rotor was disassembled, reverse the sequence to reassemble and install it *(step 1)*. Then, for either type of rotor, reconnect the power cable wires and close the rotor *(page 80)*. Plug in the rotor control and reset it by turning the dial fully in one direction, waiting for the antenna to adjust, and then in the other direction.

SERVICING THE ROTOR GEAR ASSEMBLY

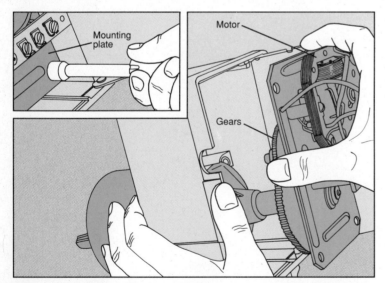

1 **Removing and disassembling the rotor.** Open the rotor, tag and disconnect the power cable wires and take down the antenna *(page 80)*. Loosen the bolts on the clamps holding the rotor and lift it up off the mast; lower the rotor to the ground. If the rotor has no door, remove the bolts holding its casing together and pry it apart; if it does not separate easily, run a putty knife around the edges to break the weatherproofing seal. If the rotor has a door, remove the clamps and U bolts from the upper shaft of the rotor, pry up the gasket and remove the bolts from the motor mounting plate *(inset)*. Pull out the mounting plate, exposing the gears on its back side *(above)*.

2 **Lubricating the gears.** If the gears are damaged, have the rotor serviced professionally. To dislodge particles from the gear teeth, use a toothpick. Lubricate the gears by applying white grease with a small stick *(above)*. If you took apart the rotor casing, reverse the sequence to reassemble it *(step 1)*. If the rotor has a door, install the mounting plate, push down the gasket, and put back the U bolts and clamps. If you took the rotor down from the roof, raise it back up carefully. Fit the rotor onto the mast, align it and tighten the clamp bolts. Install the antenna *(page 80)*, reconnect the power cable wires and close the rotor *(page 80)*. Plug in the rotor control and reset it by turning the dial fully in one direction, waiting for the antenna to adjust, and then in the other direction. If the problem persists, have the rotor serviced professionally.

REPLACING THE ANTENNA

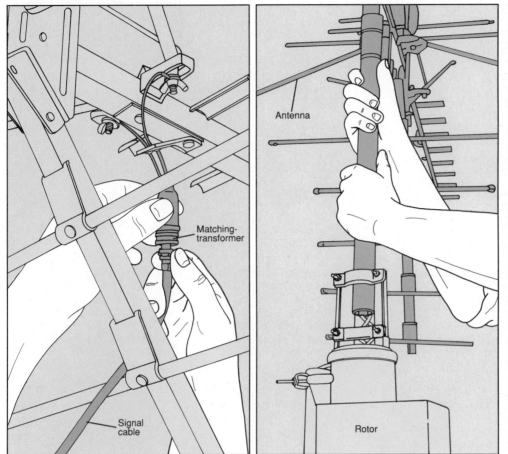

Removing a signal cable and installing a new antenna. Take down the antenna *(page 80)*. If the signal cable is coaxial, unscrew the wing nuts from the matching-transformer wires, slide down the weatherproof boot, unscrew the cable connector from the matching-transformer and remove the boot; if the signal cable is shielded twin-lead, simply unscrew the wing nuts. Remove the cable from its guides; if a connector is too big to pass through, cut it off with a utility knife. Tie a rope around the antenna and lower it to the ground.

Purchase a replacement antenna at an electronics parts supplier; consult a professional concerning the best type for your area. If you have shielded twin-lead cable, reconnect coaxial cable instead *(page 84)*. Raise the antenna to the roof with the rope. Wearing gloves, open up the antenna. Fit the cable through its guides; at the end of a new cable, install a coaxial connector *(page 133)*. Screw the matching-transformer to the antenna, slip the boot on the cable, screw the cable to the matching-transformer *(far left)* and slide up the boot. Coat all connections with weatherproofing compound. Install the antenna *(near left)*, reversing the sequence used to take down the old one *(page 80)*. Follow the manufacturer's directions to position it for best reception. Plug in the rotor control and reset it by turning the dial fully in one direction, waiting for the antenna to adjust, and then in the other direction.

CONNECTING A LOOSE CABLE

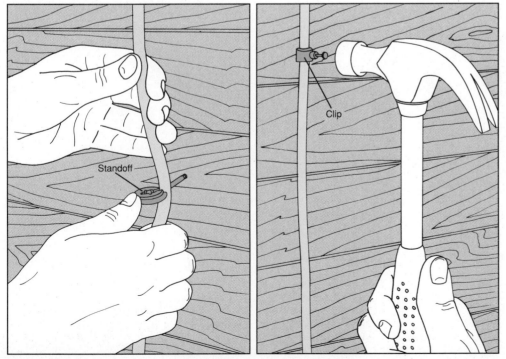

Running cable through insulated standoffs or clips. Use insulated standoffs to secure a loose cable to any type of surface; use insulated clips only to hold coaxial cable to surfaces that can accept nails. To install a standoff, screw it into the surface or into an anchor bolt set into a hole drilled in the surface. Using pliers, if necessary, turn the inner ring of the standoff, opening it to put in or take out the cable *(far left)* and closing it to lock the cable in place. To install a clip, fit the coaxial cable under it, then nail it to the surface *(near left)*. Use as many standoffs or clips as needed to hold the cable securely.

TESTING AND REPLACING THE ANTENNA SIGNAL CABLE

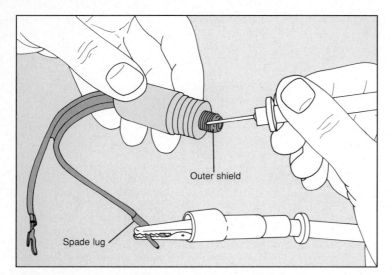

Outer shield

Spade lug

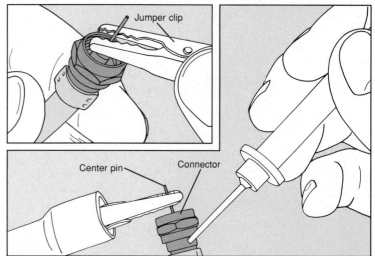

Jumper clip

Center pin   Connector

1 **Testing and replacing a matching-transformer.** Unplug the rotor control. Lower the mast or take down the antenna *(page 80)*, then unscrew the signal cable *(page 83)*. If it is shielded twin-lead, test it *(step 2)*; if it is coaxial, first remove and test the matching-transformer. Set a multitester to test continuity *(page 128)*. Touch one probe to the outer shield and touch the other probe in turn to each spade lug; there should be continuity. Then, clip one probe to a needle and gently fit it into the coaxial terminal; touch the other probe in turn to the outer shield and each spade lug *(above)*. There should be no continuity. If the matching-transformer is OK, test the cable *(step 2)*; if it is faulty, purchase an exact replacement at an electronics parts supplier and install it when you install the antenna *(page 83)* or cable *(step 3)*. Test a matching-transformer on the television or videocassette recorder the same way.

2 **Testing signal cable.** Disconnect the lower end of the cable; disconnect coaxial cable at the grounding block to test the two cable sections separately. Set a multitester to test continuity *(page 128)*. To test coaxial cable, touch one probe to the center pin and touch the other probe to the connector *(above)*; there should be no continuity. Next, connect the pin and the connector at one end of the cable with a jumper clip *(inset)*, and repeat the test at the other end. This time there should be continuity. To test a shielded twin-lead cable, first touch a probe to each wire or spade lug at one end; there should be no continuity. Next, twist together the wires or lugs at one end, and test at the other end. This time there should be continuity. If the cable is faulty, connect new cable *(step 3)*; if it is OK, have the antenna serviced.

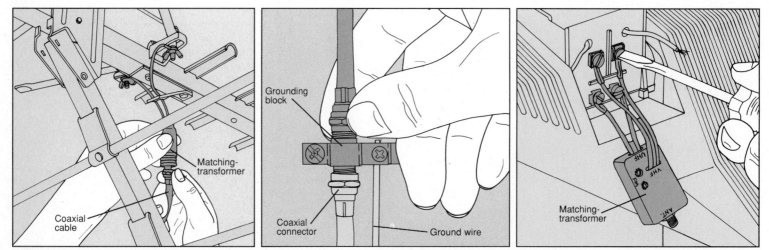

Matching-transformer

Coaxial cable

Grounding block

Coaxial connector   Ground wire

Matching-transformer

3 **Connecting coaxial signal cable.** Remove the cable from its guides; if a connector is too big to pass through, cut it off with a utility knife. Purchase matching-transformers, connectors and replacement cable at an electronics parts supplier; for best reception, replace shielded twin-lead cable with coaxial cable and also install a grounding block. Run the cable through the guides, slip on the matching-transformer boot, then install a cable connector *(page 133)*. Screw the matching-transformer wires to the antenna and screw the cable to the matching-transformer *(above, left)*; slide up the boot. Coat all connections with weatherproofing compound. Put up the antenna or raise the mast *(page 80)*. Run the new cable

down through standoffs or clips *(page 83)* to the grounding block, leaving enough slack for the antenna to turn. Then cut the cable at the block, install connectors *(page 133)* and screw on the cable *(above, center)*. At the entry point to the house, dig out the caulk and have a helper pull through the old cable. Leaving a foot-long drip loop below the grounding block, feed in the new cable and seal around it with caulk. Run the cable to the television or videocassette recorder, install a connector and connect it, using a matching-transformer, if needed *(above, right)*. Plug in the rotor control and reset it by turning the dial fully in one direction, waiting for the antenna to adjust, and then in the other direction.

ACCESS TO THE CABLE-SYSTEM INTERNAL COMPONENTS

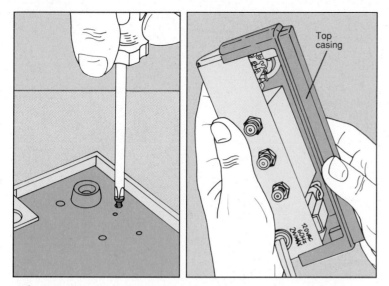

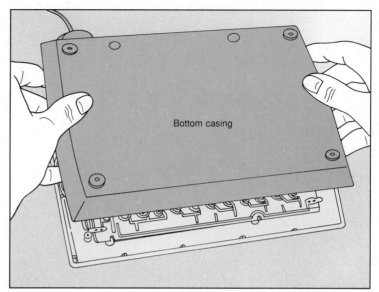

Top casing

Bottom casing

1 **Opening and closing the converter.** Unplug the converter from the wall outlet, disconnect any unit plugged into the converter and unscrew the signal cable. Check the bottom and side edges for screws securing the top casing; other screws may hold internal components in place. Remove the screws *(above, left)* and pull off the top casing *(above, right)*. After working on the converter, fit on the top casing and put back the screws. Cold check the converter for leaking voltage *(page 141)*. Screw on the signal cable, reconnect any unit unplugged from the converter and plug in the converter.

2 **Opening and closing the converter control.** If the converter control is a cordless remote, little servicing is usually required other than cleaning *(page 136)*. If the converter control is connected by a cable to the converter, unplug the converter from the wall outlet. Unscrew the bottom casing of the control and lift it up and out *(above)*, releasing any tabs securing it to the top casing. After working on the converter control, fit the casings together, put back the screws and turn the converter control upright. Plug the converter back into the wall outlet.

SERVICING THE CONVERTER-CONTROL SWITCH ASSEMBLY

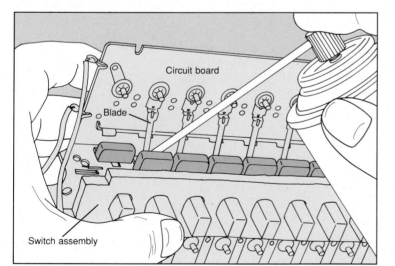

Circuit board

Blade

Switch assembly

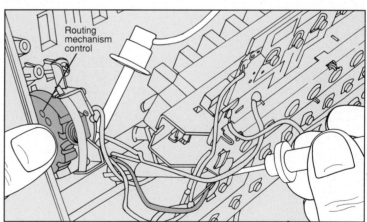

Routing mechanism control

Cleaning a switch. Open the converter control *(step above)*. Unscrew the switch assembly, prop up the circuit board and locate the switch under its control. If the spring or blade is damaged, close the converter control and take it for professional service. If the blade is dirty, run an emery board over its contact points. To clean the switch, spray electronic contact cleaner into its opening in the switch assembly. Press in and release the control to work in the cleaner *(above)*. Put back the circuit board, screw in the switch assembly and close the converter control *(step above)*.

Testing and replacing a routing mechanism. Open the converter control *(step above)*. Unscrew the switch assembly, prop up the circuit board and locate the routing mechanism under its control. If a wire is loose or broken, repair it *(page 132)*. Set a multitester to test continuity *(page 128)*. Hook a probe to the terminal contact ring on the mechanism; touch the other probe in turn to each of its wire terminals on the circuit board, turning the control to each setting *(above)*. At each setting, there should be continuity with two wires. If the mechanism is OK, test the converter control cable *(page 87)*. If the mechanism is faulty, unscrew it. Tag the wires, noting their terminal positions, and desolder them *(page 130)*. Order an exact replacement mechanism from the manufacturer, solder the wires *(page 131)* and screw the mechanism in place.

SERVICING A POTENTIOMETER

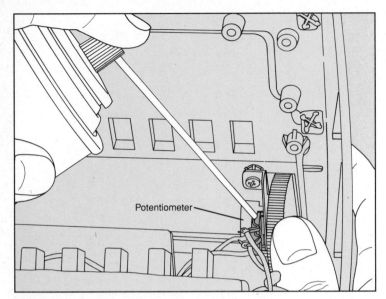

1 **Cleaning a potentiometer.** Open the converter or converter control *(page 85)*. If the potentiometer is in the converter control, unscrew the switch assembly and prop up the circuit board or support the top casing to reach it. Locate the potentiometer under or behind its control. To clean the potentiometer, spray electronic contact cleaner through the opening in its casing and rotate the control back and forth several times to work in the cleaner *(above)*. Close the converter or converter control *(page 85)*. If the problem persists, test the potentiometer wires *(step 2)*.

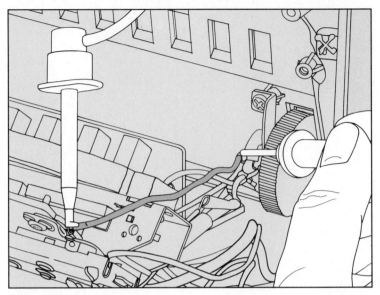

2 **Testing the wires.** Access the potentiometer as in step 1. Locate the ends of each wire connected to the potentiometer terminals. If a wire connection is loose or broken, repair it *(page 132)*. Set a multitester to test continuity *(page 128)*. Clip a probe to the end of one wire and touch the other probe to the other end of the wire *(above)*; the wire should have continuity. Test the other wires the same way. If a wire is faulty, replace it *(page 132)*. If each wire is OK, test the potentiometer *(step 3)*.

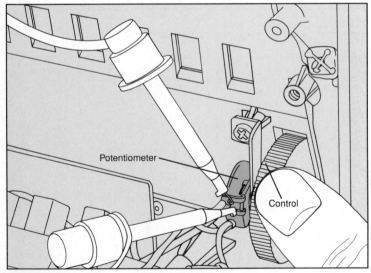

3 **Testing a potentiometer.** Set a multitester to test resistance *(page 129)*. Hook one probe to the center terminal and hook the other probe to one of the outer terminals; rotate the control fully in each direction *(above)*. There should be a variation in ohms as the control is rotated. Repeat the test between the center terminal and the other outer terminal, rotating the control fully in each direction; again there should be a variation in ohms. If the potentiometer tests OK, test the converter control cable *(page 87)*. If the potentiometer tests faulty, remove and replace it *(step 4)*.

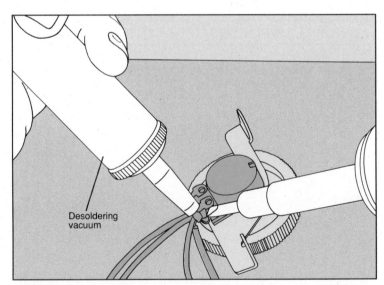

4 **Replacing a potentiometer.** Unscrew and remove the potentiometer. Tag the wires, noting their terminal positions, and desolder them *(page 130)* from the potentiometer *(above)*. Test the potentiometer again to confirm it is faulty *(step 3)*. If the potentiometer now tests OK, resolder the wires *(page 131)*. If a cable connects the converter and the converter control, test it *(page 87)*; if the converter control is a cordless remote, suspect a faulty circuit board or tuner and take the converter for professional service. If the potentiometer again tests faulty, order an exact replacement from the manufacturer. Solder the wires *(page 131)* and screw in the potentiometer. Close the converter *(page 85)* or put back the converter-control circuit board, screw in the switch assembly and close the converter control *(page 85)*.

REPLACING THE CONVERTER CONTROL CABLE

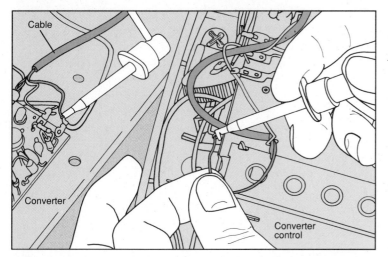

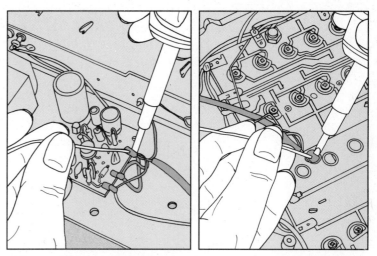

1 **Testing the cable.** Open the converter and the converter control *(page 85)*; locate the wire terminals for the cable connecting them. If a wire connection is loose or broken, repair it *(page 132)*. Set a multitester to test continuity *(page 128)*. Hook one probe to a wire terminal in the converter and hook the other probe in turn to each wire terminal in the converter control *(above)*. The multitester should register continuity once—and only once. Repeat this test at the other wire terminal in the converter. If the cable tests faulty, replace it *(step 2)*. If the cable tests OK, suspect a faulty circuit board or tuner; take the converter and the converter control for professional service.

2 **Installing a new cable.** Tag the wires, noting their terminal positions, and desolder them *(page 130)* from the converter and the converter control. Pry out the strain reliefs and slip them off the cable. Purchase an exact replacement cable at an electronics parts supplier. Slide the strain reliefs onto the ends of the cable and reinstall them. Strip back the wires and tin the leads *(page 132)*. Solder the wires to the terminals *(page 131)* in the converter *(above, left)* and the converter control *(above, right)*. Close the converter and the converter control *(page 85)*. If the problem persists, suspect a faulty circuit board or tuner and take the system for professional service.

SERVICING THE CONVERTER POWER SUPPLY

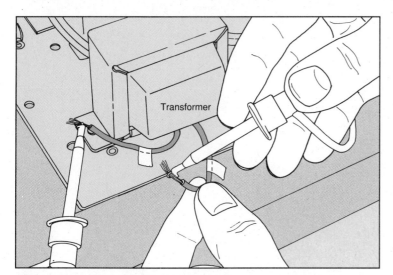

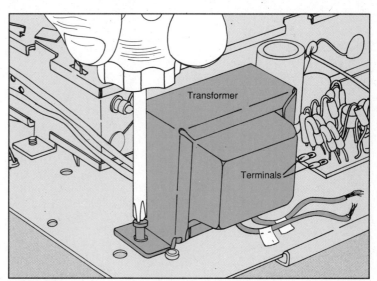

1 **Testing the transformer.** Open the converter *(page 85)* and identify the power supply components *(page 138)*. Locate the transformer wires connected to the circuit board. Tag the wires, noting their terminal positions, and desolder them from the circuit board *(page 130)*. Set a multitester to test voltage *(page 129)* and hook a probe to each wire *(above)*. Plug in the converter, record the multitester reading and unplug the converter. If no voltage is registered, replace the transformer *(step 2)*. If voltage is registered, suspect a faulty circuit board or tuner; close the converter *(page 85)* and take the system for professional service.

2 **Replacing the transformer.** Tag the transformer wires connected to the power block, noting their terminal positions, and desolder them *(page 130)*. Unscrew the transformer and remove it from the converter. Order an exact replacement transformer from the manufacturer or purchase a substitute at an electronics parts supplier. Screw in the transformer *(above)* and solder the wires *(page 131)* to the terminals on the power block and the circuit board. Close the converter *(page 85)*. If the problem persists, suspect a faulty circuit board or tuner and take the system for professional service.

VIDEOCASSETTE RECORDERS

A videocassette recorder, or VCR, can tune in a television program and show it on the television, or record it on tape, or do both at the same time. It can also play back a prerecorded tape on the television. Because the VCR and the television each has its own tuner, you can watch one program while recording another, or record a program with the television off. The audio and video heads in the VCR read and store magnetic tracks on tape, much like an audiocassette recorder.

VCRs are made in two styles, called formats: Beta and VHS. They differ mainly in how they thread the tape internally. The machine shown in this chapter is VHS; Beta components and repairs are similar. Most VCRs are programmable, meaning that their clock/timers can be preset to turn on the record function automatically.

With all these functions, the most common reason for VCR problems is simply programming errors. Check the owner's manual before consulting the Troubleshooting Guide in Entertainment Systems *(page 12)* and in this chapter *(page 89)*. Many problems can be solved by adjusting cable hookups or by cleaning and demagnetizing the tape travel components.

Cleaning supplies and most replacement parts are available at an electronics parts supplier; a motor may have to be ordered from the manufacturer. Refer to Tools & Techniques *(page 126)* before beginning any repair.

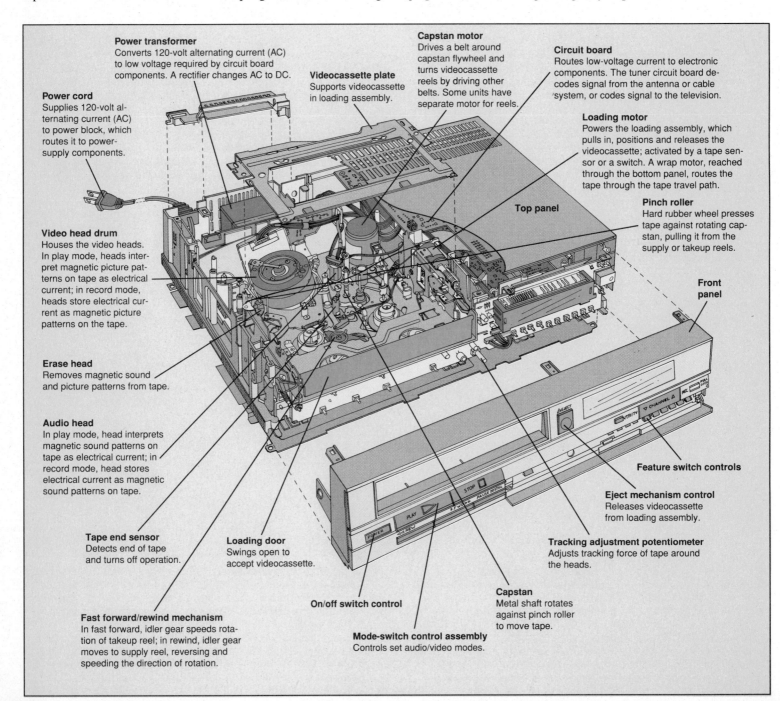

Power transformer
Converts 120-volt alternating current (AC) to low voltage required by circuit board components. A rectifier changes AC to DC.

Power cord
Supplies 120-volt alternating current (AC) to power block, which routes it to power-supply components.

Videocassette plate
Supports videocassette in loading assembly.

Capstan motor
Drives a belt around capstan flywheel and turns videocassette reels by driving other belts. Some units have separate motor for reels.

Circuit board
Routes low-voltage current to electronic components. The tuner circuit board decodes signal from the antenna or cable system, or codes signal to the television.

Loading motor
Powers the loading assembly, which pulls in, positions and releases the videocassette; activated by a tape sensor or a switch. A wrap motor, reached through the bottom panel, routes the tape through the tape travel path.

Top panel

Pinch roller
Hard rubber wheel presses tape against rotating capstan, pulling it from the supply or takeup reels.

Front panel

Video head drum
Houses the video heads. In play mode, heads interpret magnetic picture patterns on tape as electrical current; in record mode, heads store electrical current as magnetic picture patterns on the tape.

Erase head
Removes magnetic sound and picture patterns from tape.

Audio head
In play mode, head interprets magnetic sound patterns on tape as electrical current; in record mode, head stores electrical current as magnetic sound patterns on tape.

Feature switch controls

Eject mechanism control
Releases videocassette from loading assembly.

Tracking adjustment potentiometer
Adjusts tracking force of tape around the heads.

Tape end sensor
Detects end of tape and turns off operation.

Loading door
Swings open to accept videocassette.

On/off switch control

Capstan
Metal shaft rotates against pinch roller to move tape.

Mode-switch control assembly
Controls set audio/video modes.

Fast forward/rewind mechanism
In fast forward, idler gear speeds rotation of takeup reel; in rewind, idler gear moves to supply reel, reversing and speeding the direction of rotation.

TROUBLESHOOTING GUIDE

SYMPTOM	POSSIBLE CAUSE	PROCEDURE
No display lights, no picture and no sound	Videocassette recorder unplugged or off	Plug in and turn on videocassette recorder
	Remote control dirty or faulty	Service remote control (p. 136) □○
	No power to outlet or outlet faulty	Reset breaker or replace fuse (p. 10) □○; have outlet serviced
	Power cord faulty	Test and replace power cord (p. 137) □○
	Power fuse blown	Test and replace power fuse (p. 95) □○
	On/off switch faulty	Test and replace on/off switch (p. 96) ◲○
	Power supply faulty	Service power supply (p. 97) ■◓
	Circuit board faulty	Take videocassette recorder for professional service
Display lights, but no picture and no sound	Videocassette tape torn or jammed	Replace tape or have it serviced; remove jammed tape (p. 93) □○
	Television faulty	Troubleshoot entertainment system (p. 14) □○
	Drive belt loose or broken	Service drive belts (p. 94) □○
	Pinch roller faulty	Replace pinch roller (p. 95) □○
	On/off switch faulty	Test and replace on/off switch (p. 96) ◲○
	Loading motor faulty	Test and replace loading motor (p. 98) ■◓
	Wrap motor faulty	Test and replace wrap motor (p. 99) ■◓
	Capstan/reel motor faulty	Test and replace capstan/reel motor (p. 99) ■◓
	Circuit board faulty	Take videocassette recorder for professional service
Picture and sound, but no display lights	Display lights faulty	Replace display lights (p. 134) □○
Picture, but no sound; or sound, but no picture	Receiver or television faulty	Troubleshoot entertainment system (p. 14) □○
	Video or audio head or circuit board faulty	Take videocassette recorder for professional service
Sound from only one channel	Receiver or speaker faulty	Troubleshoot entertainment system (p. 14) □○
	Audio head or circuit board faulty	Take videocassette recorder for professional service
Picture and/or sound intermittent or distorted	Videocassette tape tracking poorly	Adjust tracking force control
	Television, receiver or other unit faulty	Troubleshoot entertainment system (p. 14) □○
	Tape travel path dirty	Clean and demagnetize tape travel path (p. 91) □○▲
	Drive belt dirty or loose	Service drive belts (p. 94) □○
	Pinch roller faulty	Replace pinch roller (p. 95) □○
	Capstan/reel motor faulty	Test and replace capstan/reel motor (p. 99) ■◓
	Circuit board faulty	Take videocassette recorder for professional service
Mode or feature control doesn't work	Mode or feature switch dirty or faulty	Clean, test and replace mode or feature switch (p. 96) ◲○
	Circuit board faulty	Take videocassette recorder for professional service
Videocassette tape doesn't fast forward or doesn't rewind	Fast forward/rewind mechanism dirty	Service fast forward/rewind mechanism (p. 94) □○
	Fast/forward or rewind switch dirty or faulty	Clean, test and replace switch (p. 96) ◲○
	Circuit board faulty	Take videocassette recorder for professional service
Videocassette tape can't be erased or recorded over	Videocassette safety tab removed	Restore videocassette safety tab (p. 90) □○
	Erase head or circuit board faulty	Take videocassette recorder for professional service
Videocassette tape jams or tears repeatedly	Tape travel path dirty	Clean and demagnetize tape travel path (p. 91) □○▲
	Loading assembly dirty	Clean and lubricate loading assembly (p. 93) □○
	Fast forward/rewind mechanism dirty	Service fast forward/rewind mechanism (p. 94) □○
	Pinch roller faulty	Replace pinch roller (p. 95) □○
	Wrap motor faulty	Test and replace wrap motor (p. 99) ■◓
	Capstan/reel motor faulty	Test and replace capstan/reel motor (p. 99) ■◓
Videocassette doesn't load or doesn't unload	Loading assembly dirty	Clean and lubricate loading assembly (p. 93) □○
	Videocassette tape jammed	Remove jammed tape (p. 93) □○
	Loading motor faulty	Test and replace loading motor (p. 98) ■◓

DEGREE OF DIFFICULTY: □ Easy ◲ Moderate ■ Complex

ESTIMATED TIME: ○ Less than 1 hour ◓ 1 to 3 hours ● Over 3 hours

▲ Special tool required

SERVICING VIDEOCASSETTES

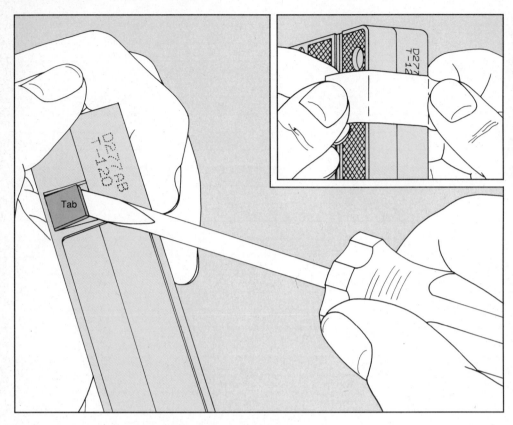

Removing and restoring the videocassette safety tab. Locate the videocassette safety tab on the top edge of the housing. To prevent the videocassette tape from being erased or recorded over, break off the safety tab using a small, flat screwdriver *(left)*; if the safety tab falls into the videocassette tape housing, remove it using long-nose pliers. To restore the ability to erase or record over the videocassette tape, cover the safety tab opening with a small piece of plastic tape *(inset)*. Avoid touching the videocassette tape with your fingers; replace the videocassette or have it serviced if the tape is damaged.

ACCESS TO THE INTERNAL COMPONENTS

Removing and reinstalling the top or bottom panel. Unload any videocassette, turn off and unplug the videocassette recorder, and disconnect the cables hooked up to it *(page 12)*. To remove the top panel, check for screws on the sides, back or bottom. Unscrew the top panel *(inset)*, slide it out from under any lip on the front panel and lift it off the frame. To remove the bottom panel, turn over the videocassette recorder, unscrew the bottom panel and lift it off *(left)*. To reinstall the top panel, slide it under any lip on the front panel and screw it to the frame. To reinstall the bottom panel, set it on the frame, put back the screws and turn the videocassette recorder upright. Cold check the videocassette recorder for leaking voltage *(page 141)* any time it has been opened. Reconnect the cables *(page 16)* and plug in the videocassette recorder.

ACCESS TO THE INTERNAL COMPONENTS (continued)

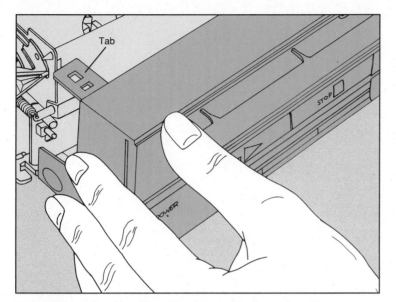

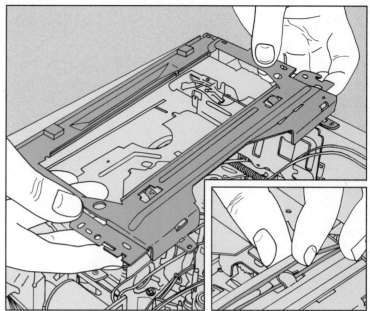

Removing and reinstalling the front panel or plate. If the machine has a front plate, remove it for access; otherwise, take off the front panel itself. Remove the top panel *(page 90)*. Check the top, sides and bottom for tabs and screws securing the front panel or plate. Pull off or unscrew any controls too large to fit through their openings. Unscrew the front panel or plate, press in the tabs at the corners and pull off the front panel or plate *(above)*. To reinstall the front panel or plate, snap it onto the frame, put back any screws, and push on or screw on the controls. Reinstall the top panel *(page 90)*.

Removing and reinstalling the videocassette plate. Remove the top panel *(page 90)* and locate the videocassette plate covering the tape travel path. Note the positions of any springs securing the videocassette plate and disconnect them from the plate using long-nose pliers or tweezers. Unhook any wires from tabs on the plate *(inset)*. Unscrew and lift out the plate *(above)*. To reinstall the videocassette plate, screw it in, hook the wires under their tabs and put back the springs. Reinstall the top panel *(page 90)*.

SERVICING THE TAPE TRAVEL PATH

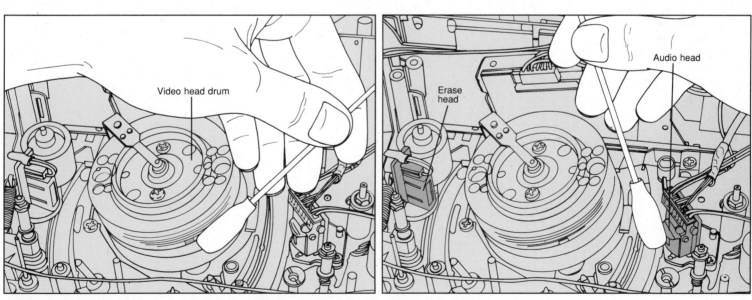

1 **Cleaning the heads.** Remove the top panel *(page 90)* and the videocassette plate *(step above)*. To clean the video heads, the audio head and the erase head, use a foam swab dipped in denatured alcohol. For VHS video heads, gently hold the swab against the upper half of the video head drum and slowly rotate the drum counterclockwise several times *(above, left)*. For Beta video heads, wipe evenly across each head. Apply extremely light pressure and wipe only horizontally; up-and-down rubbing with the swab can damage a video head. Next, use a fresh foam swab dipped in denatured alcohol to wipe in turn the entire surface of both the audio head and the erase head *(above, right)*.

SERVICING THE TAPE TRAVEL PATH (continued)

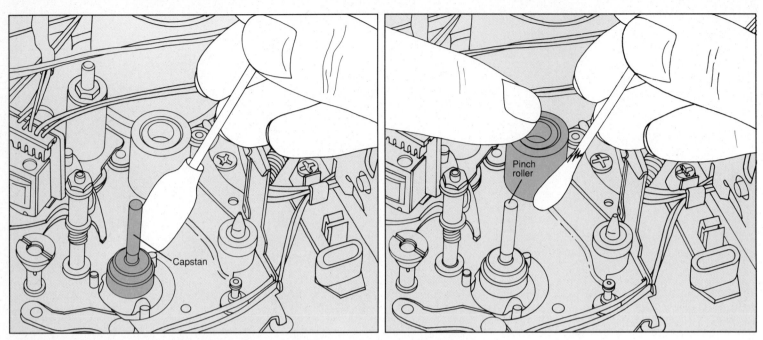

2 **Cleaning the capstan, the guides and the pinch roller.** Use a foam swab dipped in denatured alcohol to clean the entire surface of the capstan, the guides and any other metal or plastic component that contacts the videocassette tape *(above, left)*; apply only moderate pressure and change often to a fresh foam swab. To clean the pinch roller, use a fresh foam swab dipped in rubber-cleaning compound; slowly turn the pinch roller with a finger as you wipe, to reach the entire surface *(above, right)*. Check the condition of the pinch roller; if it is worn or damaged, replace it *(page 95)*.

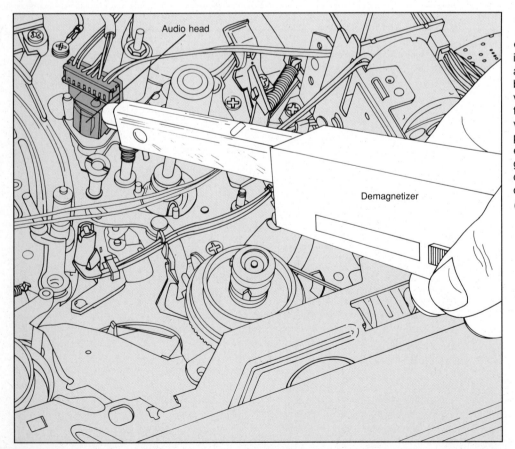

3 **Demagnetizing the tape travel path.** Purchase a demagnetizer at an electronics parts supplier. Plug the demagnetizer into a wall outlet and turn it on at least 2 feet away from the videocassette recorder. Slowly bring the demagnetizer within 1/2 inch of the video head drum, draw it about 2 feet away and turn it off; be especially careful not to touch a video head with the demagnetizer. Repeat this procedure for the audio head *(left)* and the erase head, as well as for the capstan, the guides and any other metal component that contacts a videocassette. Reinstall the videocassette plate *(page 91)* and the top panel *(page 90)*.

SERVICING THE LOADING ASSEMBLY

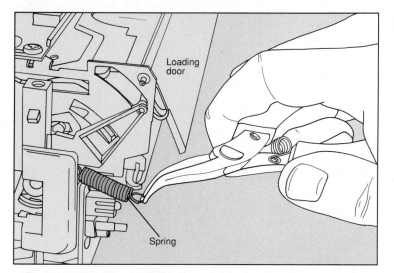

Loading door

Spring

Gears

1 **Checking the assembly.** Remove the top panel *(page 90)* and the front panel or plate *(page 91)*. Check the loading assembly and take out any obstructions. If the gears are dirty, clean and lubricate them *(step 2)*. Reconnect any unhooked spring using long-nose pliers *(above)* or tweezers; if a spring is damaged, replace it *(page 135)*. If the supply-reel drive belt is dirty, clean it with a foam swab dipped in rubber-cleaning compound; if the drive belt is worn or broken, replace it *(page 94)*. Reinstall the front panel or plate *(page 91)*, then the top panel *(page 90)*.

2 **Cleaning and lubricating the gears.** Clean the loading assembly gears using a foam swab dipped in denatured alcohol. Use a toothpick to dislodge particles from the gear teeth *(above)*. Spray gears that are difficult to reach with short bursts of compressed air. If it is necessary to turn the gears, slide in a videocassette and hold it in place. To lubricate the gears, use a toothpick to apply a little white grease. Wipe off the excess with a clean foam swab. Reinstall the front panel or plate *(page 91)* and the top panel *(page 90)*.

REMOVING A JAMMED VIDEOCASSETTE

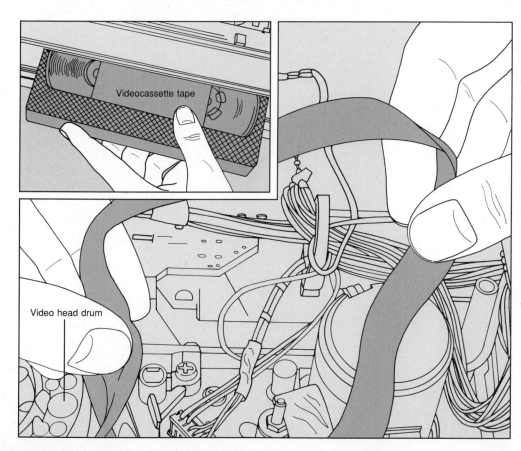

Videocassette tape

Video head drum

Retrieving jammed tape. Remove the top panel *(page 90)* and gently try to extract the videocassette tape from the tape travel path components by hand *(left)*; avoid touching the undamaged tape with your fingers or applying pressure to any components. If the tape is difficult to retrieve, cut it with scissors, making sure not to leave behind any stray scraps. Once the tape is disentangled, pull out the videocassette through the loading door *(inset)*. If the videocassette cannot be removed easily, take off the videocassette plate *(page 91)*, lift out the videocassette and put back the plate. Then reinstall the top panel *(page 90)*. If the tape has been cut or is badly damaged, replace the videocassette or have it serviced. If the tape is OK, press the button on the side of the videocassette to open the flap, and turn the takeup reel with a flat-bladed tool to rewind the tape, being careful not to twist it. Close the videocassete flap. Avoid replaying a videocassette tape that has jammed except to make a copy.

SERVICING THE FAST FORWARD/REWIND MECHANISM

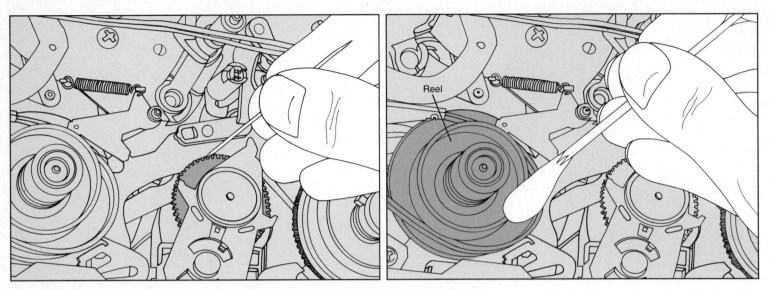

Cleaning the idler gears and the supply and takeup reels. Remove the top panel *(page 90)* and locate the idler gears and the supply and takeup reels. Clean the gears using a foam swab dipped in denatured alcohol. Use a toothpick to dislodge particles from the gear teeth *(above, left)*. Lubricate the gears by applying a little white grease with a small stick or toothpick, and wipe off any excess using a clean foam swab. To clean the reels, use a clean foam swab *(above, right)*, applying denatured alcohol if they are plastic or rubber-cleaning compound if they are rubber. Clean drive belts with rubber-cleaning compound, using a foam swab. Reinstall the top panel *(page 90)*.

SERVICING DRIVE BELTS

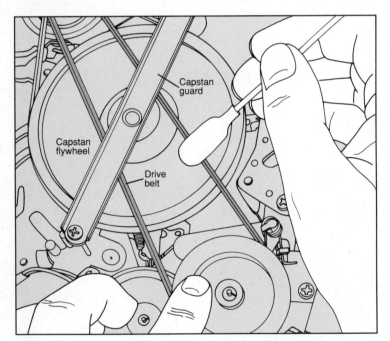

1 Cleaning a belt. Remove the bottom panel *(page 90)* and locate the drive belts on the tape transport assembly. If a belt is worn or broken, replace it *(step 2)*. If a belt is sticky or greasy, clean the belt thoroughly using a foam swab dipped in rubber-cleaning compound *(above)*. Never apply anything oily, and avoid touching the belt with your fingers. Turn the belt pulleys or the capstan flywheel with a clean foam swab to reach the entire length of the belt. Reinstall the bottom panel *(page 90)*.

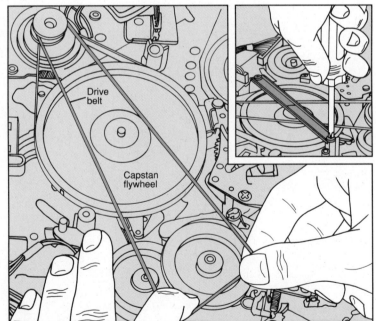

2 Removing and replacing a belt. Unscrew and remove the capstan guard *(inset)* and slip off the belt *(above)*, noting its position on the pulleys or the capstan flywheel. If necessary, use long-nose pliers or tweezers to remove any other belt in the way, being careful not to pinch it. Purchase an exact replacement belt at an electronics parts supplier. Holding the belt loosely with long-nose pliers or tweezers, wrap it around the pulleys or the capstan flywheel. Screw in the capstan guard and reinstall the bottom panel *(page 90)*.

REPLACING THE PINCH ROLLER

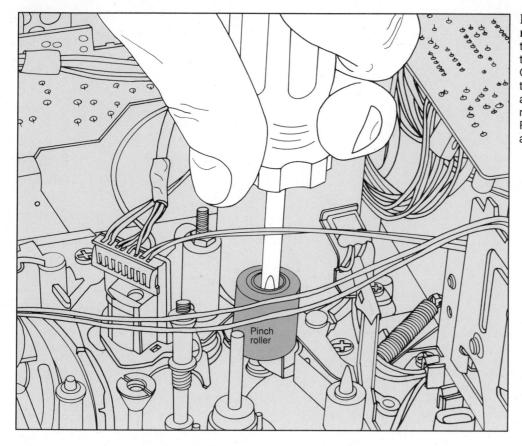

Removing and reinstalling the pinch roller. Remove the top panel *(page 90)* and the videocassette plate *(page 91)*. Unscrew the pinch roller *(left)* and lift it off the shaft. Order an exact replacement pinch roller from the manufacturer, or purchase a substitute at an electronics parts supplier. Slide the pinch roller onto the shaft and screw it into position. Reinstall the videocassette plate *(page 91)* and the top panel *(page 90)*.

Pinch roller

REPLACING THE POWER FUSE

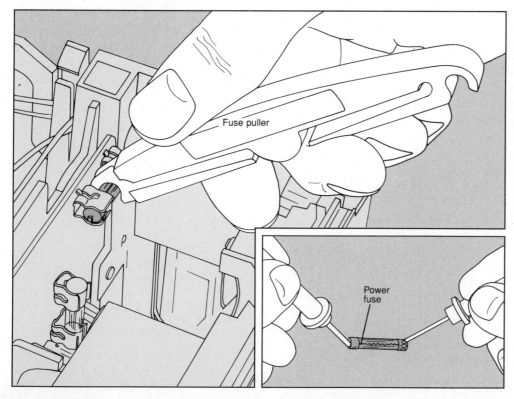

Removing and testing the fuse. Remove the top panel *(page 90)* and locate the fuse on the circuit board nearest the power supply components. Grasp the fuse with a fuse puller and gently pry it out of the retaining clips *(left)*. To test the fuse, set a multitester to test continuity *(page 128)*. Touch one probe to the cap at one end of the fuse and touch the other probe to the cap at the other end of the fuse *(inset)*. If the multitester does not register continuity, purchase an exact replacement fuse at an electronics parts supplier. If the multitester registers continuity, reinstall the fuse. Gently push the fuse into the retaining clips and reinstall the top panel *(page 90)*. If the fuse blows repeatedly, service the power supply *(page 97)*.

Fuse puller

Power fuse

SERVICING THE ON/OFF, MODE AND FEATURE SWITCHES

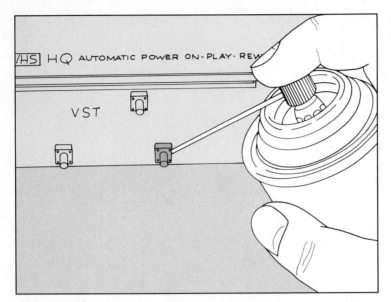

1 Cleaning a mode or feature switch. Remove the top panel *(page 90)* and the front panel or plate *(page 91)*. Find the on/off, mode and feature switches on the circuit board. If you suspect the on/off switch is faulty, test it *(step 2)*; never apply cleaner to an on/off switch. To clean a mode or feature switch, spray a small amount of electronic contact cleaner into the opening between the switch and the circuit board *(above)*. Press in and release the switch several times to work in the cleaner. Reinstall the front panel or plate *(page 91)* and the top panel *(page 90)*. If the problem persists, remove the panels again and test the switch *(step 2)*.

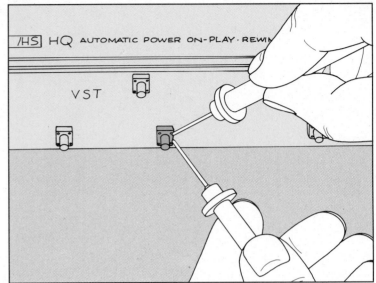

2 Testing a switch. Set a multitester to test continuity *(page 128)*. Set the switch to one position and touch a probe to each pin on one side of the switch; repeat this step with the switch set in the other position. The switch should register continuity in only one position. Repeat this procedure with the pins on the other side of the switch. If the switch tests faulty, remove it *(step 3)*. If the switch tests OK, suspect a faulty circuit board and take the videocassette recorder for professional service; reinstall the front panel or plate *(page 91)* and the top panel *(page 90)*.

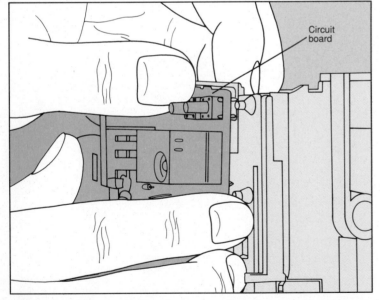

Circuit board

3 Removing a switch. Unscrew the circuit board for the switch, press in any tabs securing it to the frame *(above)*, and carefully turn it over. Desolder the switch pins *(page 130)* and pull off the switch; wiggle it to help release the pins from the circuit board. Test continuity again to confirm the switch is faulty *(step 2)*. If the switch still tests faulty, replace it *(step 4)*. If the switch now tests OK, suspect a faulty circuit board and take the videocassette recorder for professional service; put back the circuit board and reinstall the front panel or plate *(page 91)* and the top panel *(page 90)*.

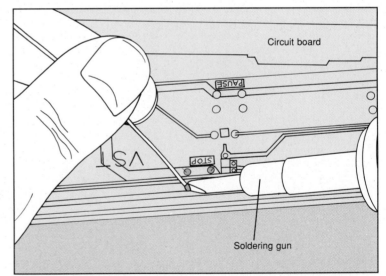

Circuit board

Soldering gun

4 Replacing a switch. Order an exact replacement switch from the manufacturer or purchase a substitute at an electronics parts supplier. Fit the switch pins into the circuit board, turn over the circuit board and solder *(page 131)* the pins *(above)*. Screw the circuit board in place. Reinstall the front panel or plate *(page 91)* and the top panel *(page 90)*. If a problem persists with the on/off switch, service the power supply *(page 97)*. If a problem persists with a mode or feature switch, suspect a faulty circuit board and take the videocassette recorder for professional service.

SERVICING THE POWER SUPPLY

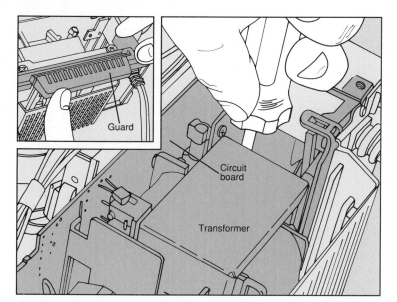

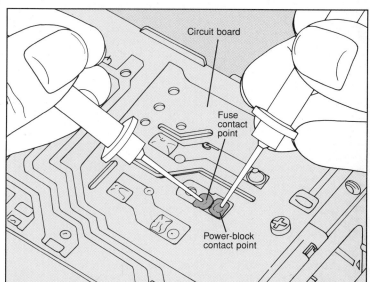

1 **Reaching the power supply components.** Remove the top panel *(page 90)* and identify the power supply components *(page 138)*. Turn over the videocassette recorder, remove any bottom panel screws securing the transformer and turn the videocassette recorder upright. Unscrew the transformer and circuit board *(above)*; disconnect any ground wire. If there is a guard *(inset)*, check the back panel for tabs securing it; press in the tabs and snap off the guard. Lift out the transformer and circuit board, avoiding damage to any wire connections.

2 **Testing between the fuse and the power block.** Locate the contact points for the fuse in the circuit board path connecting to the power block. Set a multitester to test continuity *(page 128)*. Touch one probe to a fuse contact point and touch the other probe to the power-block contact point in the path *(above)*. Repeat this step with the other fuse contact point and the power-block contact point. If the path has continuity, test between the transformer and power block *(step 3)*. If the path does not have continuity, suspect a faulty circuit board and take the videocassette recorder for professional service. Put back the power supply components, reversing the sequence used to remove them *(step 1)*, and reinstall the top panel *(page 90)*.

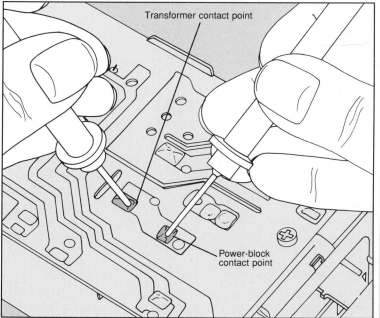

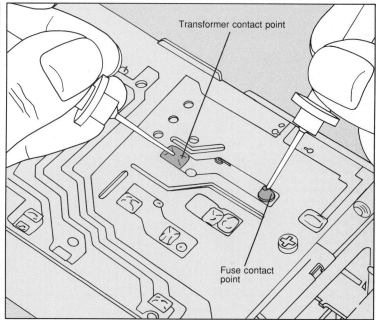

3 **Testing between the transformer and the power block.** Locate a contact point for the transformer in a circuit board path connected to the power block and in a circuit board path to the fuse. Set a multitester to test continuity *(page 128)*. Touch one probe to the transformer contact point in the path to the power block, and touch the other probe to the power-block contact point in the same path *(above, left)*. The path should have continuity. Then, touch one probe

to the transformer contact point in the path to the fuse, and touch the other probe to the fuse contact point in the same path *(above, right)*. If both paths have continuity, test the transformer *(step 4)*. If either path does not have continuity, suspect a faulty circuit board and take the videocassette recorder for professional service. Put back the power supply components, reversing the sequence used to remove them *(step 1)*, and reinstall the top panel *(page 90)*.

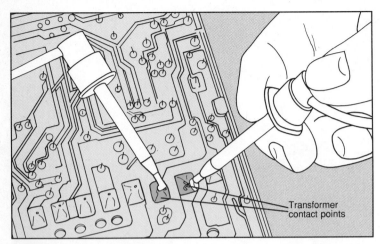

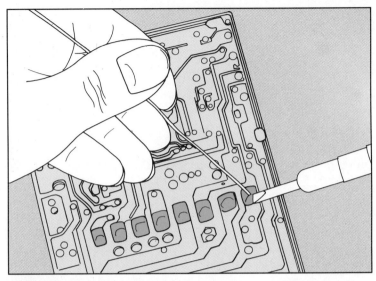

Transformer contact points

4 **Testing the transformer.** Locate the transformer contact points in paths other than to the power block or the fuse. Set a multitester to test voltage *(page 129)*. Hook each probe to one contact point *(above)*. Plug in and turn on the videocassette recorder. Note the multitester reading. Turn off and unplug the videocassette recorder. If there is no voltage, hook the second probe to another contact point and test again, continuing until one point is tested with each other point. When a pair of points has voltage, hook the probes to two different points and repeat this procedure. If you find no voltage between a particular contact point and any other contact point, replace the transformer *(step 5)*. If there is voltage between each contact point and one other contact point, suspect a faulty circuit board and take the videocassette recorder for professional service. Put back the power supply components *(step 1)*, and reinstall the top panel *(page 90)*.

5 **Replacing the transformer.** Desolder the transformer contact points *(page 130)*, carefully turn over the circuit board and pull off the transformer; wiggle it to help release the pins. Order an exact replacement transformer from the manufacturer or purchase a substitute at an electronics parts supplier. Fit the transformer into the circuit board, turn the circuit board over, and solder *(page 131)* the transformer pins *(above)*. Put back the power supply components, reversing the sequence used to remove them *(step 1)*, and reinstall the top panel *(page 90)*.

SERVICING THE LOADING MOTOR

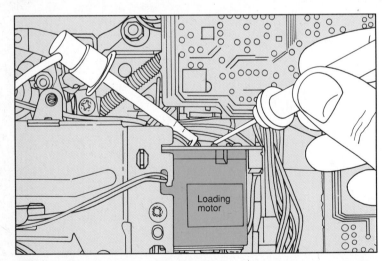

Loading motor

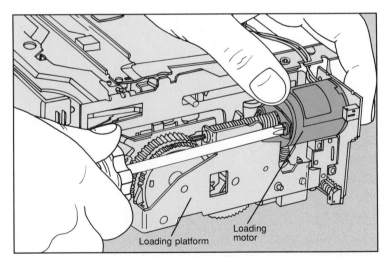

Loading platform

Loading motor

1 **Testing the motor.** Remove the top panel *(page 90)* and locate the loading-motor contact points on the circuit board. Set a multitester to test voltage *(page 129)*. Plug in and turn on the videocassette recorder. Hook a probe to one contact point and touch the other probe to the other contact point *(above)*. Load and unload a videocassette, noting the multitester reading. Turn off and unplug the videocassette recorder. If the motor has voltage, replace it *(step 2)*. If not, suspect a faulty circuit board; reinstall the top panel *(page 90)* and take the videocassette recorder for professional service.

2 **Replacing the motor.** Unscrew the loading platform. Unplug or desolder *(page 130)* the wires from the motor circuit board, noting their positions; you may need to lift the loading platform. Take out the loading platform and unscrew the motor and circuit board. Desolder the motor pins *(page 130)* and pull the motor off the circuit board. Order an exact replacement motor from the manufacturer. Solder the motor pins to the circuit board *(page 131)*, screw in the motor *(above)*, and plug in or solder *(page 131)* the wires to the circuit board. Put back the loading platform and reinstall the top panel *(page 90)*.

SERVICING THE WRAP MOTOR

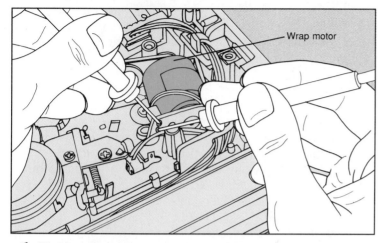

Wrap motor

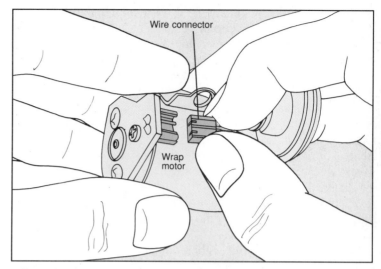

Wire connector

Wrap motor

1 **Testing the motor.** Remove the bottom panel *(page 90)* and locate the wrap-motor contact points on the circuit board. Set a multitester to test voltage *(page 129)*. Plug in the videocassette recorder, turn it on and load a videocassette. Carefully touch a probe to each motor contact point on the circuit board, avoiding any contact with other components *(above)*. Note the multitester reading and unload the videocassette. Turn off and unplug the videocassette recorder. If the multitester registers voltage, replace the motor *(step 2)*. If the multitester does not register voltage, suspect a faulty circuit board; reinstall the bottom panel *(page 90)* and take the videocassette recorder for professional service.

2 **Replacing the motor.** Note the position of the belt on the motor pulley and slip it off using long-nose pliers or tweezers. Unscrew the motor and pull the motor and circuit board from the loading assembly. Unplug or desolder *(page 130)* the wires from the motor circuit board *(above)*, noting their terminals. Order an exact replacement motor and circuit board from the manufacturer or purchase a substitute at an electronics parts supplier. Plug in or solder *(page 131)* the wires to the circuit board. Screw in the motor and circuit board, put back the belt and reinstall the bottom panel *(page 90)*.

SERVICING THE CAPSTAN/REEL MOTOR

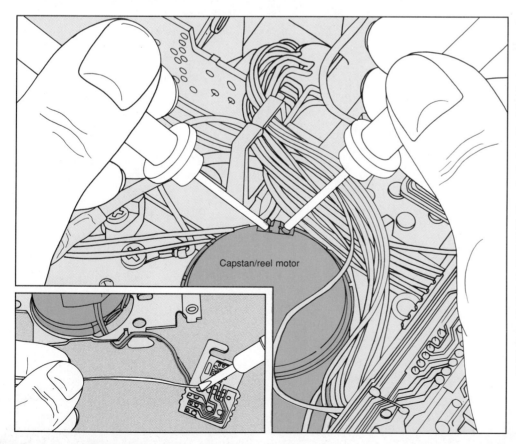

Capstan/reel motor

Testing the motor. Remove the top panel *(page 90)* and locate the capstan/reel motor terminals. Set a multitester to test voltage *(page 129)*. Plug in the videocassette recorder, turn it on and load a videocassette. Carefully touch a probe to each motor terminal, avoiding any contact with other components *(left)*. Note the multitester reading and unload the video-cassette. Turn off and unplug the videocassette recorder. If the multitester does not register voltage, suspect a faulty circuit board; reinstall the top panel *(page 90)* and take the video-cassette recorder for professional service.

If the multitester registers voltage, remove the bottom panel *(page 90)*. Using long-nose pliers or tweezers, slip the belts off the motor pulley; note the position of each belt. Unscrew the motor and lift it out of the capstan assembly. Unscrew the motor circuit board, turn it over and desolder the motor wires, noting their contact points. Order an exact replacement motor from the manufacturer or purchase a substitute at an electronics parts supplier. Solder *(page 131)* the motor wires to the circuit board, screw in the circuit board and the motor, and put back the belts. Reinstall the bottom and top panels *(page 90)*.

TELEPHONE SYSTEMS

Deregulation of the telephone industry in the United States has placed responsibility for certain telephone system maintenance into the hands of the consumer. In most cases the telephones in the house, along with the line cords, wall jacks and interior cables, are now owned by the telephone service subscriber. If your telephone bill includes a monthly service charge for maintenance of the cables and jacks, or if you are still leasing your telephone, let the telephone company handle repairs. Otherwise, you may perform routine tests and repairs yourself. In most homes, the starting point for your system is the terminal block, at or near the first-sequenced wall jack. In many systems installed since 1982, your starting point is a diagnostic jack inside the protector. Do not work on a telephone owned by the telephone company, nor on the incoming cable at the terminal block or diagnostic jack.

On telephone systems with modular components (below), parts can be swapped or replaced without the bother of disassembly. Troubleshooting a problem is often no more complicated than plugging a different telephone into a wall jack. To diagnose telephone system problems, consult the Trouble-shooting Guide at right; for the answering machine, also consult the Troubleshooting Guide in Audiocassette Recorders (page 29). Most telephone system problems can be remedied by cleaning or replacing the plug or the jack, but sometimes a telephone component may test defective. Cleaning materials and most replacement components are available at a telephone store or electronics parts supplier; some parts may have to be ordered from the telephone manufacturer.

A set of small screwdrivers, a multitester and a soldering iron make up the basic telephone system tool kit (page 126). Refer to Tools & Techniques for tips on disassembly and reassembly (page 140), for instructions on testing continuity and voltage (pages 128-129) and for directions on desoldering and soldering (pages 130-131).

Before attempting any repair to a telephone, disconnect its base from the wall jack; before working on a wall jack or the cable, either unplug your home system or take the telephone handset off the hook. Check with your local telephone company for restrictions on the use of repaired equipment; you may be required to have a telephone recertified.

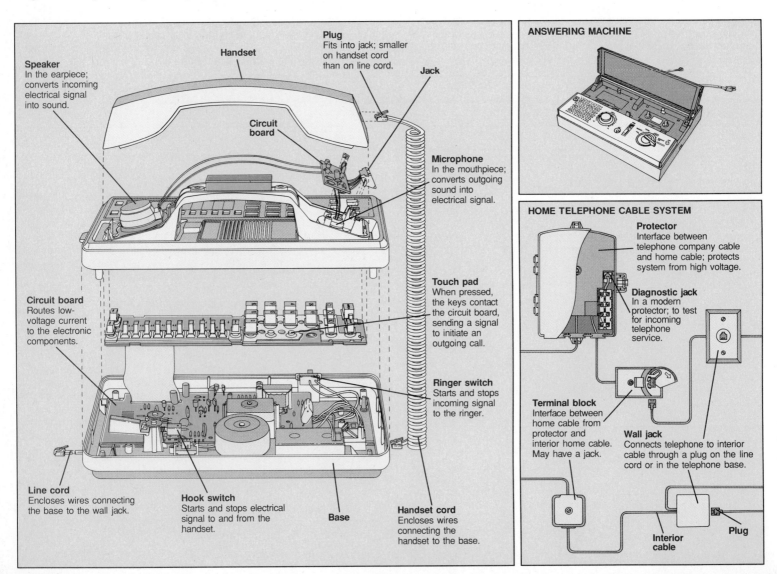

Speaker
In the earpiece; converts incoming electrical signal into sound.

Handset

Plug
Fits into jack; smaller on handset cord than on line cord.

Jack

Circuit board

Circuit board
Routes low-voltage current to the electronic components.

Line cord
Encloses wires connecting the base to the wall jack.

Hook switch
Starts and stops electrical signal to and from the handset.

Base

Microphone
In the mouthpiece; converts outgoing sound into electrical signal.

Touch pad
When pressed, the keys contact the circuit board, sending a signal to initiate an outgoing call.

Ringer switch
Starts and stops incoming signal to the ringer.

Handset cord
Encloses wires connecting the handset to the base.

ANSWERING MACHINE

HOME TELEPHONE CABLE SYSTEM

Protector
Interface between telephone company cable and home cable; protects system from high voltage.

Diagnostic jack
In a modern protector; to test for incoming telephone service.

Terminal block
Interface between home cable from protector and interior home cable. May have a jack.

Wall jack
Connects telephone to interior cable through a plug on the line cord or in the telephone base.

Interior cable

Plug

TROUBLESHOOTING GUIDE

SYMPTOM	POSSIBLE CAUSE	PROCEDURE
No dial tone in any telephone at any wall jack	Short circuit in home telephone system	Plug a telephone into diagnostic jack and listen for dial tone, or test for voltage at terminal block; replace cable (p. 108) □◕ or notify telephone company
No dial tone in any telephone at some wall jacks	Open circuit in home telephone system	Check wire connections and switch the wire positions (p. 108) ◪○
No dial tone in any telephone at one wall jack	Wall jack faulty	Test and replace wall jack (p. 104) □○
No dial tone in one telephone at any wall jack	Handset cord or line cord plug dirty or faulty	Clean and replace modular plugs (p. 103) □○▲
	Handset cord or line cord faulty	Test and replace handset cord and line cord (p. 103) □○
	Handset cord jack or base jack faulty	Test and replace telephone jacks (p. 104) □○
	Hook switch dirty or faulty	Clean hook switch (p. 106) □○; test and replace switch (p. 106) ■○
	Touch pad key dirty	Clean touch pad (p. 107) □○
	Speaker faulty	Replace speaker (p. 105) □○
	Circuit board faulty	Take telephone for professional service
No dial tone in one telephone at one wall jack	Handset off hook	Place handset on hook
	Handset cord or line cord unplugged	Plug in handset cord and line cord; try other telephones or other jacks
Dial tone, but can't call out	Hook switch dirty or faulty	Clean hook switch (p. 106) □○; test and replace switch (p. 106) ■○
	Touch pad key dirty	Clean touch pad (p. 107) □○
	Circuit board faulty	Take telephone for professional service
Dial tone, but can't receive calls	Ringer switch turned off	Turn on ringer switch
	Ringer switch faulty	Test and replace ringer switch (p. 107) □○
	Circuit board faulty	Take telephone for professional service
Ringing after handset is lifted	Hook switch dirty or faulty	Clean hook switch (p. 106) □○; test and replace switch (p. 106) ■○
	Ringer switch faulty	Test and replace ringer switch (p. 107) □○
	Circuit board faulty	Take telephone for professional service
Can't hear and/or can't be heard	Handset cord unplugged	Plug in handset cord
	Handset cord plug dirty or faulty	Clean and replace modular plugs (p.103) □○▲
	Handset cord faulty	Test and replace handset cord (p. 103) □○
	Handset cord jack faulty	Test and replace telephone jacks (p. 104) □○
	Circuit board faulty	Take telephone for professional service
	Speaker or microphone faulty	If can't hear, replace speaker (p. 105) □○; if can't be heard, replace microphone (p. 105) □○
Called party hears crackling or distortion	Handset cord or line cord plug dirty or faulty	Clean and replace modular plugs (p. 103) □○▲
	Handset cord or line cord faulty	Test and replace handset cord and line cord (p. 103) □○
	Handset cord jack or base jack faulty	Test and replace telephone jacks (p. 104) □○
	Microphone faulty	Replace microphone (p. 105) □○
	Circuit board faulty	Take telephone for professional service
Answering machine does not work at all	Answering machine unplugged from outlet	Plug in answering machine
	No power to outlet or outlet faulty	Reset circuit breaker or replace fuse (p. 10) □○; have outlet serviced
	Power cord faulty	Test and replace power cord (p. 137) □○
	Power supply faulty	Gain access to internal components (p. 109) □○; service as for audiocassette recorder (p. 29)
Recorded messages intermittent, inaudible or obscured by static	Audiocassette defective	Replace audiocassette
	Tape travel path dirty	Clean and demagnetize tape travel path (p. 109) □○▲
	Tape travel path component faulty	Gain access to internal components (p. 109) □○; service as for audiocassette recorder (p. 29)

DEGREE OF DIFFICULTY: □ Easy ◪ Moderate ■ Complex
ESTIMATED TIME: ○ Less than 1 hour ◕ 1 to 3 hours ● Over 3 hours ▲ Special tool required

ACCESS TO THE TELEPHONE SYSTEM COMPONENTS

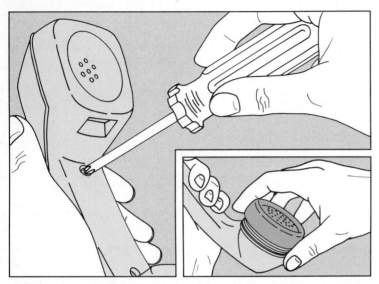

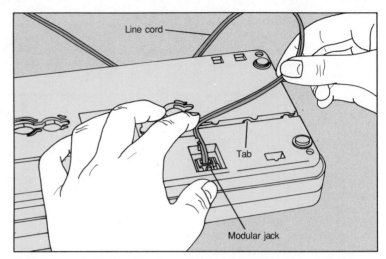

Opening and closing the handset. Disconnect the base *(right)* and unplug the handset cord from the handset. For a modern handset, remove any screws holding the top and bottom casings together *(above)*; check for hidden screws under the telephone number cover. Work the casings back and forth to unsnap the interior clips. If the casings do not separate easily, use a small putty knife to pry them apart. To close the handset, snap together the casings and put back the screws. To access a traditional handset, screw off the caps covering the speaker and microphone *(inset)*. After servicing either style, plug the handset cord into the handset and reconnect the base *(right)*.

Opening and closing the base. To disconnect a table-top base, unplug the line cord from the wall jack. To disconnect a wall-mounted base, slide the base up off the mounting plate and unplug the line cord, if any, from the wall jack. To open the base, unhook the handset cord and line cord from any tabs *(above)* and unplug both from the base. If the model has a table stand, take it off. Remove any screws in the bottom casing and turn the base upright. Lift off the top casing and turn it face down beside the bottom casing. To close the base, fit on the top casing, turn over the base and put back the screws. Plug the handset cord and the line cord into the base, hooking them under the tabs; reinstall the table stand, if any. Plug the line cord into the wall jack; slide a wall-mounted base onto the mounting plate.

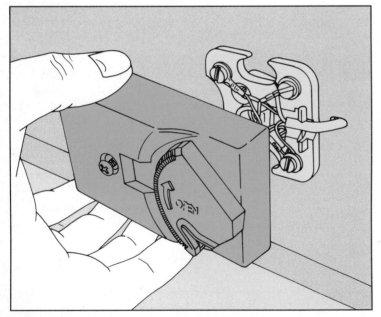

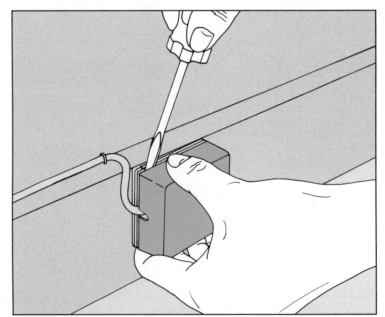

Opening and closing the terminal block. Disconnect any telephone plugged into a jack at the terminal block *(step above)*. Plug this telephone or another one into another wall jack and take the handset off the hook. If the terminal block is recessed in an outlet box behind an interface jack, unscrew the coverplate and pull it off the wall, exposing the wires connected to the back of it. If the terminal block is surface mounted, unscrew the front casing and pull it off *(above)*, exposing the wires connected to the back casing. To close the terminal block, fold back the wires and screw on the coverplate or the front casing. If you disconnected the telephone, reconnect it.

Opening and closing a wall jack. If a telephone is plugged into the wall jack, disconnect it from the jack *(step above)*. Plug this telephone or another one into a prior-sequenced wall jack and take the handset off the hook. If the wall jack is recessed in an outlet box, unscrew the coverplate and pull it off the wall, exposing the wires connected to the back of it. If the wall jack is surface mounted, slip a small screwdriver into the front casing slot and twist the screwdriver to pop off the front casing *(above)*, exposing the wires connected to the back casing. To close the wall jack, fold back the wires and screw on the coverplate or snap on the front casing. Reconnect the telephone and replace the handset.

SERVICING MODULAR PLUGS

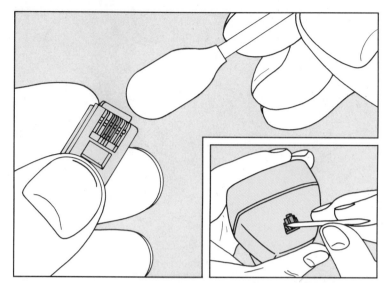

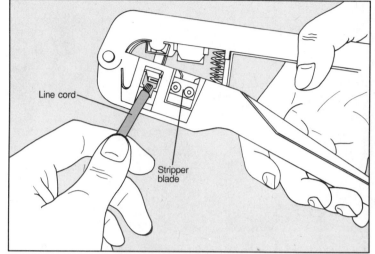

Line cord

Stripper blade

1 **Checking the modular connections.** Disconnect the telephone from the wall jack. Unplug the handset cord from the handset and the base, and unplug the line cord from the base *(page 102)*. If a plug's spring clip or one of its pins is damaged, replace the plug *(step 2)* or the cord *(below)*. Use a foam swab and denatured alcohol to clean the pins in the plugs *(above)* and in the handset and base jacks. Before cleaning the pins in the wall jack, reconnect the handset cord and line cord to the telephone, then plug in the telephone at another wall jack and take the handset off the hook. If a jack pin does not protrude enough to mate with a plug pin, gently pry it up with a toothpick *(inset)*. If a jack pin is broken, replace the jack *(page 104)*. After cleaning the pins in the wall jack, reconnect the telephone to the jack and place the handset back on the hook.

2 **Replacing a modular plug.** Purchase a modular crimping tool and a set of replacement plugs at a telephone store or an electronics parts supplier; note that the handset cord requires a smaller plug than the line cord. Snip off the old plug with wire cutters or a utility knife, making sure to cut straight across the cord. Strip 1/4 inch of insulation off the end of the cord, using the crimping tool stripper blade. Seat the new plug in the crimping tool; if the plug is for the handset cord, first install the tool adapter housed in the handle. Position the wires in the new plug in the identical color sequence as in the old plug. Pushing the wires into the new plug as far as possible, tightly squeeze the handle of the crimping tool *(above)*. Reconnect the handset cord and line cord to the telephone, then plug the telephone into the wall jack *(left)*.

SERVICING THE HANDSET CORD AND THE LINE CORD

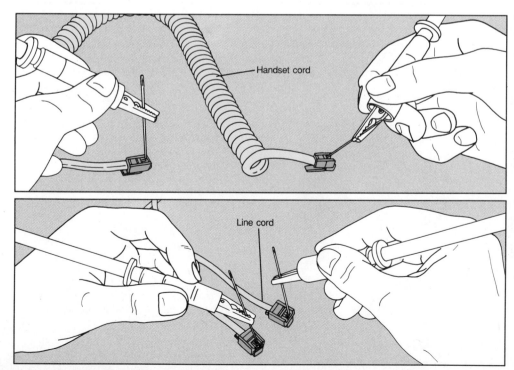

Handset cord

Line cord

Testing and replacing the handset cord and the line cord. Disconnect the telephone from the wall jack, then unplug the handset cord from the handset and the base, or unplug the line cord from the base *(page 102)*. Set a multitester to test continuity *(page 128)*. Clip a sewing needle to each probe. Touch one needle to a pin in one plug on the handset cord *(left, top)* or the line cord *(left, bottom)* and touch the other needle in turn to each pin in the other plug. The multitester should register continuity only once. Repeat this step to test each pin in one plug with each pin in the other plug. If the cord tests faulty, purchase a replacement cord at a telephone store or an electronics parts supplier. Plug the handset cord into the base and the handset, or plug the line cord into the base, then plug the telephone into the wall jack.

SERVICING TELEPHONE JACKS

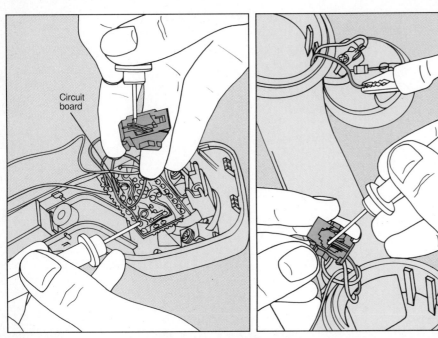

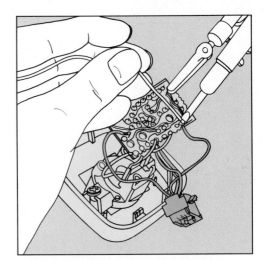

1 **Testing the handset jacks and base jack.** To test the handset jacks, open the handset and the base *(page 102)*; to test the base jack, open just the base. On a modern handset and base, unscrew the circuit board and turn it over to reach the contact points for the jack wires; for the base, first remove any parts that are in the way. On a traditional handset, lift out the speaker and the microphone along with its casing to reach the terminals of the jack wires. If a wire is loose or broken, tighten or repair it *(page 132)*. Set a multitester to test continuity *(page 128)*. Clip one probe to a wire contact pin on the jack and touch the other probe to the wire contact point on the circuit board *(above, left)* or to the wire terminal *(above, right)*. Repeat this step for each wire. If the multitester does not register continuity for each wire, replace the jack *(step 2)*. If the multitester registers continuity for each wire, screw in the circuit board and put back any other components you removed, or reinstall the speaker and the microphone along with its casing. Close the handset and the base *(page 102)*.

2 **Replacing the handset jacks and base jack.** Unclip the jack from the casing and desolder *(page 130)* or unscrew the wires, noting their positions. Purchase a replacement jack of the proper size at a telephone store or an electronics parts supplier. Screw on or solder *(page 131)* the wires *(above)* and clip the jack into the casing. Screw in the circuit board and put back any other components you removed, or reinstall the speaker and the microphone along with its casing. Close the handset and base *(page 102)*.

SERVICING WALL JACKS

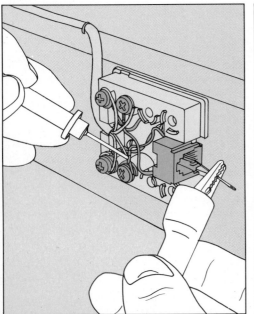

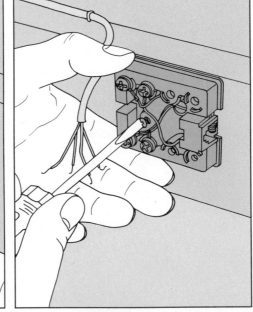

Testing and replacing a wall jack. Open the wall jack *(page 102)*. If a wire is loose or broken, tighten or repair it *(page 132)*. Set a multitester to test continuity *(page 128)*. Clip a needle to one probe and touch it to a wire contact pin on the jack; touch the other probe to the terminal at the other end of the wire *(far left)*. Repeat this step for each wire on the jack. If each wire tests OK, close the wall jack *(page 102)*.

If a wire tests faulty, loosen the terminal screws and disconnect all the jack wires; if the jack is surface mounted, as shown, disconnect the interior cable wires as well. Unclip the jack from the coverplate or unscrew the jack casing *(near left)*. Purchase a replacement jack at a telephone store or an electronics parts supplier. Clip in the jack and screw on its wires, or screw the jack casing in place and reconnect the jack wires and the interior cable wires. Close the wall jack *(page 102)*.

TESTING AND REPLACING THE TELEPHONE SPEAKER

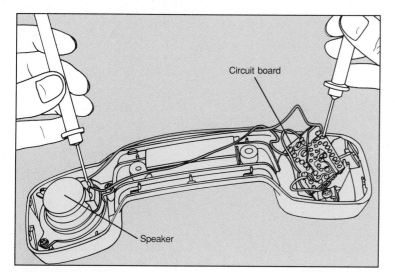

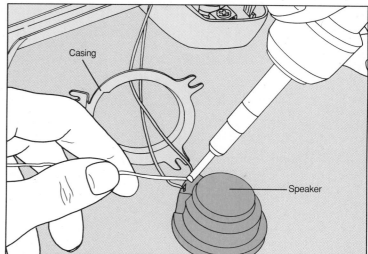

1 **Checking the wire connections.** Open the handset *(page 102)*. For a modern handset, unscrew and turn over the circuit board to reach the speaker wire contact points. For a traditional handset, lift out the speaker and the microphone with its casing to reach the speaker wire terminals and the contact pins on the jack. If a wire is loose or broken, tighten or replace it *(page 132)*. Set a multitester to test continuity *(page 128)*. Touch one probe to a wire terminal on the speaker and touch the other probe to its contact point on the circuit board *(above)* or to its contact pin on the jack. Repeat this step for the other wire. If a wire tests faulty on a modern handset, replace the wire *(page 132)*; on a traditional handset, replace the jack *(page 104)*. If each wire tests OK, replace the speaker *(step 2)*.

2 **Installing a new speaker.** Desolder *(page 130)* or unscrew the wires at the speaker terminals, remove any casing, and lift out the speaker. Purchase a replacement speaker at a telephone store or an electronics parts supplier. Fit the speaker wires through the casing, if any, and solder *(page 131)* or screw the wires to the terminals *(above)*. For a modern handset, insert the speaker along with the casing and screw in the circuit board. For a traditional handset, install the speaker and put back the microphone with its casing. Close the handset *(page 102)*. If the problem persists, suspect a faulty circuit board and take the telephone for professional service.

TESTING AND REPLACING THE TELEPHONE MICROPHONE

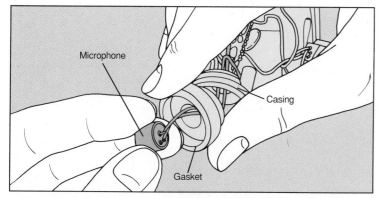

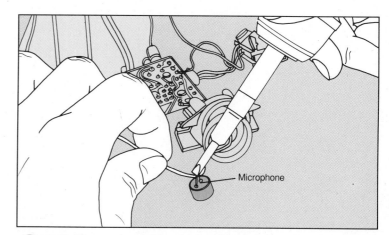

1 **Checking the wire connections.** Open the handset *(page 102)*. For a modern handset, unscrew and turn over the circuit board to reach the microphone wire contact points. Unclip the jack, unscrew the microphone casing, and pull the microphone out of the casing and its gasket, if any, to reach the microphone wire terminals *(above)*. For a traditional handset, lift out the microphone with its casing to reach the microphone wire terminals and the contact pins on the jack. If a wire is loose or broken, tighten or replace it *(page 132)*. Set a multitester to test continuity *(page 128)*. Touch one probe to a microphone wire terminal and touch the other probe to its contact point on the circuit board or its contact pin on the jack. Repeat this step for the other wire. If a wire tests faulty on a modern handset, replace the wire *(page 132)*; on a traditional handset, replace the jack and its wires *(page 104)*. If each wire tests OK, replace the microphone *(step 2)*.

2 **Installing a new microphone.** Desolder *(page 130)* the wires at the microphone terminals or lift the microphone off the contact tabs in the casing. Purchase a replacement microphone at a telephone store or an electronics parts supplier. For a modern handset, solder *(page 131)* the microphone wires to the terminals *(above)*. Push the microphone into the gasket, if any, and the casing, screw in the casing, clip in the jack, and screw in the circuit board. For a traditional handset, seat the microphone on the contact tabs in the casing. Close the handset *(page 102)*. If the problem persists, suspect a faulty circuit board and take the telephone for professional service.

SERVICING THE TELEPHONE HOOK SWITCH

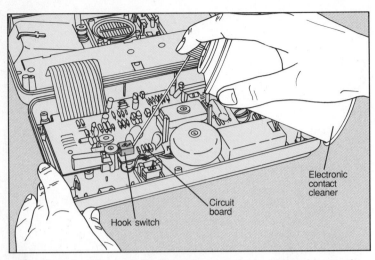

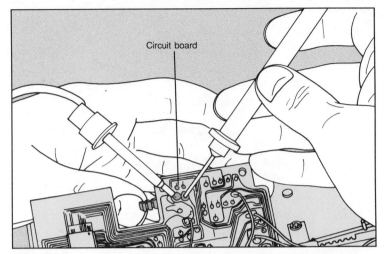

1 **Cleaning the switch.** Open the base *(page 102)* and locate the hook switch on the circuit board in the bottom casing. Using electronic contact cleaner, direct the nozzle into the openings on the top of the hook switch and spray in a little cleaner *(above)*. Work in the cleaner by depressing and releasing the hook several times. If the lever slides poorly or the spring is damaged, unscrew the circuit board, remove any parts that are in the way and turn over the circuit board. Desolder the hook switch pins *(page 130)* and replace the hook switch *(step 4)*. If the lever and the spring function smoothly, close the base *(page 102)*. If the problem persists, reopen the base and test the hook switch *(step 2)*.

2 **Testing the switch.** Unscrew the circuit board and turn it over to reach the hook switch pins; if required, remove the hook and any other obstructions. Set a multitester to test continuity *(page 128)* and follow the technique for testing a multi-pole switch *(page 136)*. Hook one probe to a switch pin and touch the other probe in turn to the other switch pins *(above)*, pressing and releasing the lever for each test. Repeat this step until each switch pin is tested with each other switch pin, checking for a continuity pattern. If the switch does not have a continuity pattern, remove it *(step 3)*. If the switch has a continuity pattern, screw in the circuit board, put back the hook and any other components you removed, and close the base *(page 102)*.

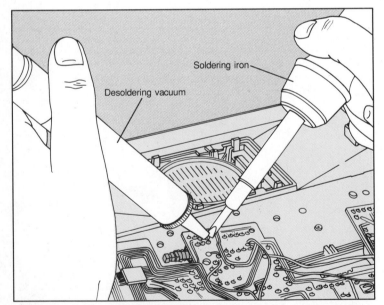

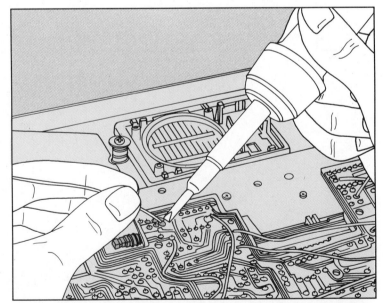

3 **Removing the switch.** Desolder *(page 130)* the switch pins from the circuit board *(above)*. Gently wiggle the switch from the top of the circuit board to free the pins. Confirm that the switch is faulty by testing it again for continuity while out of circuit *(step 2)*. If the switch now has a continuity pattern, suspect a problem with the circuit board and take the telephone for professional service. If the switch still does not have a continuity pattern, replace it *(step 4)*.

4 **Replacing the switch.** Order a replacement hook switch from the telephone manufacturer or purchase a hook switch at a telephone store or an electronics parts supplier. Slip the pins of the switch into the top of the circuit board. Supporting the switch in place, turn over the circuit board and solder *(page 131)* the pins *(above)*. Screw in the circuit board, put back the hook and any other components you removed, and close the base *(page 102)*. If the problem persists, suspect a faulty circuit board and take the telephone for professional service.

SERVICING THE TELEPHONE TOUCH PAD

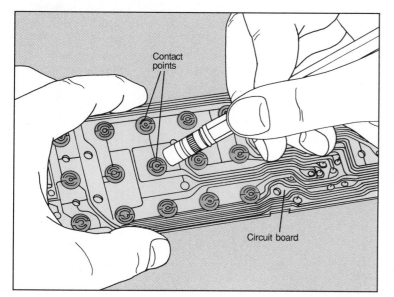

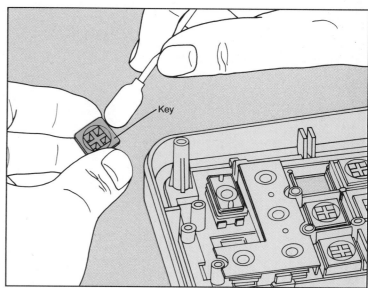

1 **Cleaning the contacts.** Open the base or the handset *(page 102)*. Unscrew the circuit board in the upper casing and turn it over to reach the contact points of the touch-pad keys. Clean dirt from each contact point on the circuit board, rubbing gently with the eraser end of a pencil *(above)* or wiping lightly with a foam swab sprayed with a little electronic contact cleaner.

2 **Cleaning the keys.** Lift off the pads covering the bottom of the keys. Inspect each key for dirt and grime, removing and replacing one key at a time. Clean the keys using a foam swab dipped in alcohol *(above)*. Put the pads back on the bottom of the keys and screw in the circuit board. Close the base or the handset *(page 102)*. If the problem persists, suspect a faulty circuit board and take the telephone for professional service.

TESTING AND REPLACING THE RINGER SWITCH

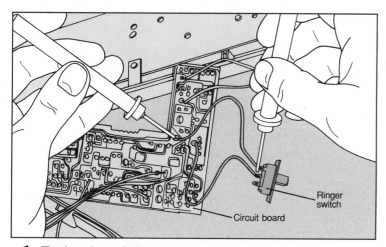

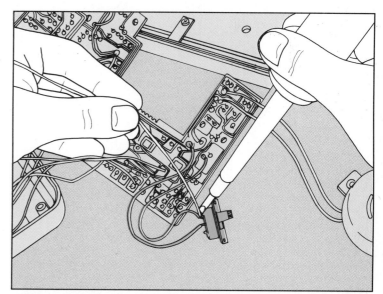

1 **Testing the switch.** Open the base or the handset *(page 102)*. Unscrew the circuit board in the lower casing, remove any parts in the way, and turn over the circuit board to reach the ringer-switch wire contact points. If a wire is loose or broken, secure or replace it *(page 132)*. Set a multitester to test continuity *(page 128)*. Touch one probe to a switch wire terminal and touch the other probe to the wire's contact point on the circuit board *(above)*. Repeat this step for the other wire. If a wire does not have continuity, replace it *(page 132)*. Next, with the switch in the ON position, touch a probe to each switch wire terminal; the switch should have continuity. With the switch in the OFF position, there should be no continuity. If the switch tests faulty, replace it *(step 2)*. If the switch tests OK, screw in the circuit board, put back any other components and close the base or handset *(page 102)*.

2 **Replacing the switch.** Desolder the wires from the switch terminals *(page 130)*, tagging one with its position for reassembly. Confirm that the switch is faulty by testing it for continuity again, while out of circuit *(step 1)*. If the switch now tests OK, suspect a problem with the circuit board and take the telephone for professional service. If the switch still tests faulty, purchase a replacement switch at a telephone store or an electronics parts supplier. Solder the wires *(page 131)* to the terminals of the switch *(above)*. Screw in the circuit board, put back any other components and close the base or handset *(page 102)*.

REPAIRING AN OPEN TELEPHONE CIRCUIT

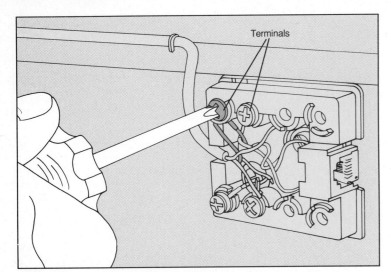

Terminals

1 Checking the wire connections. Of the wall jacks that have no dial tone, open the one *(page 102)* that is nearest in sequence to the terminal block. Check the wire connection at each terminal. If a wire is loose or broken, tighten *(above)* or repair it *(page 132)*. If the problem persists, repeat this step at the prior-sequenced wall jack. If the problem still persists, switch the wire positions *(step 2)* or replace the cable *(below)* connecting the two wall jacks. If you cannot determine the wall jack sequence, check each wall jack; if there is still no dial tone at one or more wall jacks, call for service.

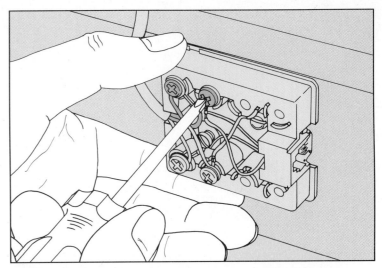

2 Switching wire connections. Reopen the wall jack and remove the incoming cable's wires from their terminals. Reconnect the red wire to the black terminal, the black wire to the red terminal, the green wire to the yellow terminal and the yellow wire to the green terminal *(above)*. Reopen the prior-sequenced wall jack, remove the outgoing cable's wires from their terminals and reconnect them, making the identical substitution. If you cannot distinguish the outgoing and incoming wires, consult a telephone service professional. Close the wall jacks *(page 102)*. If there is still no dial tone, replace the cable *(below)*.

REPAIRING A SHORTED TELEPHONE CIRCUIT

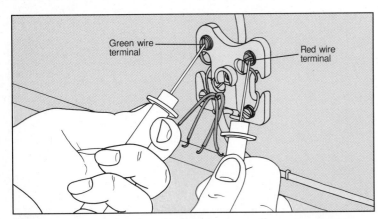

Green wire terminal

Red wire terminal

1 Testing voltage at the terminal block. Open the terminal block *(page 102)* and disconnect the wires leading to the further-sequenced wall jacks. If the terminal block has no jack, set a multitester to test voltage *(page 129)*. Touch the negative probe to the red wire terminal and the positive probe to the green wire terminal *(above)*. If there is no voltage, notify the telephone company. If there is voltage, reconnect the wires and close the terminal block. If the terminal block has a jack, wrap the disconnected wires with electrical tape, close the terminal block *(page 102)* and plug in a working telephone. If you hear no dial tone, notify the telephone company. If you hear a dial tone, unplug the telephone, open the terminal block, reconnect the wires and close the terminal block. When a terminal block tests OK, open the wall jack next in sequence *(page 102)* and do the telephone test there. If there is no dial tone, replace the cable between that wall jack and the terminal block *(step 2)*. If there is a dial tone, repeat the test at the next jack until the faulty length of cable is located.

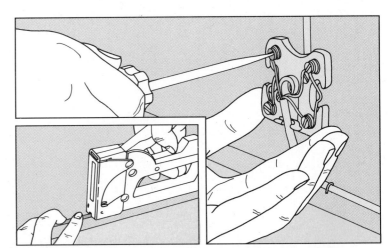

2 Replacing the interior cable. Reopen the jacks between which the cable is faulty *(page 102)* and remove the wires of the cable connecting them. Pull out the staples securing a surface cable using pliers; for a cable that runs behind the wall, wrap the wire ends with electrical tape and leave the cable hidden. Purchase telephone cable, insulated wire staples and spade lug connectors at a telephone or electronics store. If the jacks are in recessed outlet boxes, unscrew and pull out the outlet boxes and drill a small hole beside each wall opening through which to thread the new cable. Crimp spade lug connectors to the wires at one end of the cable *(page 132)* and connect the wire terminals in one jack *(above)*. Run the cable as unobtrusively as possible to the other jack, securing it with the staples *(inset)*. Cut the cable to length using wire cutters, crimp on spade lug connectors and connect the wires to the jack terminals. Close the jacks *(page 102)*.

SERVICING THE ANSWERING MACHINE

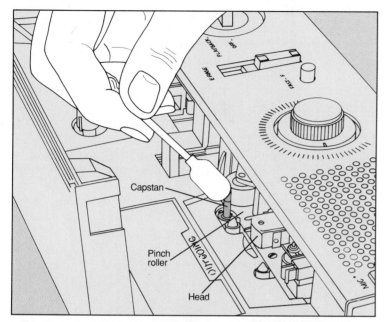

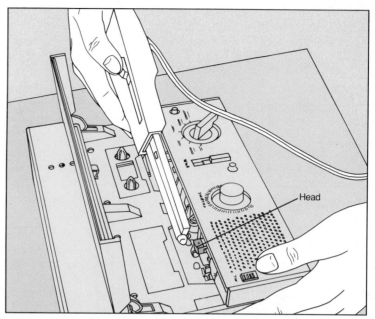

1 **Cleaning the tape travel paths.** Turn off the answering machine and unplug it from the wall outlet. Unplug the line cords to the wall jack and to the telephone. Open the loading doors and unload the audiocassettes to reach the tape travel paths. Using a foam swab and denatured alcohol, clean the audio heads, the capstans *(above)*, the guides and other metal parts that contact an audiocassette. Clean the pinch rollers with rubber-cleaning compound; rotate them with a finger as you clean. Repeat this step every three months to prevent a buildup of dirt.

2 **Demagnetizing the tape travel paths.** Purchase a demagnetizer at an electronics parts supplier. Plug the demagnetizer into a wall outlet and turn it on at least 2 feet away from the answering machine. Slowly bring the demagnetizer within 1/2 inch of an audio head *(above)*, gradually draw it about 2 feet away and turn it off. Repeat this step for the other audio head as well as for the capstans, the guides and other metal parts that contact an audiocassette. Reconnect the line cords. Plug the answering machine into the wall outlet and reload the audiocassettes. To prevent static interference in recordings, demagnetize after each cleaning.

ACCESS TO THE ANSWERING MACHINE COMPONENTS

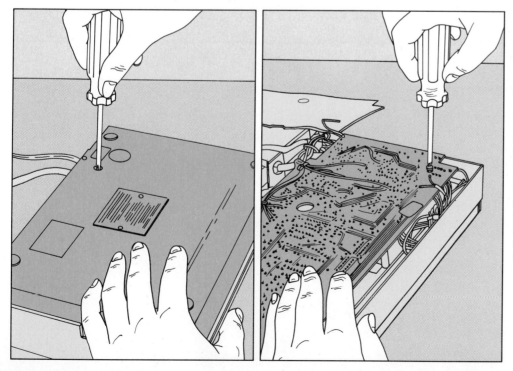

Removing the bottom panel. Unload the audiocassettes, turn off the answering machine and unplug it from the wall outlet. Unplug the line cords to the wall jack and to the telephone. Pull off or unscrew any control too large to pass through its opening in the top and side panels. Turn over the answering machine, remove any screws securing the bottom panel *(far left)* and lift it off. Unscrew the circuit board if it obstructs access to internal components *(near left)*. To service the internal components, consult Audiocassette Recorders *(page 28)*. To close the answering machine, put back any components removed, reinstall the circuit board, screw on the bottom panel, and put back any controls taken off. Cold check the answering machine for leaking voltage *(page 141)*. Reconnect the line cords. Plug the answering machine into the wall outlet, turn it on and reload the audiocassettes.

COMPUTERS AND PRINTERS

By following programmed instructions, your computer can analyze and compile data, or perform complex calculations in seconds. The touch of a finger to a key sends an electronic code to the central processing unit (CPU). A silicon microchip located on the motherboard, the CPU is the workhorse of the computer. The CPU carries out simple tasks commanded by a program, the computer's brain. Programs are stored in memory — integrated circuits (IC) on a circuit board. When you use the video display, the CPU sends characters in the form of electronic codes to the monitor (CRT), where they are translated into their alphabetical equivalent and beamed onto the screen. When you use the printer, the CPU moves codes out of the disk, memory or keyboard and delivers them to the printer, where they are translated into their alphabetical equivalent and sent through the print head to paper. The CPU also tells the read/write head whether to read from or store on a disk.

All personal computers work this way, but their styles vary. Your system may have a main unit with built-in disk drives and a separate keyboard, monitor and printer (below); or it may have a main unit with a built-in keyboard, independent disk drive and power supply units, and a television. Most computers perform a self-test each time they boot up; for many computers, diagnostic programs are also available. For additional help, consult the Troubleshooting Guide (page 112). Many computer problems can be remedied by adjusting cable hookups or by cleaning the key switches, read/write and print heads, and peripheral-card edge connectors. Supplies and most replacement parts are available at a computer or electronics parts supplier. Refer to Tools & Techniques (page 126) for the basic tools and methods required to do repairs.

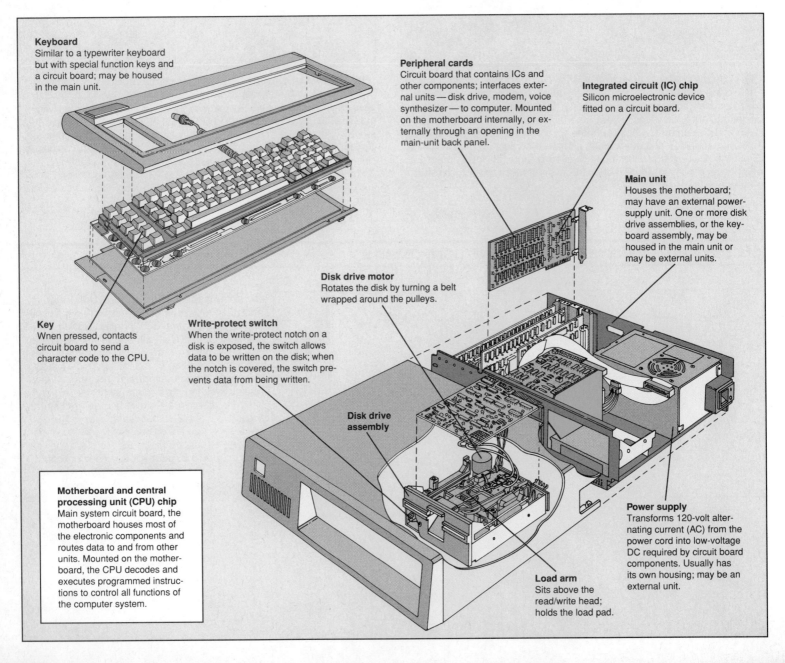

Keyboard
Similar to a typewriter keyboard but with special function keys and a circuit board; may be housed in the main unit.

Peripheral cards
Circuit board that contains ICs and other components; interfaces external units — disk drive, modem, voice synthesizer — to computer. Mounted on the motherboard internally, or externally through an opening in the main-unit back panel.

Integrated circuit (IC) chip
Silicon microelectronic device fitted on a circuit board.

Main unit
Houses the motherboard; may have an external power-supply unit. One or more disk drive assemblies, or the keyboard assembly, may be housed in the main unit or may be external units.

Disk drive motor
Rotates the disk by turning a belt wrapped around the pulleys.

Key
When pressed, contacts circuit board to send a character code to the CPU.

Write-protect switch
When the write-protect notch on a disk is exposed, the switch allows data to be written on the disk; when the notch is covered, the switch prevents data from being written.

Disk drive assembly

Motherboard and central processing unit (CPU) chip
Main system circuit board, the motherboard houses most of the electronic components and routes data to and from other units. Mounted on the motherboard, the CPU decodes and executes programmed instructions to control all functions of the computer system.

Load arm
Sits above the read/write head; holds the load pad.

Power supply
Transforms 120-volt alternating current (AC) from the power cord into low-voltage DC required by circuit board components. Usually has its own housing; may be an external unit.

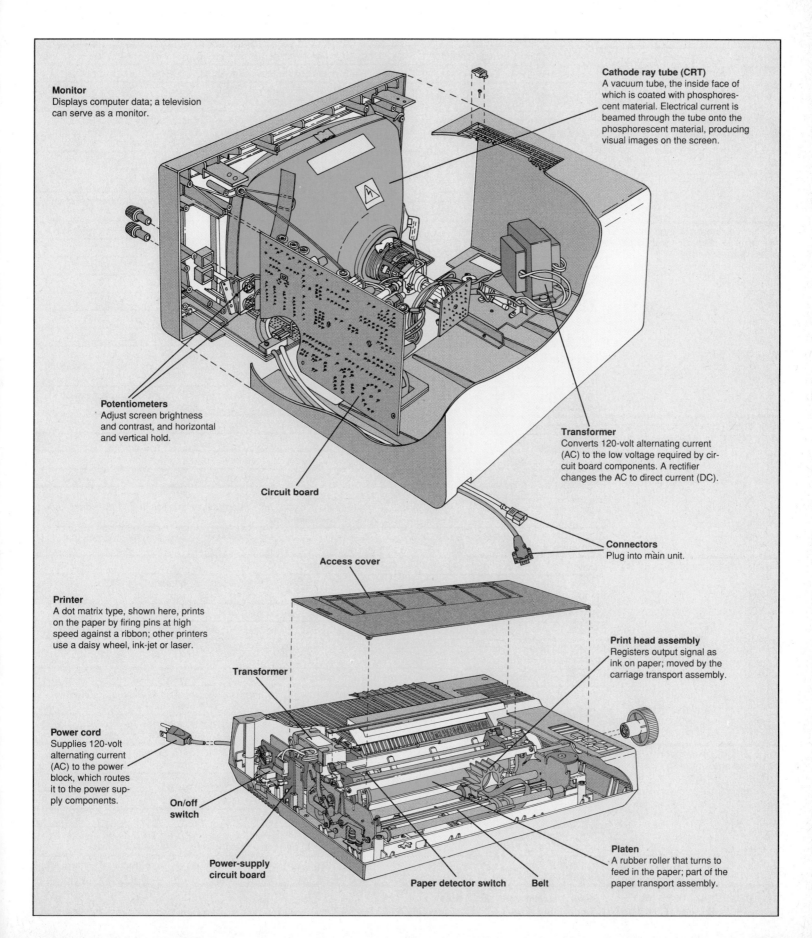

Monitor
Displays computer data; a television can serve as a monitor.

Cathode ray tube (CRT)
A vacuum tube, the inside face of which is coated with phosphorescent material. Electrical current is beamed through the tube onto the phosphorescent material, producing visual images on the screen.

Potentiometers
Adjust screen brightness and contrast, and horizontal and vertical hold.

Circuit board

Transformer
Converts 120-volt alternating current (AC) to the low voltage required by circuit board components. A rectifier changes the AC to direct current (DC).

Connectors
Plug into main unit.

Access cover

Printer
A dot matrix type, shown here, prints on the paper by firing pins at high speed against a ribbon; other printers use a daisy wheel, ink-jet or laser.

Transformer

Print head assembly
Registers output signal as ink on paper; moved by the carriage transport assembly.

Power cord
Supplies 120-volt alternating current (AC) to the power block, which routes it to the power supply components.

On/off switch

Power-supply circuit board

Paper detector switch

Belt

Platen
A rubber roller that turns to feed in the paper; part of the paper transport assembly.

TROUBLESHOOTING GUIDE

SYMPTOM	POSSIBLE CAUSE	PROCEDURE
Computer system does not boot up	Computer system unplugged or turned off	Plug in and turn on computer system
	No power to outlet or outlet faulty	Reset breaker or replace fuse (p. 10) □○; have outlet serviced
	Main unit, disk drive unit or power-supply unit cable hookup faulty	Service cable hookups (p. 134) □○
	Main unit, disk drive unit or power-supply unit power fuse blown	If power fuse mounted externally, test and replace it (p. 118) □○; if power fuse mounted internally, take main unit or disk drive unit, or disk drive unit and power supply unit, for professional service
	CPU or IC chip faulty	Test and replace CPU and IC chips (p. 117) ■○; if you cannot locate faulty IC chip, take main unit, or main unit and disk drive unit, for professional service
	Power supply in main unit or disk drive unit, or external power-supply unit, faulty	Take main unit or disk drive unit, or disk drive unit and power supply unit, for professional service
Disk drive does not read from nor write to disk, or reads and writes intermittently	Disk loaded incorrectly or faulty	Reload disk; replace disk
	Disk-drive unit cable hookup faulty	Service cable hookups (p. 134) □○
	Disk-drive read/write head dirty	Service disk-drive read/write head (p. 114) □○
	Disk drive belt dirty or faulty	Service disk drive belt (p. 115) □○
	Disk drive motor runs too fast or too slow	Adjust disk-drive motor speed (p. 115) ◨○
	Disk-drive write-protect switch faulty	Test and replace disk-drive write-protect switch (p. 116) □○
	Peripheral-card edge connector dirty	Clean peripheral-card edge connectors (p. 116) □○
	CPU or IC chip faulty	Test and replace CPU and IC chips (p. 117) ■○; if you cannot locate faulty IC chip, take main unit, or main unit and disk drive unit, for professional service
	Disk drive assembly, peripheral card or motherboard faulty	Take main unit, or main unit and disk drive unit, for professional service
Disk drive reads from but does not write to disk	Disk write-protect notch covered	Uncover disk write-protect notch
	Disk faulty	Replace disk
	Disk-drive write-protect switch faulty	Test and replace disk-drive write-protect switch (p. 116) □○
	Peripheral-card edge connector dirty	Clean peripheral-card edge connectors (p. 116) □○
	CPU or IC chip faulty	Test and replace CPU and IC chips (p. 117) ■○; if you cannot locate faulty IC chip, take main unit, or main unit and disk drive unit, for professional service
	Disk drive assembly, peripheral card or motherboard faulty	Take main unit, or main unit and disk drive unit, for professional service
No display on monitor	Monitor unplugged from main unit	Plug in monitor
	Monitor brightness or contrast potentiometer set incorrectly	Adjust monitor brightness and contrast controls
	Monitor cable hookup faulty	Service cable hookups (p. 134) □○
	Monitor power fuse blown	Test and replace power fuse (p. 118) □○
	Monitor brightness or contrast potentiometer dirty or faulty	Service potentiometers (p. 118) □○
	Peripheral-card edge connector dirty	Clean peripheral-card edge connectors (p. 116) □○
	CPU or IC chip faulty	Test and replace CPU and IC chips (p. 117) ■○; if you cannot locate faulty IC chip, take monitor and main unit for professional service
	Picture tube, peripheral card or motherboard faulty	Take monitor and main unit for professional service
Keyboard does not work, or works intermittently	Keyboard-assembly unit cable unplugged or hookup faulty	Plug in keyboard assembly unit; service cable hookups (p. 134) □○
	Keyboard assembly dirty	Service keyboard assembly (p. 120) □○
	Keyboard cable faulty	Test and replace keyboard cable (p. 120) □○
	Peripheral-card edge connector dirty	Clean peripheral-card edge connectors (p. 116) □○
	CPU or IC chip faulty	Test and replace CPU and IC chips (p. 117) ■○; if you cannot locate faulty IC chip, take main unit for professional service
	Keyboard assembly, peripheral card or motherboard faulty	Take keyboard unit, or keyboard assembly and main unit, for professional service

DEGREE OF DIFFICULTY: □ **Easy** ◨ **Moderate** ■ **Complex**
ESTIMATED TIME: ○ **Less than 1 hour** ◖ **1 to 3 hours** ● **Over 3 hours**

SYMPTOM	POSSIBLE CAUSE	PROCEDURE
Printer does not light up nor print	Printer unplugged or turned off	Plug in and turn on printer
	Printer controls set incorrectly	Adjust printer controls
	No power to outlet or outlet faulty	Reset breaker or replace fuse *(p. 10)* □○; have outlet serviced
	Printer cable hookups faulty	Service cable hookups *(p. 134)* □○
	Printer power fuse blown	Test and replace power fuse *(p. 118)* □○
	Printer power cord faulty	Test and replace power cord *(p. 137)* □○
	Printer on/off switch faulty	Test and replace on/off switch *(p. 124)* □○
	Printer power supply faulty	Service power supply *(p. 124)* ◰○
	Printer circuit board faulty	Take printer for professional service
Printer lights up but prints poorly or not at all	Ribbon worn or faulty	Replace ribbon cartridge
	Carriage transport assembly dirty	Service carriage transport assembly *(p. 122)* □○
	Carriage transport-assembly belt faulty	Replace carriage transport-assembly belt *(p. 123)* □○
	Print head dirty or faulty	Clean and replace print head *(p. 123)* □○
	Peripheral-card edge connector dirty	Clean peripheral-card edge connectors *(p. 116)* □○
	CPU or IC chip faulty	Test and replace CPU and IC chips *(p. 117)* ■○; if you cannot locate faulty IC chip, take main unit and printer for professional service
	Printer circuit board, peripheral card or motherboard faulty	Take main unit and printer for professional service
Printer lights up but paper feeds poorly or not at all	Paper loaded incorrectly	Reload paper
	Paper transport assembly jammed	Unjam paper transport assembly *(p. 121)* □○
	Paper transport assembly dirty	Service paper transport assembly *(p. 122)* □○
	Printer circuit board faulty	Take printer for professional service

DEGREE OF DIFFICULTY: □ **Easy** ◰ **Moderate** ■ **Complex**
ESTIMATED TIME: ○ **Less than 1 hour** ◓ **1 to 3 hours** ● **Over 3 hours**

ACCESS TO THE MAIN-UNIT INTERNAL COMPONENTS

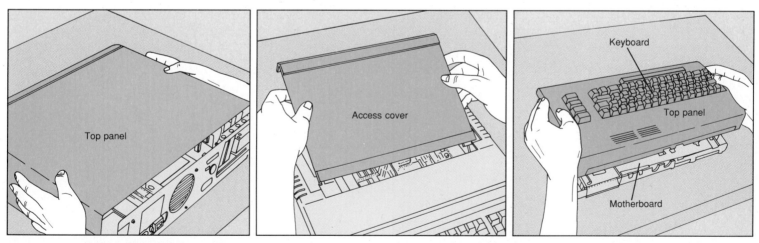

Removing and reinstalling the top panel. Turn off the computer system. Unplug the main unit, disconnect the cables hooked up to it *(page 12)* and remove any external peripheral cards *(page 116)*. For a main unit with an external keyboard unit, check for top panel screws on the back panel edges and remove them. If there are tabs on the top panel sides, press them and raise the top panel; push the hinge to lock the top panel open. If there are no tabs, slide the top panel out from under any lip on the front or back panel and lift it off the frame *(above, left)*. For a main unit with an internal keyboard assembly, check for tabs securing an access cover; press them and lift off the access cover *(above, center)*.

If there are no tabs or if further disassembly is required, check for top panel screws on the bottom panel edges and remove them. Carefully turn the main unit upright and lift up the top panel *(above, right)*. If the cable wires connecting the keyboard and the motherboard are soldered, carefully turn the top panel face down; if the cable has a connector at the keyboard assembly or motherboard, note its position, unplug it, and lift off the top panel. After working on the main unit, reverse the sequence to reinstall the top panel. Cold check for leaking voltage *(page 141)*. Reconnect the cables and any peripheral cards removed, plug in the main unit and turn on the computer system.

ACCESS TO THE DISK DRIVE

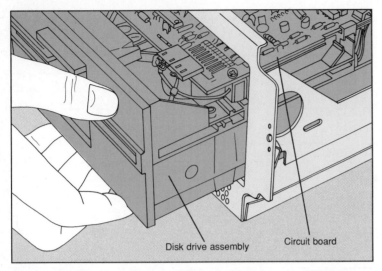

Disk drive assembly   Circuit board

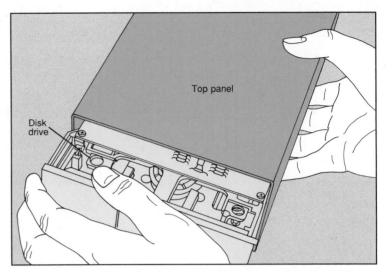

Top panel

Disk drive

Removing and reinstalling an internal disk-drive assembly. Remove the main-unit top panel *(page 113)* and locate the disk drive assembly. Unscrew the disk drive assembly from the frame, slide it forward and unplug the connectors from the back of it, noting their terminals. Gently pull the disk drive assembly out through the opening in the front panel *(above)*. Repeat the procedure to remove a second disk-drive assembly. After working on the disk drive assembly, reverse the sequence to reinstall it. Then reinstall the main-unit top panel *(page 113)*.

Opening and closing an external disk-drive unit. Turn off the computer system, unplug the disk drive unit and disconnect the cables hooked up to it. Check for top panel screws along the edges of the bottom panel and remove them. Carefully turn the disk drive unit upright, slide the top panel out from under any lip on the front or back panel, and slide or lift it off the frame *(above)*. After working on the disk drive unit, reverse the sequence to close it. Cold check for leaking voltage *(page 141)*. Reconnect the cables and plug in the disk-drive unit.

SERVICING THE READ/WRITE HEAD

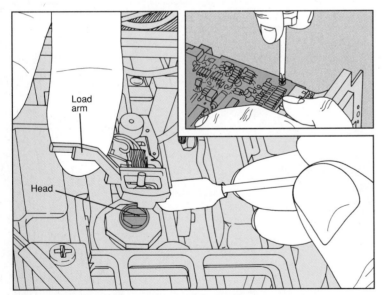

Load arm

Head

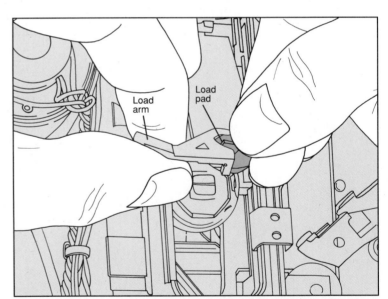

Load arm   Load pad

1 **Cleaning the head.** Gain access to the disk drive assembly *(step above)*. Unscrew the circuit board or plate above the disk drive *(inset)* and turn it over. Unplug the connector for any cable in the way, noting its position. If there is a load arm above the read/write head, carefully lift it up, exposing the head below it and the load pad on its underside. If the load pad is damaged, replace it *(step 2)*. If the load pad is dirty, use a brush with soft bristles to wipe it lightly. To clean the head, rub it gently using a foam swab moistened with denatured alcohol *(above)*. Reinstall or close the disk drive assembly *(step above)*.

2 **Replacing the load pad.** If the load pad is held to the load arm by a pin, as shown in step 1, twist the pad using long-nose pliers to work out the pin, and remove the pad. If the load pad is not held to the load arm by a pin, slide the pad out from under the arm *(above)*. Order an exact replacement load pad from the manufacturer or purchase a substitute at a computer parts supplier. If the load pad is secured with a pin, position the pad under the load arm and push the pin into place. If the load pad is not secured with a pin, slide the pad under the load arm. Reinstall or close the disk drive assembly *(step above)*.

SERVICING THE DISK DRIVE BELT

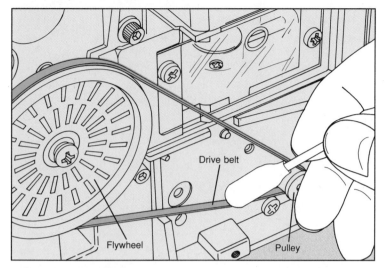
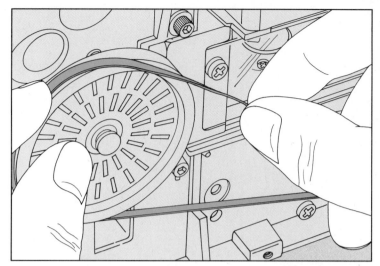

Drive belt

Flywheel

Pulley

1 **Cleaning the belt.** Gain access to the disk drive assembly *(page 114)*. To reach the drive belt, carefully turn the disk drive assembly on its side. If the belt is damaged, replace it *(step 2)*. If the belt is sticky or greasy, clean it thoroughly using a foam swab lightly moistened with rubber-cleaning compound *(above)*. Never apply anything oily and avoid touching the belt with your fingers. Turn the belt pulley or the flywheel with a clean foam swab to reach the entire length of the belt. Reinstall or close the disk drive assembly *(page 114)*.

2 **Removing and replacing the belt.** Note the position of the drive belt for reference, and slip it off the flywheel and the pulley *(above)*. Purchase an exact replacement belt at a computer parts supplier. Holding the belt loosely with long-nose pliers or tweezers, wrap it around the flywheel and the pulley. Reinstall or close the disk drive assembly *(page 114)*.

ADJUSTING THE DISK-DRIVE MOTOR SPEED

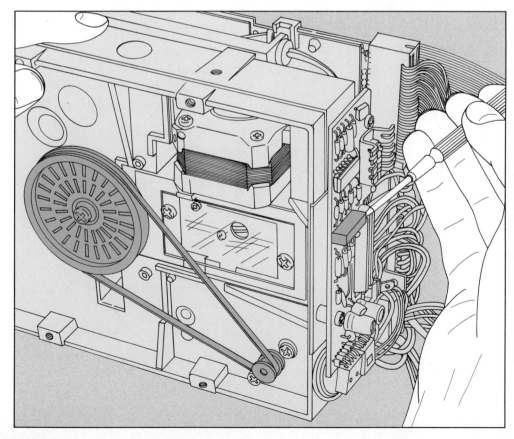

Resetting the motor speed. Gain access to the disk drive assembly *(page 114)*. Carefully turn the disk drive assembly on its side and locate the disk-speed adjustment screw. Reconnect the cables to the disk drive assembly and plug in the main unit or the external disk-drive assembly unit.

If the disk drive assembly is not equipped with a built-in strobe disc, turn on the computer system and boot up a disk-speed test program disk ordered from the manufacturer. Following the test program instructions, use a small screwdriver to adjust the screw *(left)* until the monitor shows that the disk is turning at the speed specified by the manufacturer, usually 300 rpm.

If the disk drive assembly is equipped with a built-in strobe disc, turn on the computer system, boot up a blank disk and reset the computer by pressing the reset control or the Ctrl, Alt and Del keys. Shine a fluorescent light on the disk drive and observe the strobe disc markings. Using a small screwdriver, adjust the screw to the exact point at which the markings appear as a solid, motionless band. Remove the disk and reinstall or close the disk drive assembly *(page 114)*.

SERVICING THE DISK DRIVE WRITE-PROTECT SWITCH

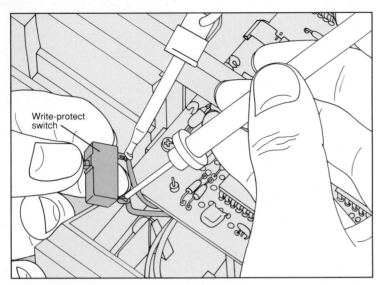

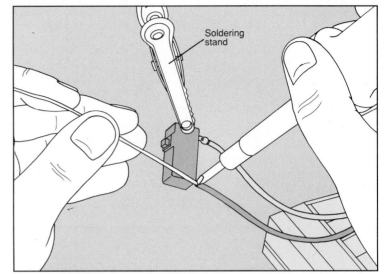

1 **Testing the switch.** Gain access to the disk drive assembly *(page 114)* and locate the write-protect switch. If it has an optical detector and emitter instead of a switch, take the unit for service. Unplug or desolder *(page 130)* the switch wires from the circuit board; if the switch terminals are not accessible, unscrew the switch and pull it away from the assembly. Set a multitester to test continuity *(page 128)*. Touch a probe to each switch terminal *(above)*. Set the switch in each position; there should be continuity in only one position. If the switch tests faulty, replace it *(step 2)*. If the switch tests OK, reinstall or close the disk drive assembly *(page 114)* and take the unit for professional service.

2 **Removing and replacing the switch.** Plug in or resolder *(page 131)* the write-protect switch wires to the circuit board. If the switch is still mounted on the disk drive assembly, unscrew it and pull it away from the assembly. Support the switch in a soldering stand and desolder the wires *(page 130)* from the switch terminals. Order an exact replacement switch from the manufacturer. Support the switch in the soldering stand and solder the wires *(page 131)* to the switch terminals *(above)*. Screw the switch into place on the disk drive assembly. Reinstall or close the disk drive assembly *(page 114)*. If the problem persists, suspect a faulty circuit board and take the unit for professional service.

SERVICING THE PERIPHERAL CARDS

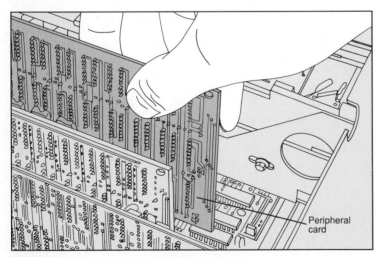

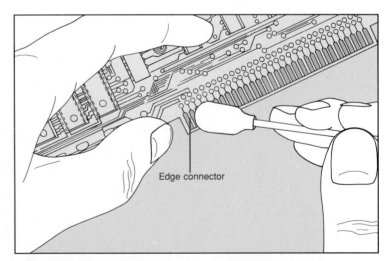

1 **Removing a peripheral card.** If the peripheral cards are externally mounted, turn off the computer system; if they are internally mounted, also remove the main-unit top panel *(page 113)* and locate them on the motherboard. To take out a card, unplug or unscrew any connector from it, noting its terminals. Note the card position, gently wiggle it to release the edge connectors *(above)* and pull it off the motherboard. Avoid touching the edge connectors with your fingers. If the edge connectors are not damaged, clean them *(step 2)*. If an edge connector is damaged, take the card and main unit for professional service.

2 **Cleaning the edge connectors.** Carefully lay the peripheral card flat. To clean off oxidation buildup, gently rub each edge connector with a pencil eraser. Turn over the peripheral card and repeat the procedure on the other side of each edge connector. Then, wipe both sides of each edge connector using a foam swab moistened with denatured alcohol *(above)*. Put back the card, ensuring that each edge connector fits snugly, and plug in or screw on any connectors removed from it. If there is more than one peripheral card, remove *(step 1)* and clean each of them, one at a time. Close the main-unit top panel *(page 113)*.

REPLACING THE CPU AND IC CHIPS

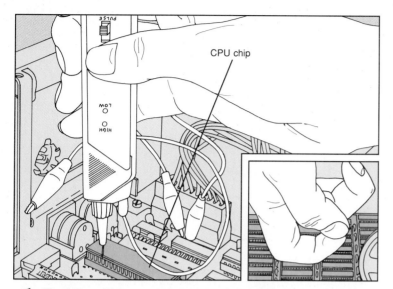

CPU chip

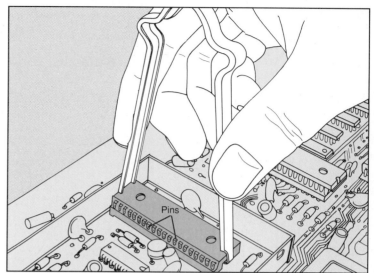

Pins

1 **Testing a chip.** Remove the main-unit top panel *(page 113)*. If an IC chip feels extremely hot *(inset)*, suspect it is faulty; replace it *(step 2)* or have it tested professionally. To test the CPU chip, check the motherboard markings or the schematic diagram to locate a 5-volt source on the motherboard *(page 138)*. Clip the ground wire of a logic probe to the main unit frame and clip one of the other wires to each terminal on the 5-volt source. Set the logic probe to PULSE and TTL/LS. Plug in and turn on the main unit. Touching the logic probe to only one pin at a time, carefully test each chip pin *(above)*. The logic probe should flash when some pins are touched. If the CPU chip tests faulty, replace it *(step 2)*. If the CPU chip tests OK, suspect a faulty motherboard. and take the main unit for professional service.

2 **Installing a new chip.** If the IC or CPU chip pins are soldered to the motherboard, do not attempt to remove the chip; reinstall the top panel *(page 113)* and take the main unit for professional service. If the pins are not soldered to the motherboard, note their positions and remove the chip. Using a chip extractor, grasp the chip securely at each end *(above)*, gently wiggle it to release the pins, and pull it off the motherboard. Purchase an exact replacement IC or CPU chip at a computer parts supplier. Grounding one hand on the main unit frame, pick up the chip and gently fit the pins into the motherboard, being careful not to bend the pins. Reinstall the main-unit top panel *(page 113)*. If the problem persists, suspect a faulty circuit board or motherboard and take the main unit for professional service.

ACCESS TO THE MONITOR INTERNAL COMPONENTS

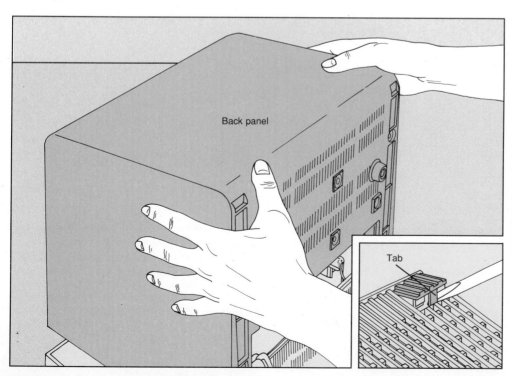

Back panel

Tab

Removing and reinstalling the back panel. Turn off the computer system, unplug the main unit and disconnect the cables from the monitor; if the cables cannot be unplugged from the monitor, disconnect them from the main unit. Wait at least 24 hours to allow the cathode ray tube to discharge stored voltage. Remove any back panel screws from the top, sides and bottom; there also may be screws hidden under tabs *(inset)*. Pull off any controls, and unscrew any locknuts, too large to fit through their openings in the front panel. Carefully turn the monitor face down and lift off the back panel *(left)*, avoiding damage to any wire connections. After working on the monitor, reverse the sequence to reinstall the back panel. Reconnect the cables and plug in the main unit.

REPLACING THE FUSE

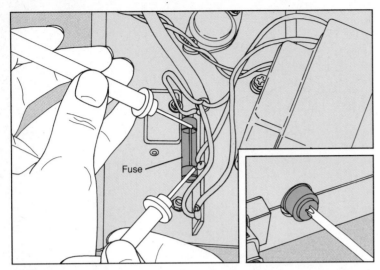

Fuse

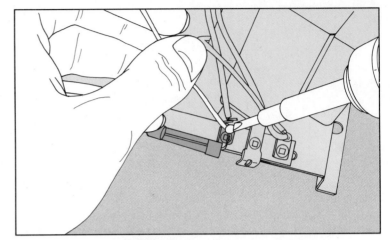

1 **Testing the fuse.** For a fuse inside the monitor, remove the monitor back panel *(page 117)* to locate it. For a fuse inside the printer, remove the top panel *(page 121)* and the power-supply circuit board. If the fuse is held by retaining clips, pull it out with a fuse puller. If the fuse caps are soldered to posts, test the fuse in place. Set a multitester to test continuity and touch a probe to each fuse cap *(above)*. The fuse should have continuity. If it tests faulty, replace it *(step 2)*; if it tests OK, push it back into the clips if you removed it and reinstall the back or top panel. For a fuse mounted externally on a disk drive or power supply unit, unplug the unit, unscrew the fuse *(inset)* and test it the same way.

2 **Installing a new fuse.** If the fuse caps are soldered, de-solder them *(page 130)* and test the fuse again to confirm it is faulty *(step 1)*; if it now tests OK, resolder the fuse caps *(page 131)* and reinstall the monitor back panel *(page 117)* or the printer power-supply circuit board and top panel *(page 121)*. When any fuse tests faulty, purchase an exact replacement at an electronics parts supplier. For a fuse inside the monitor or the printer, gently push the new fuse into the retaining clips or solder the caps *(page 131)* to the posts *(above)*, and reinstall the monitor back panel *(page 117)* or the printer power-supply circuit board and top panel *(page 121)*. For a fuse mounted externally on a disk drive unit or power supply unit, screw in the fuse and plug in the unit. If a fuse blows repeatedly, take the unit for professional service; for the printer, service the power supply *(page 124)*.

SERVICING A POTENTIOMETER

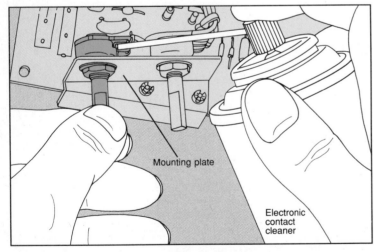

Mounting plate

Electronic contact cleaner

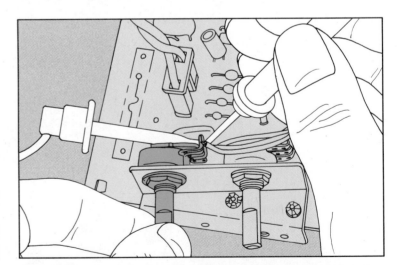

1 **Cleaning the potentiometer.** Remove the monitor back panel *(page 117)* and locate the potentiometer on the mounting plate behind its shaft; for better access to the potentiometer, unscrew and take out the circuit board. To clean the potentiometer, spray short bursts of electronic contact cleaner into the opening in the potentiometer casing. Rotate the shaft back and forth several times to work in the cleaner *(above)*. Reposition the circuit board and screw it back in. Reinstall the monitor back panel *(page 117)*. If the problem persists, test the potentiometer *(step 2)*.

2 **Testing the potentiometer.** Remove the monitor back panel *(page 117)*. Unscrew and take out the circuit board. Set a multitester to test resistance *(page 129)*. Hook a probe to the center potentiometer pin. Touch the other probe in turn to each outer potentiometer pin, rotating the shaft back and forth each time *(above)*. The multitester should register a variation in ohms for each pin. If there is no ohms variation, remove the potentiometer *(step 3)*. If there is an ohms variation, suspect a faulty circuit board. Put back the circuit board, reinstall the monitor back panel *(page 117)* and take the monitor for professional service.

SERVICING A POTENTIOMETER (continued)

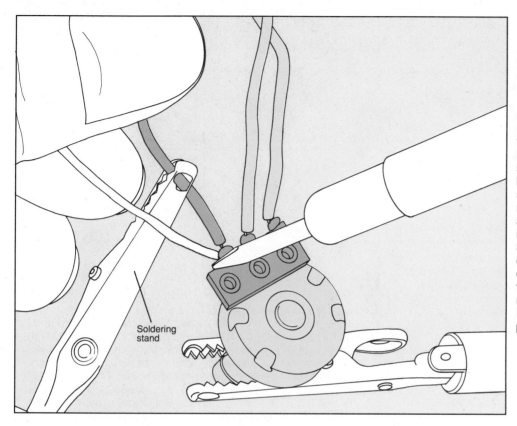

Soldering
stand

3 **Removing and replacing the potentiometer.** Unscrew the locknut securing the potentiometer shaft to the mounting plate and slip out the shaft. Tag the potentiometer wires, noting their terminal positions. Desolder the wires from the potentiometer *(page 130)*; if necessary, support it in a soldering stand. Test the potentiometer again to confirm it is faulty *(step 2)*. If the potentiometer now tests OK, suspect a faulty circuit board and take the monitor for professional service; resolder the wires *(page 131)*, put back the potentiometer and the locknut, screw in the circuit board and reinstall the monitor back panel *(page 117)*. To replace a faulty potentiometer, purchase an exact replacement at an electronics parts supplier. Solder the wires *(page 131)* to the potentiometer terminals *(left)*, slip the shaft through the opening in the mounting plate and screw on the locknut. Put back the circuit board and reinstall the monitor back panel *(page 117)*. If the problem persists, take the monitor for professional service.

ACCESS TO THE KEYBOARD INTERNAL COMPONENTS

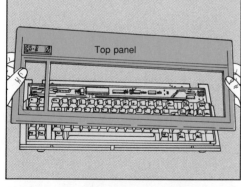

Top panel

Opening and closing an external keyboard assembly unit. Turn off the computer system, unplug the main unit and disconnect the cable from the keyboard or main unit. Unscrew the keyboard bottom panel, carefully turn the unit upright and lift off the top panel *(above)*. Turn over the unit, unscrew the bottom plate and remove it. If further disassembly is required, turn the unit upright again, unscrew the keyboard assembly and gently lift it off the circuit board. After working on the keyboard assembly, reverse the sequence to reinstall it, reconnect the cable and plug in the main unit.

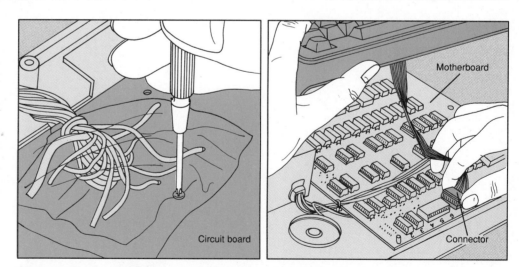

Circuit board

Motherboard

Connector

Removing and reinstalling an internal keyboard assembly. Remove the main-unit top panel *(page 113)*. For a main unit with no access cover, unscrew the keyboard-assembly circuit board from the underside of the top panel *(above, left)* and gently lift it out. For a main unit with an access cover, turn over the unit and remove the bottom panel screws. Carefully turn the main unit upright and lift up the top panel. If the cable wires connecting the keyboard and the motherboard are soldered, gently turn the top panel face down; if the cable has a connector at the keyboard assembly or motherboard, note its position, unplug it *(above, right)* and lift off the top panel. If further disassembly is required, unscrew the keyboard-assembly circuit board from the underside of the top panel and gently lift it out. After working on the keyboard assembly, reverse the sequence to reinstall it and the main-unit top panel *(page 113)*.

SERVICING THE KEYBOARD ASSEMBLY

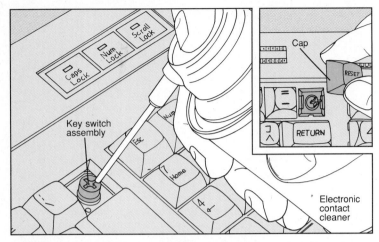

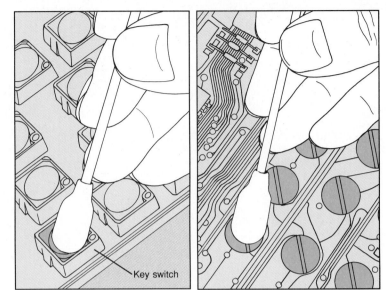

Key switch

Cleaning a key switch. Turn off the computer system and unplug the main unit; for an external keyboard, disconnect the cable from the keyboard or main unit. Pull off the key cap *(inset)*; if needed, gently use a screwdriver to pry it up. If the key switch assembly is inaccessible this way, clean the keyboard assembly *(step right)*. If the key switch assembly is held by tabs, press them and lift out the assembly, exposing the circuit board contact point. Gently rub the contact point with a pencil eraser, then wipe it using a foam swab moistened with denatured alcohol. If the key switch assembly cannot be removed, spray in short bursts of electronic contact cleaner *(above)*; press and release the switch to work in the cleaner. Push on the key cap, reconnect any cables and plug in the main unit. If the problem persists, clean the keyboard assembly *(step right)*.

Cleaning the keyboard assembly. Gain access to the keyboard assembly *(page 119)*. For a keyboard assembly with individual key switches soldered to the circuit board, clean each key switch individually *(step left)*. Otherwise, clean the underside of each key switch *(above, left)* as well as the key-switch contact point on the circuit board *(above, right)*. Gently rub them with a pencil eraser and then wipe them using a foam swab moistened with denatured alcohol. Reinstall or close the keyboard assembly *(page 119)*. If the problem persists, suspect a faulty circuit board and take the main unit or keyboard assembly unit for professional service.

REPLACING THE KEYBOARD CABLE

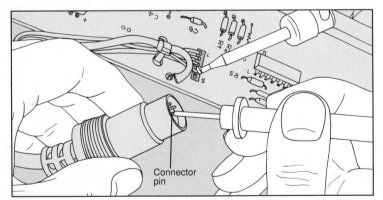

Connector pin

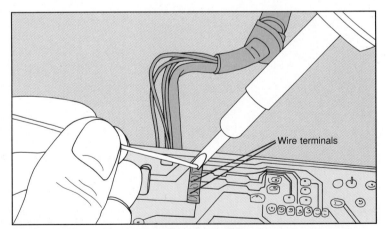

Wire terminals

1 **Testing the cable.** Gain access to the keyboard assembly *(page 119)*; for a cable that has a connector plug at one end, unplug the cable. Locate the wire terminals at the other end of the cable; if required, unscrew and turn over the circuit board or unplug the wire connectors. Set a multitester to test continuity *(page 128)*. Hook one probe to one wire terminal on the circuit board and touch the other probe in turn to each connector pin in the plug *(above)*. The multitester should register continuity once—and only once. Repeat the test for the other wires. If the cable has a connector plug at each end, test from each pin at one end to each pin at the other end, in turn. If the cable tests faulty, replace it *(step 2)*. If the cable tests OK, suspect a faulty circuit board; reinstall or close the keyboard assembly *(page 119)* and take the unit for professional service.

2 **Installing a new cable.** Unscrew and turn over the circuit board, if required, to reach the soldered contact points of the cable wires. Tag the wires, noting their terminals for reference, desolder them *(page 130)* and pull them off the circuit board. Purchase an exact replacement keyboard cable at a computer parts supplier. Thread the cable wires through the circuit board and solder them *(page 131)* to the terminals *(above)*, or push on their connectors. Reinstall or close the keyboard assembly *(page 119)*; for an external unit with a cable that has plug connectors at each end, plug the cable into the keyboard and the main unit. If the problem persists, suspect a faulty circuit board and take the unit for professional service.

ACCESS TO THE PRINTER INTERNAL COMPONENTS

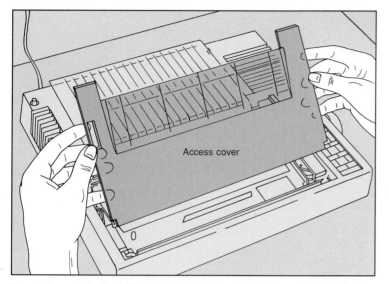

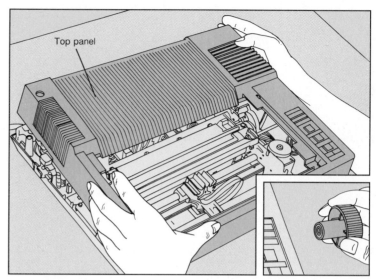

Top panel

Removing and reinstalling the access cover. Turn off the computer system. To reach the paper transport assembly or the carriage transport assembly on most printers, there is an access cover that can be raised and lowered. To remove the access cover, lift it up and press in on the side edges to free it from the hinges *(above)*. Release the ribbon from the print head and pull the ribbon cartridge out of the printer. After working on the paper transport assembly or the carriage transport assembly, reverse the sequence to reinstall the access cover.

Removing and reinstalling the top panel. Turn off the computer system, unplug the printer and disconnect the cables hooked up to it *(page 12)*. Remove the access cover *(step left)* and pull off or unscrew the paper-advance control *(inset)*. Check for top panel screws on the top, sides or bottom, remove them and lift off the top panel *(above)*. After working on the printer, reverse the sequence to put back the top panel, reinstall the access cover and reconnect the cables. Cold check for leaking voltage *(page 141)*, then plug in the printer.

UNJAMMING THE PRINTER PAPER-TRANSPORT ASSEMBLY

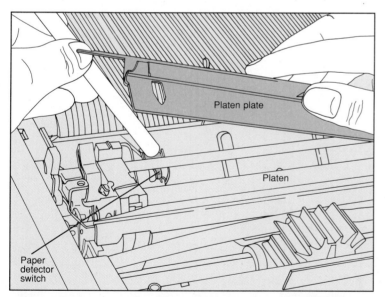

Platen plate

Platen

Paper detector switch

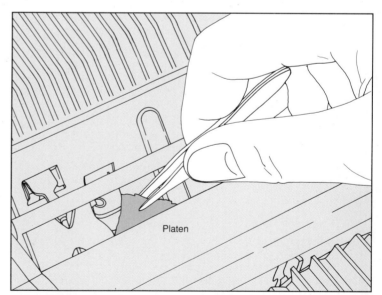

Platen

1 **Removing and reinstalling the platen plate and the platen.** Remove the access cover *(step above)*. Unscrew and lift off the platen plate; depress the paper detector switch *(above)* to disengage it. If the obstruction can easily be reached, remove it *(step 2)*. If the obstruction cannot easily be taken out, remove the top panel *(step above)* and locate the screws for the platen mounting assembly. Unscrew the mounting assembly and lift the platen out of the printer. Take out the obstruction, fit in the platen and screw on the mounting assembly. Then reinstall the platen plate.

2 **Removing an obstruction.** Remove the platen plate *(step 1)*, locate the obstruction and pull it out using tweezers *(above)*. To help dislodge the obstruction, spray compressed air around and under the platen, or reinstall the paper-advance control and turn the platen. If the obstruction is still difficult to reach or take out, remove the platen mounting assembly *(step 1)*; do not probe under the platen with a sharp object. After taking out the obstruction, reinstall the platen and the platen plate *(step 1)*. Then reinstall the top panel *(step above)*.

CLEANING THE PRINTER PAPER-TRANSPORT ASSEMBLY

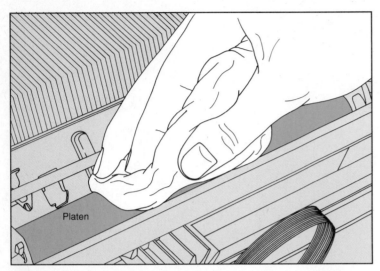

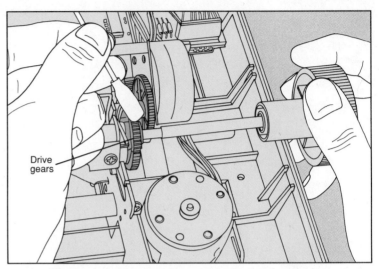

1 **Cleaning the platen.** Unscrew and lift off the platen plate. If the platen is badly pitted or damaged, order an exact replacement from the manufacturer; remove the old one and install the new one *(page 121)*. To clean the platen, rub it using a clean, lint-free cloth moistened with rubber-cleaning compound *(above)*; rotate the paper-advance control to reach the entire surface. Use another cloth moistened with denatured alcohol to clean the platen plate. Clean other metal components with a foam swab and denatured alcohol. Screw on the platen plate.

2 **Cleaning the gears.** For easiest access to the paper-transport assembly gears, remove the printer top panel *(page 121)*. If a gear looks damaged, take the printer for professional service. To clean the gears, use a foam swab moistened with denatured alcohol; reinstall the paper-advance control and rotate it to turn the gear assembly *(above)*. Dislodge dirt between the gear teeth with a toothpick. To lubricate the gears, apply a little white grease with a small stick or toothpick; wipe off any excess lubricant using a clean foam swab. Pull off the paper-advance control and reinstall the top panel or the access cover *(page 121)*.

SERVICING THE PRINTER CARRIAGE-TRANSPORT ASSEMBLY

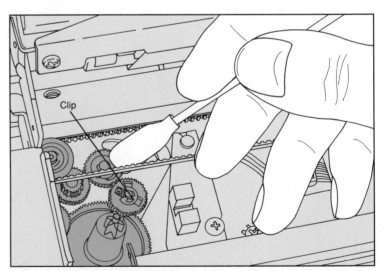

1 **Cleaning the belt and guide rail.** Remove the printer access cover *(page 121)*. If the carriage-transport assembly belt is damaged, replace it *(page 123)*. Wipe the belt using a clean, lint-free cloth moistened with rubber-cleaning compound. Wrap your fingers with the cloth and lightly tug on the belt to reach its entire length. Clean the print-head guide rail using another cloth moistened with denatured alcohol *(above)*; gently slide the print head assembly by hand to reach its entire length. Use a foam swab and denatured alcohol to clean any other metal components. Lubricate the guide rail with a clean cloth moistened with light machine oil; avoid dripping oil onto any other components.

2 **Cleaning and replacing the gears.** To reach the carriage-transport assembly gears, remove the printer top panel *(page 121)*. Clean the gears using a foam swab and denatured alcohol *(above)*; turn the gears by hand, if necessary. Dislodge dirt between the gear teeth with a toothpick. To lubricate the gears, apply a little white grease with a small stick or toothpick. Wipe off any excess lubricant using a clean foam swab. If a gear is damaged, pry off its clip with a screwdriver and lift the gear off its shaft. Order an exact replacement from the manufacturer or purchase a substitute at a computer parts supplier. Slide the gear onto the shaft and push on the clip. Reinstall the top panel *(page 121)*.

REPLACING THE PRINTER CARRIAGE-TRANSPORT ASSEMBLY BELT

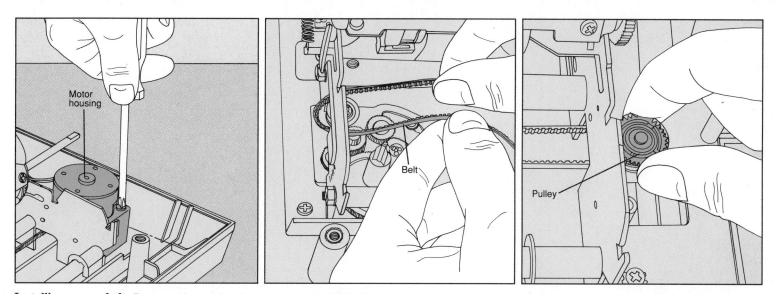

Installing a new belt. Remove the printer top panel *(page 121)*. To reach the belt pulley under the motor, unscrew the motor housing *(above, left)* and lift it off. Pry the clip off the pulley using a screwdriver, lift the pulley off its shaft and release the belt from around it. Tug down sharply on the belt to release it from the clips on the print head assembly *(above, center)*; for best access, gently slide the print head assembly by hand along the guide rail. Slip the belt off the pulley at the end of the printer opposite the motor. Order an exact replacement carriage-transport assembly belt from the manufacturer or purchase a substitute at a computer parts supplier. Loop the belt around the pulley at the end of the printer opposite the motor. Without stretching the belt, fit it around the pulley that sits under the motor, then slide the pulley back onto its shaft *(above, right)*. Put the clip back on the pulley and screw the motor housing into place. Pull up firmly on the belt to snap it into the clips on the print head assembly. Reinstall the top panel *(page 121)*.

SERVICING THE PRINTER PRINT-HEAD ASSEMBLY

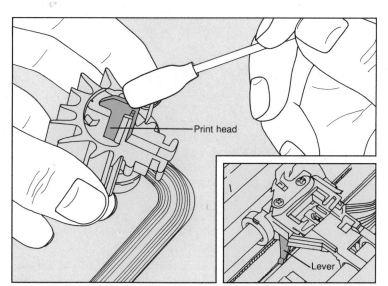

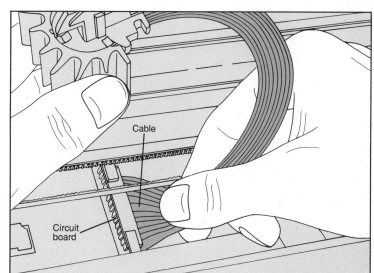

1 **Removing the assembly and cleaning the head.** Remove the printer access cover *(page 121)*; for best access to the print head, gently slide the print head assembly by hand along the guide rail. Shift the lever on the carriage to unlock the assembly and slide it off the carriage *(inset)*, avoiding any damage to the cable connected to it. To clean the print head, gently wipe across it just above the cable connection using a foam swab moistened with denatured alcohol *(above)*. Slide the assembly back onto the carriage and shift the lever until it clicks locked. Reinstall the access cover *(page 121)*. If the problem persists, replace the print head *(step 2)*.

2 **Replacing the assembly.** Remove the print head assembly *(step 1)*. If the print head is clipped to the assembly, gently push it off and pull off the cable from under it. If the print head cannot be pushed off, locate the end of the cable at the circuit board, note its terminals and disconnect it; remove the top panel *(page 121)* if necessary to reach it. Order an exact replacement print-head assembly from the manufacturer or purchase a substitute at a computer parts supplier. Connect the cable to the circuit board *(above)* or the print head and push the print head into the assembly. Slide the assembly onto the carriage and shift the lever to lock it. Reinstall the top panel or access cover *(page 121)*.

SERVICING THE PRINTER ON/OFF SWITCH

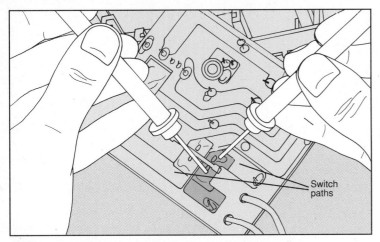

Switch paths

1 **Testing the switch.** Remove the printer top panel *(page 121)* and locate the on/off switch on the circuit board behind its control. Unscrew and lift out the circuit board, unplug the wires from it, and locate the four switch-contact points. Set a multi-tester to test continuity *(page 128)*. Touch a probe to each switch contact point in one circuit-board path *(above)*, and set the switch ON, then OFF. There should be continuity in the ON position, and no continuity in the OFF position. Test the two switch-contact points in the other path the same way. If the switch tests faulty, remove it and test again *(step 2)*. If the switch tests OK, service the power supply *(below)*.

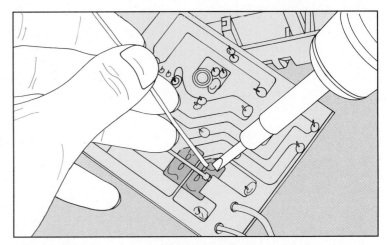

2 **Removing and replacing the switch.** Desolder the switch pins from the circuit board *(page 130)* and pull off the switch; wiggle it to help release the pins. Test the switch again to confirm it is faulty *(step 1)*. If the switch now tests OK, suspect a faulty circuit board and take the printer for professional service. If the switch again tests faulty, order an exact replacement from the manufacturer or purchase a substitute at a computer parts supplier. Fit the switch into the circuit board and solder *(page 131)* the pins *(above)*. Reconnect the wires and screw in the circuit board. Reinstall the top panel *(page 121)*.

SERVICING THE PRINTER POWER SUPPLY

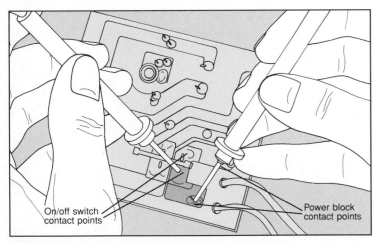

On/off switch contact points

Power block contact points

1 **Testing between the on/off switch and the power block.** Remove the printer top panel *(page 121)* and identify the power supply components *(page 138)*. Unscrew the circuit board, lift it out and unplug the wires from it. Locate the contact points for the on/off switch in the circuit board paths to the power block. Set a multitester to test continuity *(page 128)*. Touch one probe to a switch contact point and touch the other probe to the power-block contact point in the same path *(above)*. The multitester should register continuity. Repeat the test with the other switch contact point and the power-block contact point in its path. If both paths have continuity, test between the fuse and the on/off switch *(step 2)*. If a path does not have continuity, suspect a faulty circuit board and take the printer for professional service; put back the circuit board and reinstall the top panel *(page 121)*.

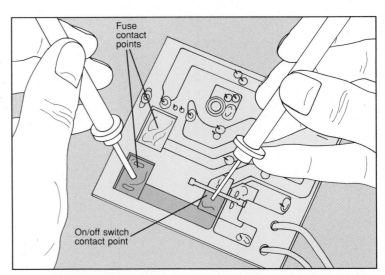

Fuse contact points

On/off switch contact point

2 **Testing between the fuse and the on/off switch.** Locate the contact point for the fuse in the circuit board path to the on/off switch. Set a multitester to test continuity *(page 128)*. Touch one probe to the fuse contact point and touch the other probe to the on/off switch contact point in the same path *(above)*. The multitester should register continuity. If the path has continuity, test between the transformer and the coil *(step 3)*. If the path does not have continuity, suspect a faulty circuit board and take the printer for professional service; put back the circuit board and reinstall the top panel *(page 121)*. To test the fuse, touch a probe to each fuse contact point, in different paths. There should be continuity; if not, replace the fuse *(page 118)*.

SERVICING THE PRINTER POWER SUPPLY (continued)

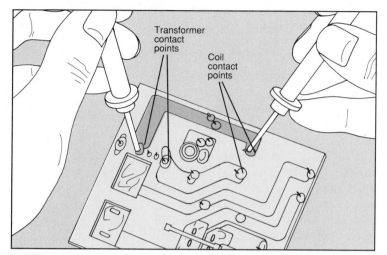

3 **Testing between the transformer and the coil.** Locate the transformer contact points in the circuit board paths to the coil. Set a multitester to test continuity *(page 128)*. Touch one probe to a transformer contact point and touch the other probe to the coil contact point in the same path *(above)*. The multitester should register continuity. Repeat the test with the other transformer contact point and the coil contact point in its path. If both paths have continuity, test between the coil, fuse and on/off switch *(step 4)*. If a path does not have continuity, suspect a faulty circuit board and take the printer for professional service; put back the circuit board and reinstall the top panel *(page 121)*.

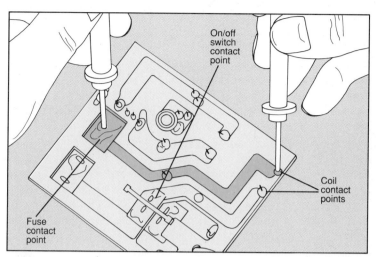

4 **Testing between the coil and the fuse and the on/off switch.** Locate the coil contact points in the circuit board paths to the fuse and to the on/off switch. Set a multitester to test continuity *(page 128)*. Touch one probe to the fuse contact point and touch the other probe to the coil contact point in the same path *(above)*. The multitester should register continuity. Repeat the test with the on/off switch contact point and the coil contact point in its path. If both paths have continuity, test the transformer *(step 5)*. If a path does not have continuity, suspect a faulty circuit board and take the printer for professional service; put back the circuit board and reinstall the top panel *(page 121)*.

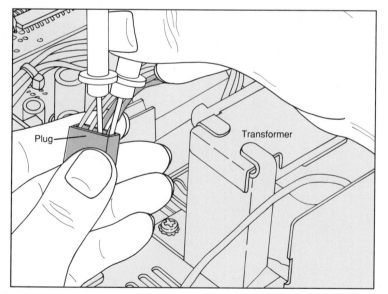

5 **Testing the transformer.** Plug the wires back into the power-supply circuit board. Locate the transformer wires that connect to other than the power-supply circuit board and unplug them. Set a multitester to test voltage *(page 129)*. If there are matching-colored wire pairs, fit a probe against each wire contact point in a matching pair *(above)*. Plug in and turn on the printer. The multitester should register voltage. Turn off and unplug the printer. Repeat the test with the other matching pair of wires. If there is one odd-colored wire, test it with each other wire the same way. If there is no voltage registered in a test, replace the transformer *(step 6)*. If there is voltage registered in each test, suspect a faulty circuit board and take the printer for professional service; put back the circuit board and reinstall the top panel *(page 121)*.

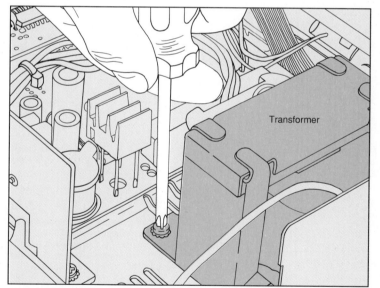

6 **Removing and replacing the transformer.** Unscrew the transformer, unplug the wires connecting it to the power-supply circuit board, noting their terminals, and lift out the transformer. Order an exact replacement transformer from the manufacturer or purchase a substitute at a computer parts supplier. Install the transformer *(above)* and plug the wires into the power-supply circuit board and into the other circuit board. Reinstall the top panel *(page 121)*. If the problem persists, suspect a faulty circuit board and take the printer for professional service.

TOOLS & TECHNIQUES

This section introduces basic tests and procedures that are common to almost all home electronics repairs, from testing continuity, resistance and voltage to repairing loose or broken wire connections and replacing damaged connectors. Checking springs, servicing gear assemblies and replacing display lights are typical repairs for units that, although possibly still functioning, may not be performing at their best. The electrical heart of an electronic unit, the power supply is a likely source of total unit failure. Principles of the power supply, along with several standard configurations of power-supply components, are included. Information on reading circuit boards and schematic diagrams, the road maps of an electronic unit, are presented on pages 138-139. Advice on purchasing replacement parts, and on how to deal with a professional when your own efforts fail, appears on page 141.

You can handle most home electronics repairs with the basic kit of tools and supplies shown below. For the best results, always purchase the highest-quality tools you can afford and use the right tool for the job. A set of metric screwdrivers is an asset for repairs to many imported electronic units, although it is usually possible to substitute conventional screwdrivers. Take the time to care for and store your tools properly. Clean metal tools — but never their handles — using a cloth moistened with light machine oil. To remove rust from a tool, rub it with fine steel wool. Protect tools in a sturdy plastic or metal toolbox, with a secure lock if stored around children. A multitester *(pages 128-129)* is virtually a must for testing components inside an electronic unit. Multitesters can often be rented from the same electronics parts supplier from whom you purchase replacement components.

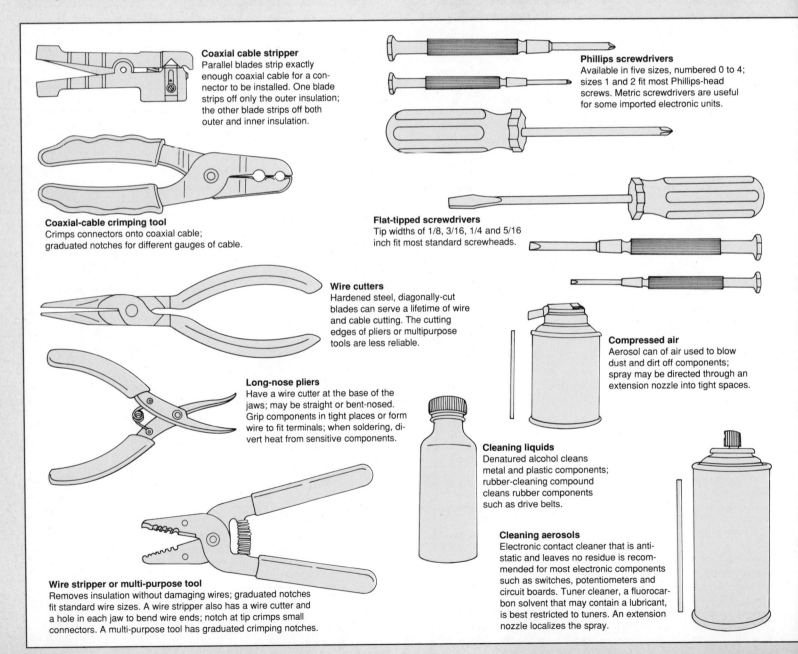

Coaxial cable stripper
Parallel blades strip exactly enough coaxial cable for a connector to be installed. One blade strips off only the outer insulation; the other blade strips off both outer and inner insulation.

Coaxial-cable crimping tool
Crimps connectors onto coaxial cable; graduated notches for different gauges of cable.

Long-nose pliers
Have a wire cutter at the base of the jaws; may be straight or bent-nosed. Grip components in tight places or form wire to fit terminals; when soldering, divert heat from sensitive components.

Wire stripper or multi-purpose tool
Removes insulation without damaging wires; graduated notches fit standard wire sizes. A wire stripper also has a wire cutter and a hole in each jaw to bend wire ends; notch at tip crimps small connectors. A multi-purpose tool has graduated crimping notches.

Phillips screwdrivers
Available in five sizes, numbered 0 to 4; sizes 1 and 2 fit most Phillips-head screws. Metric screwdrivers are useful for some imported electronic units.

Flat-tipped screwdrivers
Tip widths of 1/8, 3/16, 1/4 and 5/16 inch fit most standard screwheads.

Wire cutters
Hardened steel, diagonally-cut blades can serve a lifetime of wire and cable cutting. The cutting edges of pliers or multipurpose tools are less reliable.

Compressed air
Aerosol can of air used to blow dust and dirt off components; spray may be directed through an extension nozzle into tight spaces.

Cleaning liquids
Denatured alcohol cleans metal and plastic components; rubber-cleaning compound cleans rubber components such as drive belts.

Cleaning aerosols
Electronic contact cleaner that is antistatic and leaves no residue is recommended for most electronic components such as switches, potentiometers and circuit boards. Tuner cleaner, a fluorocarbon solvent that may contain a lubricant, is best restricted to tuners. An extension nozzle localizes the spray.

Review the owner's manual for the unit before undertaking any repair; even a quick and simple job may void the warranty provided by the manufacturer. Prevent accidents while working on a unit by unplugging it and disconnecting the cables and any wires hooked up to it. Set up for a job on a clean work surface that is well lit and free of clutter. Work patiently and methodically; never take short cuts. Keep in mind that even seemingly complicated tasks are seldom more than a sequence of easy steps. Check for hidden screws and tabs, for example, rather than trying to force panels or casings apart. Magnetize screwdrivers to avoid time-consuming hunts for a screw dropped inside the unit. Always substitute a faulty component with an identical replacement. Perform a cold check for leaking voltage *(page 141)* before plugging a unit back in, to ensure that no wires are crossed or disconnected.

Throughout this book, the use of a multitester, also known as a volt-ohmmeter, is called for to test continuity, resistance and voltage. Be aware that although you may be performing the same test using the same procedure, the purpose of the test may vary from one instance to another. In one situation, continuity may mean a component is OK; in another situation, continuity may mean a component is faulty. Or, for example, when testing the resistance of a potentiometer in circuit, the purpose is to confirm that the potentiometer is not the problem; when testing the resistance of the potentiometer out of circuit, the purpose is to confirm that the potentiometer is the problem. Likewise, when testing voltage, the purpose for the test may differ: with a transformer, the results of the test show the voltage coming out of the transformer; with a motor, the results of the test show the voltage going to the motor.

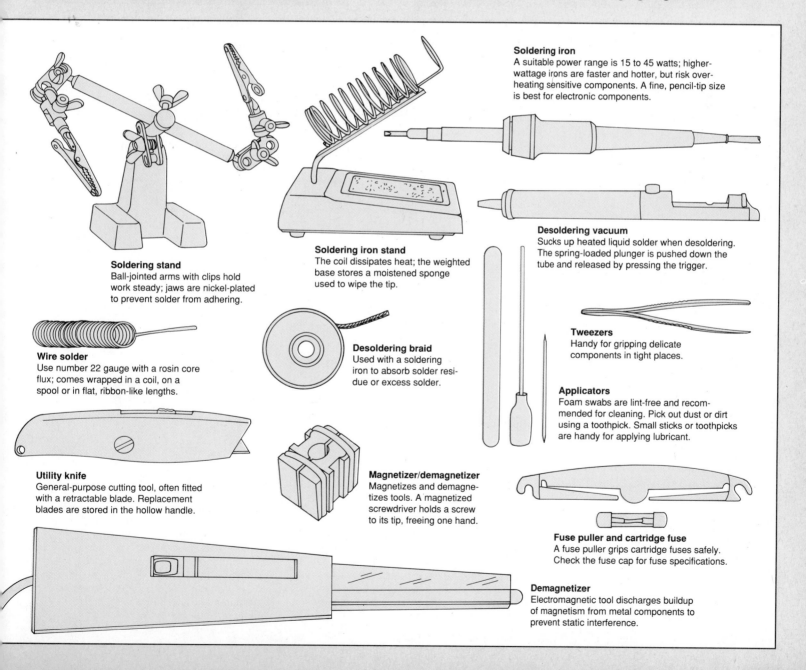

Soldering iron
A suitable power range is 15 to 45 watts; higher-wattage irons are faster and hotter, but risk overheating sensitive components. A fine, pencil-tip size is best for electronic components.

Desoldering vacuum
Sucks up heated liquid solder when desoldering. The spring-loaded plunger is pushed down the tube and released by pressing the trigger.

Soldering iron stand
The coil dissipates heat; the weighted base stores a moistened sponge used to wipe the tip.

Soldering stand
Ball-jointed arms with clips hold work steady; jaws are nickel-plated to prevent solder from adhering.

Tweezers
Handy for gripping delicate components in tight places.

Wire solder
Use number 22 gauge with a rosin core flux; comes wrapped in a coil, on a spool or in flat, ribbon-like lengths.

Desoldering braid
Used with a soldering iron to absorb solder residue or excess solder.

Applicators
Foam swabs are lint-free and recommended for cleaning. Pick out dust or dirt using a toothpick. Small sticks or toothpicks are handy for applying lubricant.

Utility knife
General-purpose cutting tool, often fitted with a retractable blade. Replacement blades are stored in the hollow handle.

Magnetizer/demagnetizer
Magnetizes and demagnetizes tools. A magnetized screwdriver holds a screw to its tip, freeing one hand.

Fuse puller and cartridge fuse
A fuse puller grips cartridge fuses safely. Check the fuse cap for fuse specifications.

Demagnetizer
Electromagnetic tool discharges buildup of magnetism from metal components to prevent static interference.

TROUBLESHOOTING WITH A MULTITESTER

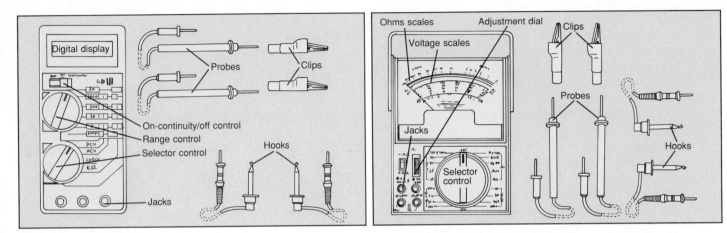

Using a multitester. To test continuity, resistance or voltage, a digital *(above, left)* or an analog *(above, right)* multitester is required. Their operating principles are the same, but the digital multitester, more expensive than the analog, is easier to use and read. For an accurate reading, the analog multitester must be "zeroed" after the selector control is set to the specified scale: Clip the probes together and turn the adjustment dial to align the needle as closely as possible with the zero on the scale, then unclip the probes. When testing continuity or resis-

tance, the multitester sends a low-voltage electrical current from its batteries through the component being tested. The multitester then registers the precise amount of resistance to the electrical current. Zero ohms, total lack of resistance, indicates a completed circuit or continuity. Infinite ohms indicates total resistance, no completed circuit, or an absence of continuity. A component may have resistance between these two extremes. When testing voltage, the multitester registers the precise amount of electrical current flowing in a completed circuit.

TESTING CONTINUITY

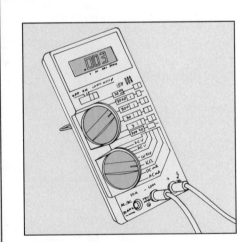

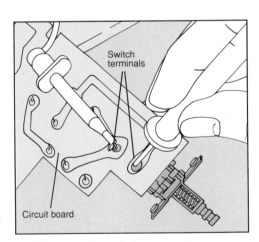

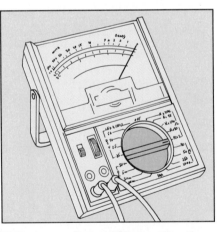

Using a digital multitester. Plug the probe cables into the jacks; if required, connect hooks or clips to the probes. Set the on-continuity/off control to CONTINUITY. Turn the range control to its lowest setting and turn the function control to its ohms setting. Touch each probe to the terminals indicated *(above, center)*. If you hear a beep, there is continuity. If there is no beep, there is no continuity.

Testing continuity. In this example, a switch on a circuit board is being tested *(above)*. When each probe contacts a switch terminal, the multitester tries to send low-voltage electrical current from its batteries through one probe. If the current passes through the switch to the other probe, there is a complete circuit and continuity. If the current does not pass through to the other probe, there is no complete circuit and no continuity.

Using an analog multitester. Plug the probe cables into the jacks; if required, connect hooks or clips to the probes. Set the selector control to the RX1 ohms setting; zero the multitester *(step above)*. Touch each probe to the terminals indicated *(above, center)*. If the needle swings to zero ohms, there is continuity. If the needle does not swing from infinite ohms, there is total resistance and no continuity.

TESTING RESISTANCE

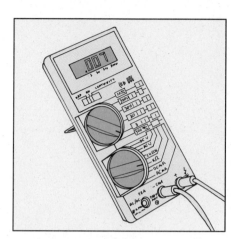

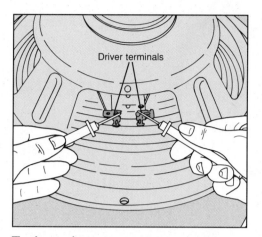

Driver terminals

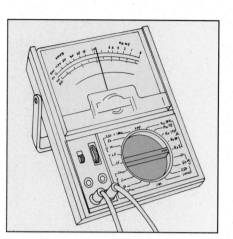

Using a digital multitester. Plug the probe cables into the jacks; if required, connect hooks or clips. Set the on-continuity/off control to ON. Turn the range control to its lowest setting and turn the function control to its ohms setting. Touch each probe to a terminal *(above, center)*. Read the display for the resistance in the circuit.

Testing resistance. When each probe contacts a driver terminal *(above)*, the multitester tries to send low-voltage electrical current from its batteries through one probe. The amount of electrical current that passes through the driver to the other probe is limited by the driver circuitry; this is displayed, in ohms, as a measurement of resistance to the electrical current.

Using an analog multitester. Plug the probe cables into the jacks; if required, connect hooks or clips. Set the selector control to the RX1 ohms setting; zero the multitester *(page 128)*. Touch each probe to a terminal *(above, center)*. Check the needle position on the scale for the amount of resistance the circuit has.

TESTING VOLTAGE

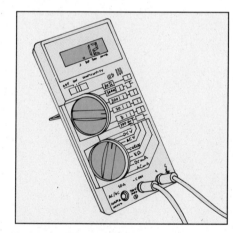

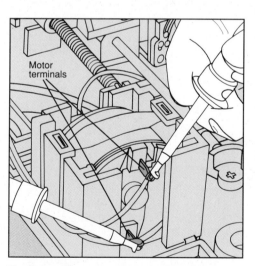

Motor terminals

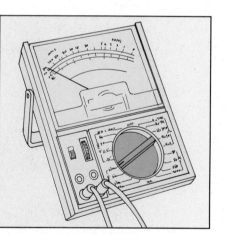

Using a digital multitester. Plug in the cables and connect hooks or clips. Set the on-continuity/off control to ON and the range control to 30. Turn the selector control to ACV for a transformer, or a motor not connected to a circuit board; use DCV for a motor connected to a circuit board. Clip or hook each probe to a terminal *(above, center)*. Read the display for the amount of voltage flowing in the circuit.

Testing voltage. In this example, the power to a DC motor from a circuit board is being tested *(above)*. With each probe contacting a motor terminal, a low-voltage electrical current is sent through the multitester by plugging the electronic unit into a wall outlet and turning it on. The amount of electrical current flowing through the multitester is registered on the display.

Using an analog multitester. Plug in the cables and connect hooks or clips. Set the selector control to 50 ACV for a transformer, or a motor not connected to a circuit board; use DCV for a motor connected to a circuit board. Zero the multitester *(page 128)*. Hook each probe to a terminal *(above, center)*. Check the needle position on the scale for the amount of voltage flowing in the circuit.

PREPARING A SOLDERING IRON

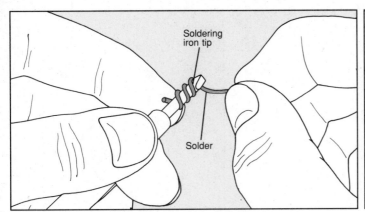

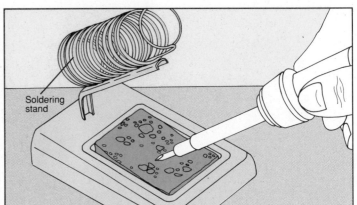

Setting up for soldering. Dampen a sponge and place it in the tray on the base of the soldering iron stand. Tie the soldering-iron power cord around a leg of the work table; leave enough slack for the soldering iron to be used comfortably, but not enough for it to travel very far if it is knocked off its stand.

If the soldering iron is new, tin the tip by tightly wrapping a short length of solder in a spiral around it *(above, left)*; use just enough to coat the entire tip evenly. Plug the soldering iron into a wall outlet and allow the solder to melt; turn the handle to help spread it. Lightly wipe the tip across the sponge to distribute the solder smoothly and remove any excess *(above, right)*.

If the soldering iron has been used before, plug it into a wall outlet and wait several minutes. After the soldering iron heats up, wipe the tip across the sponge to remove any old solder and dirt. Keep the soldering iron in its stand until you are ready to use it; wipe the tip on the sponge frequently as you use it. Unplug the soldering iron when you take a break.

If you have never used a soldering iron before, practice soldering *(page 131)* and desoldering *(steps below)* on lengths of scrap wire or discarded components before undertaking repairs to an electronic unit. After using the soldering iron, wipe the tip on the sponge, unplug the soldering iron and untie the power cord from the table leg.

DESOLDERING

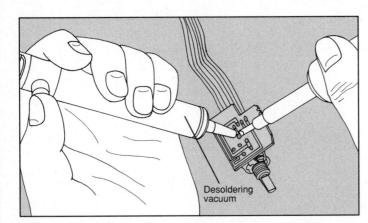

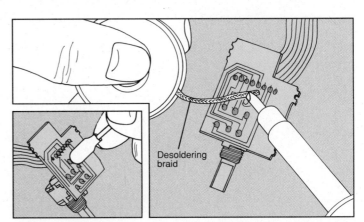

1 Removing old solder. Prepare a soldering iron *(step above)*. Lightly touch its tip against the old solder for a few seconds, until it begins to melt; if the iron is held any longer, the heat generated may damage nearby components. Push down the plunger in the desoldering vacuum, position it over the solder and press the trigger *(above)*, sucking up the solder as it melts. Repeat the procedure until the solder is completely removed from the terminals. If the old solder does not come off easily, solder *(page 131)* and then desolder. Clean up stubborn traces of solder *(step 2)*.

2 Cleaning up solder and flux residue. To lift off remaining solder, use desoldering braid. Place the braid over the old solder, gently touch the soldering iron tip against the braid for a few seconds *(above)* and pull up the braid. Repeat the procedure as required. To clean off flux residue left by the old solder, rub gently using a foam swab moistened with denatured alcohol or with flux-cleaning solvent *(inset)*. Perform the same procedure to clean up accidental solder drops that occur while soldering.

SOLDERING

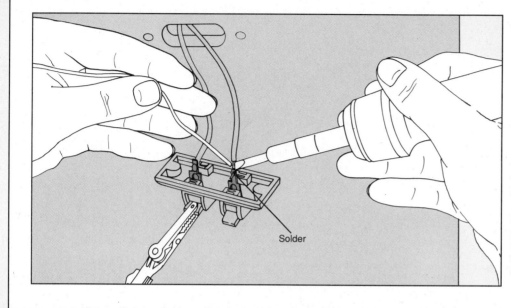

Solder

Connecting parts with solder. Prepare a soldering iron *(page 130)*; before soldering wire ends, strip back the insulation *(page 132)*. If required, first clean up old solder traces and flux residue from the terminals *(page 130)*. Always use rosin-core solder; never apply an acid-core solder.

To solder a wire, hold it against the terminal or twist it clockwise around it. Lightly touch the soldering iron tip to the wire for a few seconds *(left)* and then touch the solder to the wire; avoid touching solder directly to the soldering iron. Apply just enough solder to coat the connection evenly. Perform the same procedure for each wire in a cable or for each pin on a switch or potentiometer. Avoid holding the soldering iron against a wire or pin for more than a few seconds; the heat can damage electronic components.

REPLACING WIRES AND CABLES

Choosing the right wire and cable. Most electronics parts suppliers stock a wide assortment of wires and cables. Purchase the correct gauge, which is a grading of diameter or thickness usually marked on the insulation. When buying coaxial cable, refer to its ohms rating. Wires for an electronic unit generally fall between 16 and 24 gauge, with the thicker wire having a smaller number. Wires narrower than 18 are usually unmarked. When in doubt, snip off a length of the old wire and take it with you. Never install replacement wire or cable of a smaller gauge; if necessary, use a larger gauge.

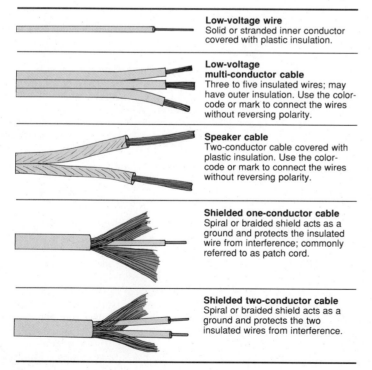

Low-voltage wire
Solid or stranded inner conductor covered with plastic insulation.

Low-voltage multi-conductor cable
Three to five insulated wires; may have outer insulation. Use the color-code or mark to connect the wires without reversing polarity.

Speaker cable
Two-conductor cable covered with plastic insulation. Use the color-code or mark to connect the wires without reversing polarity.

Shielded one-conductor cable
Spiral or braided shield acts as a ground and protects the insulated wire from interference; commonly referred to as patch cord.

Shielded two-conductor cable
Spiral or braided shield acts as a ground and protects the two insulated wires from interference.

Coaxial cable
Stranded or solid center conductor protected by foam insulation. Spiral or braided outer conductor acts as a ground. Outer insulation protects the cable from weather.

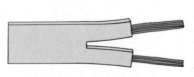

Shielded twin-lead cable
Two inner conductors protected by foam insulation; may contain an inner foil sheathing to protect the inner conductors from interference. Outer insulation protects the cable from weather.

Ribbon cable
Multi-conductor; low-voltage wires within plastic insulation. Ribbon cable connectors pierce the insulation to contact the wires.

Telephone cable
Four insulated wires; use the color code to connect the wires without reversing polarity.

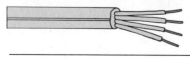

Ground wire
Solid 10-gauge wire; often uninsulated.

REPAIRING DAMAGED WIRE CONNECTIONS

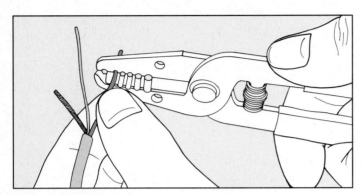

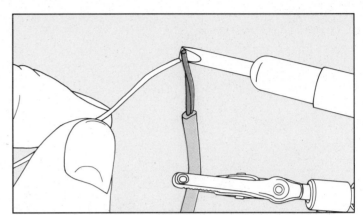

1 **Stripping back wire ends.** If a wire connection is loose or broken and the wire is long enough to be reconnected, desolder *(page 130)* and cut off the end. If a wire or cable tested faulty or is too short to be reconnected, desolder *(page 130)* and replace it *(page 131)*. To prepare a wire for soldering or for a connector, use a wire stripper to remove 1/4 inch of insulation. Fit the wire into the notch for its gauge, squeeze the handles and pull off the insulation. If the wire is solid, solder it *(page 131)* or install a connector *(steps below)*. If the wire is stranded, first tin the leads *(step 2)*.

To prepare a cable, cut off the outer insulation with a utility knife, then strip back the insulation from each wire as above; the amount stripped depends on the connector *(page 133)*.

2 **Tinning wire leads.** Prepare a soldering iron *(page 130)*. Support the wire in a soldering stand and twist the strands together clockwise between your thumb and fore-finger. Hold the soldering iron tip against the wire for a few seconds, then touch the solder to the wire *(above)*. Apply just enough solder to coat the wire strands evenly; snip off any protruding untinned wire strands using wire cutters. After tinning the wire leads, solder the wire *(page 131)* or install a wire connector *(steps below)*. If you are preparing a cable, repeat the procedure for each wire, then solder them *(page 131)* or install a cable connector *(page 133)*.

INSTALLING WIRE CONNECTORS

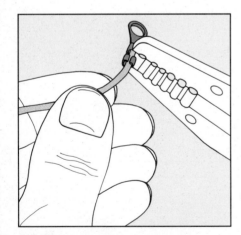

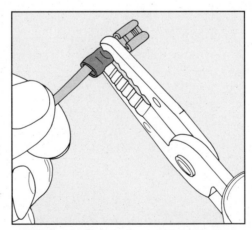

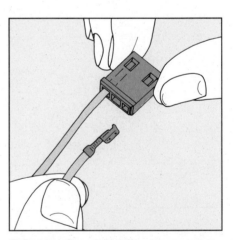

Crimping a connector. Purchase crimp, or solderless, connectors at an electronics parts supplier; be sure they are appropriate to the terminals and the wire gauge. To install a crimp connector, strip back the wire *(step above)*, fit it into the connector sleeve and crimp it using the outer notch on a wire stripper *(above)*. Gently tug the wire to ensure it is held securely.

Soldering and crimping a spade lug. Purchase spade lugs to fit the terminals and the wire at an electronics parts supplier. To install a spade lug, strip back the wire *(step above)* and prepare a soldering iron *(page 130)*. Fit the wire into the spade lug sleeve. Hold the soldering iron tip to the sleeve for a few seconds, touch the solder to the wire inside the sleeve, then crimp it with a wire stripper *(above)*.

Crimping for a plug. Purchase a plug, and crimp connectors to fit its terminals and the wires, at an electronics parts supplier. Strip back each wire *(step above)* and install a crimp connector *(far left)*. Snap each crimp connector into the plug *(above)*. Gently tug each wire to ensure it is held securely. If you install a plug at the other end of the wires, take care not to cross them.

INSTALLING AUDIO AND VIDEO CABLE CONNECTORS

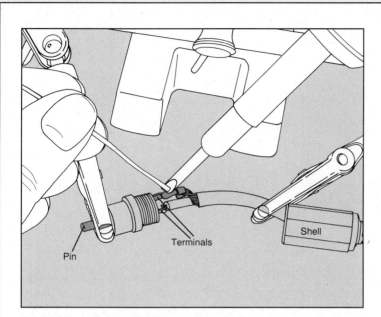

Pin — Terminals — Shell

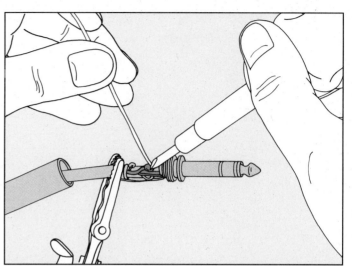

Replacing a phono plug. Snip off the old plug using wire cutters or a utility knife. Purchase an exact replacement plug at an electronics parts supplier. Unscrew the shell and slide it onto the cable. If the plug pin is solid, cut off 1/2 inch of outer insulation, strip back 1/4 inch of wire insulation *(page 132)* and solder *(page 131)* the insulated wire to the terminal closest to the plug tip. If the plug pin has a hole, cut off 1 1/2 inches of outer insulation and strip back 3/4 inch of wire insulation. Insert the insulated wire into the pin and solder the wire to the pin tip. Solder the uninsulated wire to the remaining terminal *(above)* or to a plug clip. Using pliers, squeeze the plug clips together to secure the cable. Screw the shell onto the plug.

Replacing a 1/8- or 1/4-inch plug. Snip off the old plug using wire cutters or a utility knife. Purchase an exact replacement plug at an electronics parts supplier. Unscrew the shell and slide it and any insulating sleeve onto the cable. Cut 1 1/2 inches of outer insulation off the cable and strip back 1/2 inch of insulation from the wires *(page 132)*. Solder *(page 131)* the uninsulated wire to the terminal farthest from the plug tip, and solder the insulated wires to the other plug terminals *(above)*. Using pliers, squeeze the plug clips together to secure the cable. Slide any insulating sleeve and the shell over the plug and screw on the shell.

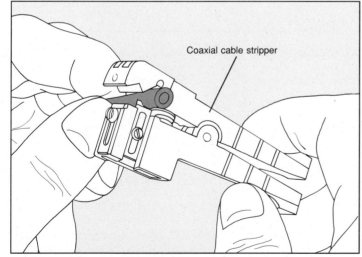

Coaxial cable stripper

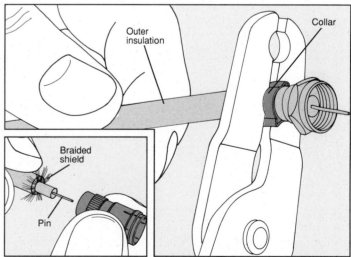

Outer insulation — Collar

Braided shield — Pin

Replacing a coaxial connector. Cut off the old connector using wire cutters or a utility knife. Purchase an exact replacement connector at an electronics parts supplier. Slide the collar onto the cable, then fit the cable into a coaxial cable stripper, with the longer blade 1/2 inch from the end. Squeeze the handles and turn the stripper around the cable *(above, left)*, cutting it

in two places. Pull the outer insulation off the second cut, exposing the braided shield, and pull the braided shield off the first cut, exposing the pin. Unravel the braided shield and fold it back over the outer insulation. Push the connector onto the cable *(inset)* and slide the collar over the connector. Crimp the collar securely using a coaxial-cable crimping tool *(above, right)*.

SERVICING COMPUTER CABLE HOOKUPS

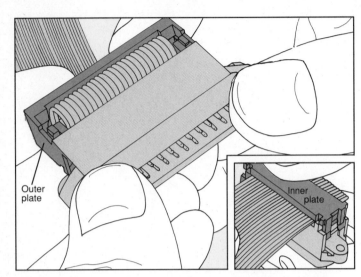

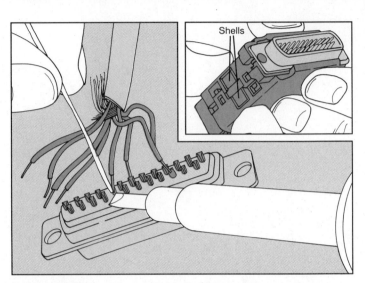

Servicing ribbon cable connections. Remove the connector from the terminal at each end of the cable. To clean the pins and terminals, use a foam swab moistened with denatured alcohol. To test the cable, set a multitester to test continuity *(page 128)*. Hook one probe to a pin on one connector and touch the other probe in turn to each pin on the other connector; there should be continuity once—and only once. Repeat the test with each pin on the connector. If the cable tests faulty or if a pin is damaged, cut off the connector with a utility knife. Purchase an exact replacement cable or connector at a computer parts supplier. Use a screwdriver to unclip the connector's outer and inner plates. Fit the cable over the terminals, leaving 1/2 inch of overlap, and snap on the inner plate *(inset)*. Fold the cable over the inner plate and snap on the outer plate *(above)*.

Servicing DB25 cable connections. Remove the connector from the terminal at each end of the cable. Unscrew and pry apart the connector shells. If a wire is loose or broken, repair it *(page 132)*; reinstall the connector shells. To test the cable, set a multitester to test continuity *(page 128)*. Hook one probe to a pin on one connector and touch the other probe in turn to each pin on the other connector; there should be continuity once—and only once. Repeat the test with each pin on the connector. If the cable tests faulty, replace it; if a pin is damaged, cut off the connector with a utility knife. Purchase an exact replacement cable or connector at a computer parts supplier. Cut off 1 1/2 inches of outer insulation, and strip 1/2 inch of insulation off the wires *(page 132)*. Solder *(page 131)* the wires to the terminals *(above)*, snap the shells together *(inset)* and install the screws.

REPLACING DISPLAY LIGHTS

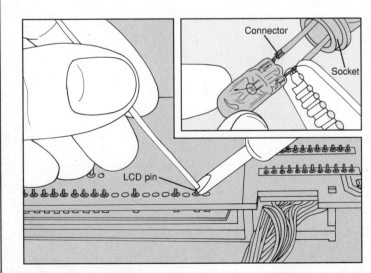

Replacing a liquid-crystal display (LCD), a light-emitting diode (LED) or a bulb. Consult the chapter on the unit to remove any panels. Locate an LCD or LED on its circuit board; unscrew and take out the circuit board to reach its pins. Desolder *(page 130)* the pins and pull off the LCD or LED; wiggle it to help release the pins. Order an exact replacement from the manufacturer or purchase a substitute at an electronics parts supplier. Fit the pins into the circuit board and solder *(page 131)* the pins. Reinstall any components removed and cold check for leaking voltage *(page 141)*.

To replace a bulb, locate the bulb and unscrew or wiggle it out of its socket. If there are wires held by connectors to the back of the bulb, pull off the wires. Order an exact replacement bulb from the manufacturer or purchase a substitute at an electronics parts supplier. Screw or press the bulb into its socket, push on the connectors and crimp them using the outer notch of a wire stripper *(inset)*. Reinstall any components removed and cold check for leaking voltage *(page 141)*.

SERVICING SPRINGS

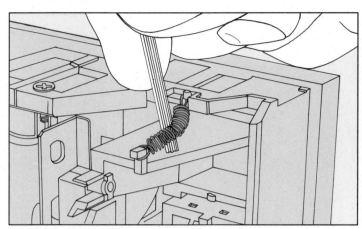
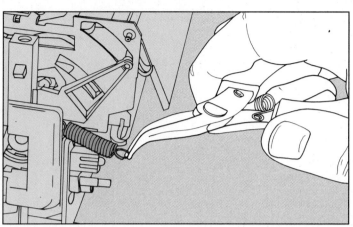

Removing and installing springs. Consult the chapter on the unit to access the spring. If a spring is unhooked at one end, reconnect it using long-nose pliers or tweezers. To check spring tension, use a small stick to tug on it gently *(above, left)*. If the spring does not snap back tautly into a straight position when released, note its connection points and use long-nose pliers or tweezers to unhook it. Snip off a few spring windings with wire cutters. Bend the cut end of the spring into a hook using long-nose pliers and reconnect the spring. If a damaged spring cannot be shortened and reconnected, order an exact replacement from the manufacturer or buy a substitute at an electronics parts supplier. Use long-nose pliers or tweezers to install the spring, being careful not to stretch it *(above, right)*. Reinstall any components removed and cold check for leaking voltage *(page 141)*.

SERVICING GEAR ASSEMBLIES

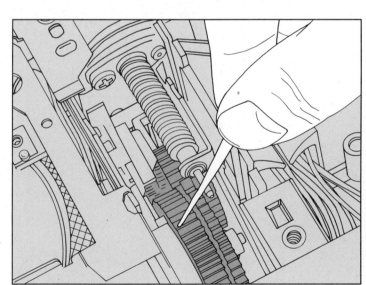
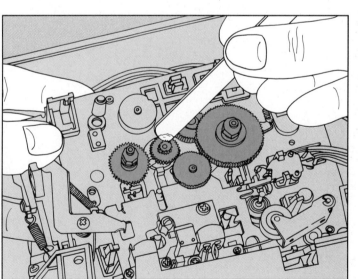

Servicing gear assemblies. Consult the chapter on the unit to access the gears. To clean a gear assembly, wipe off each gear using a foam swab moistened with alcohol. Use a toothpick to dislodge dirt from between the gear teeth *(above, left)*. To reach the entire gear assembly, try gently turning a gear by hand; too much force can break or strip the gear teeth. If gears are difficult to reach and cannot be turned, spray them with short bursts of compressed air or electronic contact cleaner. To lubricate a gear assembly, apply a little white grease to each gear with a small stick *(above, right)*; use a clean foam swab to wipe off excess lubricant. If a gear is damaged, note its position and remove it, saving any clip, washer or screw holding it in place. Order an exact replacement from the manufacturer or purchase a substitute at an electronics parts supplier. Fit the gear in place and install its fastener. Reinstall any components removed and cold check for leaking voltage *(page 141)*.

SERVICING SWITCHES AND POTENTIOMETERS

Testing multi-pole switches and potentiometers. Switches and potentiometers play a key role in routing, reducing or stopping electrical current through circuits. A switch closes a circuit, letting current flow, or opens a circuit, keeping current from passing. A potentiometer varies the amount of resistance to current. Some typical switches and potentiometers are shown at right.

Testing a multi-pole switch or a double potentiometer is sometimes a challenge, since they function in more than one circuit. However, by reading a circuit board *(page 138)*, you can locate pairs or multiples of pins in the same path and test between or among them. Determining the operating pattern of the switch or potentiometer then becomes much easier. Tests performed between pins in the same path and another pin should register the same result in each switch position.

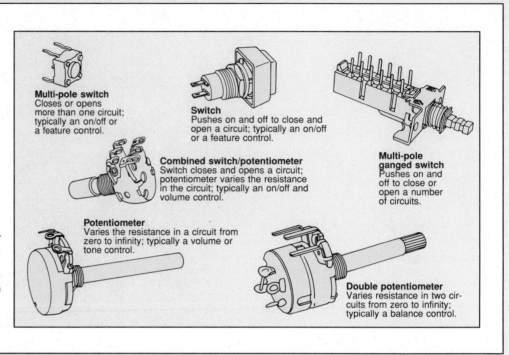

Multi-pole switch
Closes or opens more than one circuit; typically an on/off or a feature control.

Switch
Pushes on and off to close and open a circuit; typically an on/off or a feature control.

Combined switch/potentiometer
Switch closes and opens a circuit; potentiometer varies the resistance in the circuit; typically an on/off and volume control.

Multi-pole ganged switch
Pushes on and off to close or open a number of circuits.

Potentiometer
Varies the resistance in a circuit from zero to infinity; typically a volume or tone control.

Double potentiometer
Varies resistance in two circuits from zero to infinity; typically a balance control.

SERVICING A REMOTE CONTROL

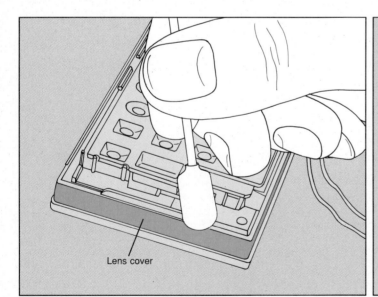

Lens cover

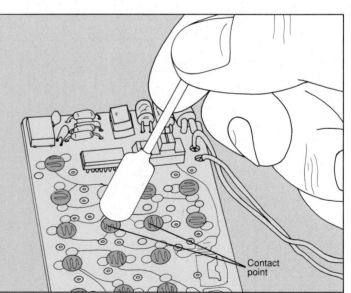

Contact point

Cleaning a remote control. To clean the outside of the lens cover, wipe with a damp, lint-free cloth. Check the battery terminals each time you change the batteries; if the terminals are dirty, rub them gently using a pencil eraser or spray them with short bursts of electronic contact cleaner. To clean inside the remote control, remove the screws holding the top and bottom casings together; check for hidden screws inside the battery compartment or under the manufacturer's label. If the casings do not separate easily, gently pry them apart using a small putty knife. Unscrew and lift out the circuit board. Use a foam swab moistened with denatured alcohol to clean the inside of the lens cover *(above, left)*. To reach the key assembly, remove the key pad from the circuit board. Clean the key-assembly contact points by gently rubbing them with a pencil eraser and then wiping them using a clean foam swab moistened with denatured alcohol *(above, right)*. Reinstall the circuit board and the pad, snap the casings back together and reinstall the screws.

REPLACING A FUSE

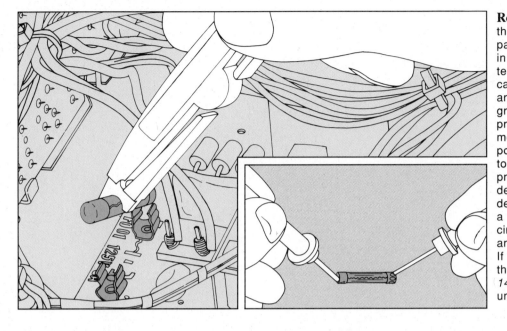

Removing and replacing a fuse. Consult the chapter on the unit to remove any panels. If the fuse is externally mounted in the back panel, turn the fuse cap counterclockwise and pull the fuse out of its casing. If the fuse is internally mounted and its caps are held in retaining clips, grip the fuse with a fuse puller and gently pry it out *(left)*. If the fuse is internally mounted and its caps are soldered to posts, leave it in place. Set a multitester to test continuity *(page 128)*. Touch a probe to each fuse cap *(inset)*. If a soldered fuse does not register continuity, desolder it *(page 131)* and test again. If a fuse does not register continuity out of circuit, purchase an exact replacement at an electronics parts supplier and install it. If you removed any panels, reinstall them, then cold check for leaking voltage *(page 141)*. If a fuse blows repeatedly, take the unit for professional service.

TESTING AND REPLACING A POWER CORD

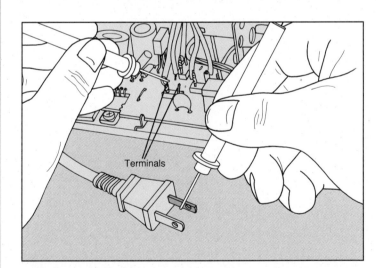

Terminals

1 **Testing the power cord.** Consult the chapter on the unit to remove any panels, and locate the power cord terminals. If the power cord wires are soldered, note their positions and desolder one wire *(page 130)*; if they are connected to other wires under a cap insulator, cut one wire with wire cutters. Set a multitester to test continuity *(page 128)*. Touch one probe to a plug prong and touch the other probe in turn to the end of each power cord wire *(above)*. The multitester should register continuity once—and only once. Repeat the test with the other plug prong and each wire. If the power cord tests OK, reinstall it *(step 2)*; refer to the chapter on the unit for servicing the power supply or take the unit for professional service.

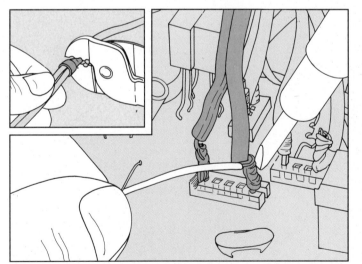

2 **Replacing the power cord.** If the power cord tests faulty, desolder the other wire *(page 130)* or use wire cutters to cut the other wire. Pry out any strain relief with pliers and remove the power cord from the strain relief. Purchase an exact replacement power cord and plug at an electronics parts supplier. To install the power cord, strip back 3/4 inch of insulation from each wire *(page 132)*. Solder the wires *(page 131)* to the terminals *(above)* or twist them together and crimp on a cap insulator *(inset)*. Fit the power cord into the strain relief, if you removed it, and push the strain relief firmly into place. Reinstall the panels and cold check for leaking voltage *(page 141)*.

SERVICING POWER SUPPLIES

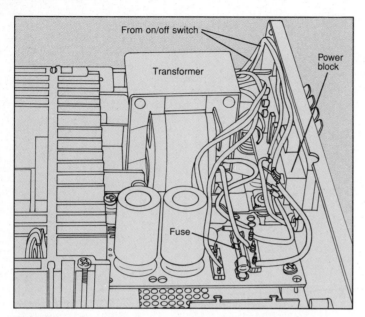

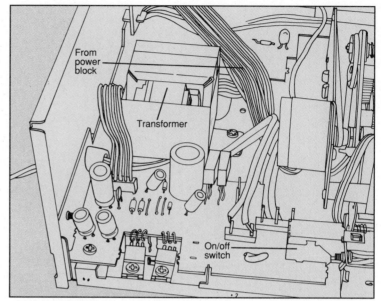

Identifying and testing power-supply components. Power supplies vary in their specific components, as well as in the sequence and way the components are connected. However, their operating principles are fundamentally the same. Four typical power supplies found in electronic units are shown above and on page 139.

The power supply provides electrical current to electronic components in the unit. The power cord routes 120-volt alternating current (AC) to the power block from an outlet. The on/off switch starts the flow of AC by closing a circuit in the unit. The transformer steps down the 120-volt AC to the low voltage required by circuit board components. A rectifier then changes the AC to direct current (DC). Usually, a fuse protects the parts from voltage spikes.

Simple tests can determine whether the power supply functions correctly. By testing the continuity *(page 128)* of the power cord, fuse, and on/off switch, as well as the wires and paths between these components and between them and the transformer, you can determine whether current reaches the transformer; by testing the low-voltage output *(page 129)* of the transformer, you can determine whether current is being delivered to electronic components.

The power-supply components are arranged in three typical sequences: fuse to on/off switch to transformer; on/off switch to fuse to transformer; and on/off switch to transformer. A variation, commonly found in a receiver, has a fuse, on/off switch and transformer each connected to the power block.

Wires and circuit board paths *(step below)* are often used in combination to connect two components. It can be difficult to

READING A CIRCUIT BOARD

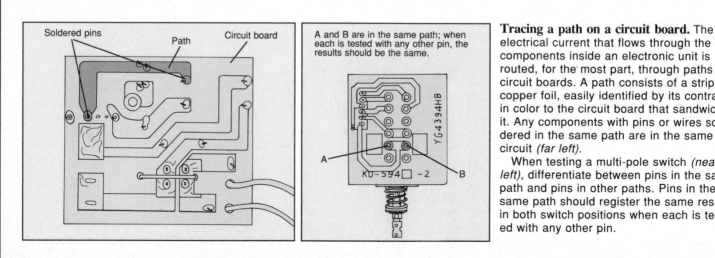

Tracing a path on a circuit board. The electrical current that flows through the components inside an electronic unit is routed, for the most part, through paths on circuit boards. A path consists of a strip of copper foil, easily identified by its contrast in color to the circuit board that sandwiches it. Any components with pins or wires soldered in the same path are in the same circuit *(far left)*.

When testing a multi-pole switch *(near left)*, differentiate between pins in the same path and pins in other paths. Pins in the same path should register the same result in both switch positions when each is tested with any other pin.

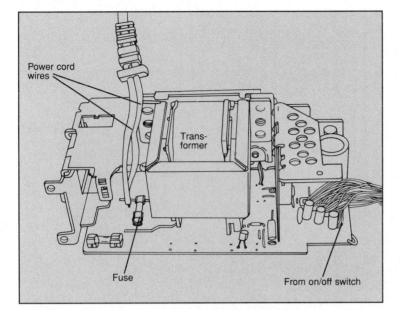

Power cord wires

Trans-former

Fuse

From on/off switch

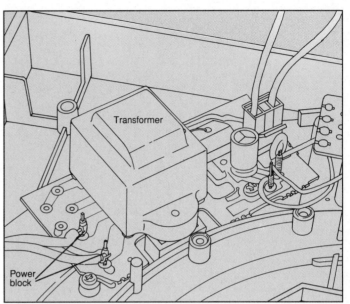

Transformer

Power block

figure out which wire or path goes where and to remember whether or not it has been tested. But orienting yourself to one power-supply component at a time assures you of testing each connection between them. In the first example *(page 138, left)*, the power-supply components include an on/off switch, a fuse and a transformer. By following the two wires from the fuse, for instance, you would discover that the power-supply component to which they connect is the power block; you could then test the wires between them. Following this procedure from the on/off switch would lead you to test the wires between it and the power block. And, by following the two wires from the transformer, you would discover that the power-supply component to which its wires connect is also the power block. Finally, you would locate the transformer wires leading away from the power-supply components and test for low voltage.

The same procedure would lead to different, but equally thorough, testing of the connections between components in any other power supply. In the second example *(page 138, right)*, you would test between the on/off switch and the power block and between the transformer and the on/off switch; there is no fuse. The final test would be for low voltage from the transformer. In the third example *(above left)*, by tracing the circuit board path you would test between the on/off switch and the fuse, the fuse and the power block, and the transformer and the on/off switch; then test for low voltage from the transformer. In the fourth example *(above, right)*, you test between the transformer and the power block, then for low voltage from the transformer; the on/off switch here is not directly connected to the power supply components.

READING A SCHEMATIC DIAGRAM

COMPONENT	SYMBOL	COMPONENT	SYMBOL
SWITCH	⚬—⚬ OR ⚬—⚬	LIGHT EMITTING DIODE (LED)	▶▮
POTENTIOMETER	—⎍⎍⎍— OR —⎍⎍⎍—	LIQUID CRYSTAL DISPLAY (LCD)	L C D
FUSE	—⚬⚬— OR —▭—	BULB	⊏◖ OR ⊏◯
TRANSFORMER	⫩⫨ OR ⫩⫨	SPEAKER	◁ OR ◁)))
MOTOR	⚬Ⓜ⚬ OR ⚬Ⓜ⚬	ANTENNA	Ⴤ OR Ⴤ OR Ⴤ
POWER PLUG	⊐→ OR ⊐	GROUND	⏚ OR ⏚ OR ↓

Identifying schematic diagram symbols.
A schematic diagram uses symbols to show how the components of a unit are connected. Some symbols are standard; others vary depending on the manufacturer. Typical basic symbols you are likely to find on a schematic diagram are shown at left.

Component specifications are sometimes listed right on the schematic diagram; or, there may be a part number for use as reference in a schematic diagram manual. When ordering a replacement part from the manufacturer or purchasing a substitute at an electronics parts supplier, be sure to state the component specifications and manufacturer part number.

TIPS ON DISASSEMBLY AND REASSEMBLY

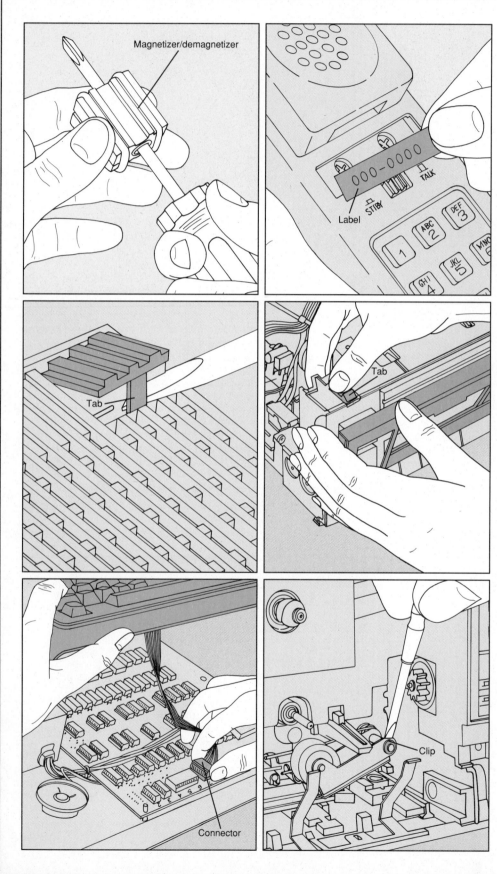

Magnetizer/demagnetizer

Label

000-0000

STBY

TALK

Tab

Tab

Connector

Clip

Working methodically and safely.
Adhering to a few simple disassembly and reassembly guidelines ensures that your experiences in home electronics repair are rewarding and accident-free. Keep in mind the warnings you are likely to find on the back and bottom panels of a unit *(page 9)*. Before undertaking a major repair, review the owner's manual and check whether the unit is still under warranty.

Set up for repairs on a clean, well-lit work table; a wooden surface is ideal. Protect the unit from scratches by covering the table with a clean, insulating pad; an old blanket will do.

Magnetize screwdrivers before you start to work by passing their heads through a magnetizer/demagnetizer *(top left)*. Keep screws and other small parts in labeled trays, jars or film containers.

Discharge any static buildup from yourself by touching an exposed, unpainted metal surface on the unit, such as a screw; hold the frame to ground yourself before handling circuit boards and, especially, a computer CPU chip.

Study the unit panels before beginning, to determine the sequence in which they were installed. Check for hidden screws under labels *(top right)* and recessed screws covered by a tab *(center left)*. To release a stubborn screw, press the screwdriver firmly into the screwhead and snap any glue seal with a sharp counter-clockwise twist. Pull or slide off panels gently; never force them. If a panel resists being removed, check the edges for tabs securing it to another panel or to the frame *(center right)*.

Disassemble only what is needed to reach parts being repaired. Refer to the unit service manual, if it is available from the manufacturer or an electronics parts supplier. Write down your sequence of disassembly steps for reference in reassembly.

As you remove a panel, check behind it for wires connecting it to internal components. Before unplugging a connector *(bottom left)*, note its terminal positions; soldered connections rarely need to be removed.

Unscrew circuit boards using as little pressure as possible; they are very easily damaged. Carefully pry any small clip off a component *(bottom right)*; keep one hand ready to catch it.

Before reinstalling panels, check that no tools are left inside and that all components are back in place. After reassembly, but before plugging in the unit, perform a cold check for leaking voltage *(page 141)*.

A COLD CHECK FOR LEAKING VOLTAGE

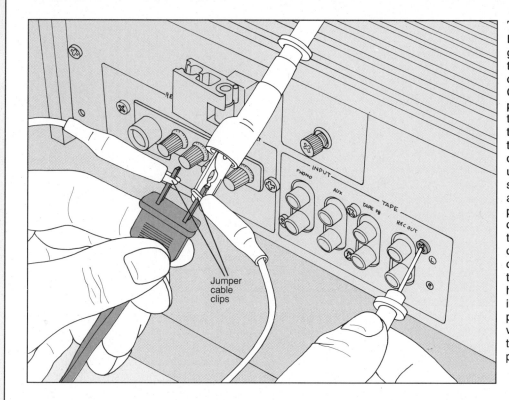

Jumper cable clips

Testing for a potential electrical hazard.
Before plugging in a unit that has undergone an internal repair, perform a simple test to confirm that no internal electrical circuits have been damaged or shorted. Clip a jumper cable to the prongs on the power cord plug and set the on/off control to the ON position. Set a multitester to test continuity *(page 128)*. Clip one multitester probe to a plug prong and touch the other probe in turn to at least two or three unpainted metal surfaces on the unit *(left)*; screws through the panels into the frame, and cable terminals, make ideal test points. In each test, there should be *no* continuity. Unclip the jumper cable and a touch a probe to each prong on the power cord plug; in this test, there *should* be continuity. If the unit tests faulty in any test, do not plug it into an outlet until you have located the problem and remedied it; if you cannot determine the cause of the problem, take the unit for professional service. If the unit tests OK in each test, set the on/off control to the OFF position and plug the unit into an outlet.

GETTING HELP WHEN YOU NEED IT

MODEL NO.	ZAB-500	BRAND ®
∿ 120 V 12 W 60 Hz		
SER. NO. 2580516630264		MADE IN U.S.A. 14568490974

Learning what you need to know for effective repairs. The key to obtaining the correct replacement component, schematic diagram or owner's manual for your unit is the model and serial numbers, usually stamped on a plate or a sticker *(above)* on the back or bottom panel. If you cannot locate it, consult the manufacturer.

If individual components are not listed in the owner's manual, consult the schematic diagram. It can be ordered from the manufacturer or may also be available at your local electronics parts supplier. Typical schematic-diagram symbols are presented on page 139.

Some parts carry their own serial numbers, either stamped on them or listed in the owner's manual or service manual. The reference number for a circuit board component may be marked on the circuit board or listed in the schematic diagram. Any component found within a shaded area on a schematic diagram must be ordered from the manufacturer.

Armed with this information, call your local electronics parts supplier to check whether the part is in stock. Electronics parts suppliers often have comparison lists of equivalent substitute components. If possible, take the faulty component with you.

When purchasing a replacement component, you have several sources from which to choose:
Electronics parts suppliers. If a store does not carry a part the dealer may be able to order it or tell you where to find it.
Audio/video stores and computer stores. Many do not sell more than basic supplies such as cables, cleaners or software. A dealer may be able to help you locate other sources.
Hardware stores. Many stock cable, tools and basic audio and video supplies, but their salespeople are not specialized.
Manufacturers. Get the address and telephone number of the manufacturer from your owner's manual, or by asking an electronics parts supplier.

If you require professional service, choose carefully. Ask friends for references, or consult your electronics parts supplier. Your local Better Business Bureau or consumer rights office may also help you select a reputable technician. Be sure the technician is trained to service your brand.
You and your warranty. Before attempting any repair, check the warranty provided by the manufacturer. If the warranty is still in effect, you will void it if you undertake the repair yourself. Only an authorized service technician should make the needed repairs.

INDEX

Page reference in *italics* indicates an illustration of the subject mentioned. Page reference in **bold** indicate a Troubleshooting Guide for the subject mentioned.